THE
NEW
ELIZABETHANS
SIXTY PORTRAITS OF OUR AGE

JAMES NAUGHTIE

Collins

First published in 2012 by Collins

HarperCollins*Publishers*
77–85 Fulham Palace Road
London W6 8JB

www.harpercollins.co.uk

1 3 5 7 9 10 8 6 4 2

Endpaper photographs courtesy of Getty Images, with the exception of
Elizabeth David, Alan Sainsbury, Ralph Robins, Richard Doll and
Vladimir Raitz, courtesy of PA Photos. Illustration of Talaiasi Labalaba
by Nicolette Caven.

Extracts from *The Complete Poems* by Philip Larkin reproduced with
permission by Faber and Faber Limited.

A catalogue record for this book is
available from the British Library

ISBN: 978-0-00-748650-2

Printed and bound in Great Britain by
Clays Ltd, St Ives plc.

MIX
Paper from
responsible sources
FSC™ C007454

Contents

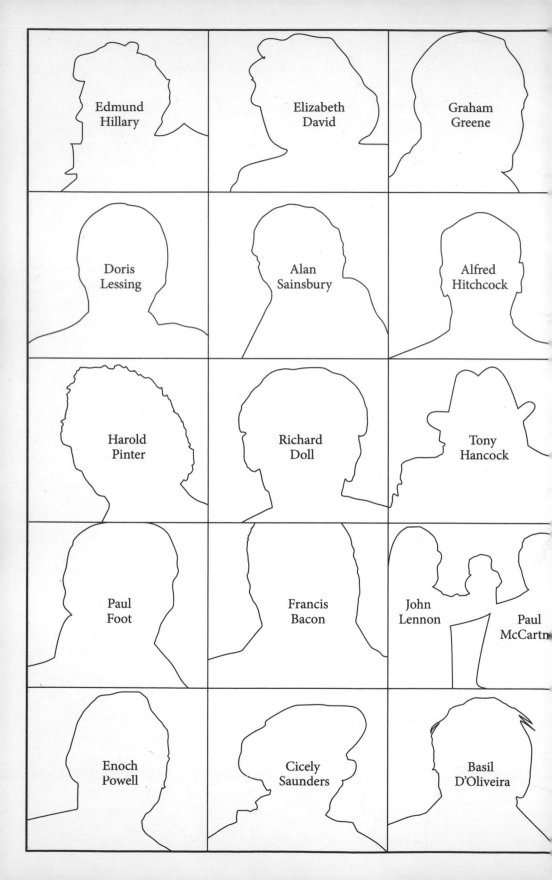

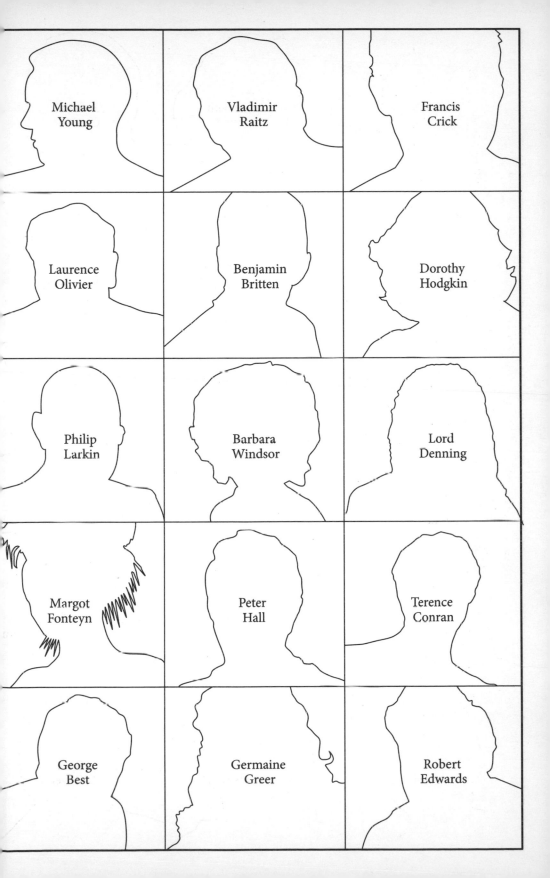

Michael Young

Vladimir Raitz

Francis Crick

Laurence Olivier

Benjamin Britten

Dorothy Hodgkin

Philip Larkin

Barbara Windsor

Lord Denning

Margot Fonteyn

Peter Hall

Terence Conran

George Best

Germaine Greer

Robert Edwards

Introduction: Our Age

WHEN THE OLYMPIC GAMES opened in London for the third time in the modern era, there was a surprising outburst of national self-confidence. It was unexpected because a weary habit of apology seemed to have taken hold, over the course of many years, and the relentless flow of dark economic news, rolling in with every tide, might easily have sapped any appetite for celebration. But no. The summer of 2012 turned out to be a festival of confidence, stirring up memories of a time when the country had a sharper sense of itself, and when we imagine that the trains ran on time. Maybe that belief in resilience will turn out to have been another self-deception, but with the coincidence of the Diamond Jubilee to give the era a time-frame, there seemed to be a surprising amount to cherish from years that could too easily add up to an age of decline.

These sixty portraits are reminders of some of the people who shaped these decades, and whose voices were the soundtrack that we all heard. They take us back to the early fifties, and the last days of wartime rationing, into the tumult of the sixties, and then through years that swung from economic crisis to seasons of optimism, and back again.

These people made their mark in a time when our feeling for the past was shot through with self-doubt. In an era of change, when national ingenuity would be tested, a fear of weakness began to spread. British governments since the fifties have had to deal with the awkwardness of an imperial legacy which bequeathed powers that were often illusory. Economic power waned, and the currency – always a token of national strength – shrivelled with the growth of more prosperous rivals. On Coronation Day in 1953, a pound bought nearly twelve Deutschmarks; forty years later, it would get you two and a half. The Royal Navy at the start of the twenty-first century seemed like a flotilla compared with the armada that might have assembled to mark the end of the war in Europe in 1945. And in this new century, after the long era of American dominance, all Europe was preparing for the economic and political consequences of a decisive shift in power to the East. It is natural in an atmosphere of such relentless transition to search for solid ground, and footholds that will guarantee some respite and a chance for reflection.

The subjects of these portraits are useful guides, because their feats – and, of course, their failures – are a reminder of the character of our time. They explain why we were inspired or deflated, why we laughed or wondered, how the age of deference gave way to the culture of youth, how a Prime Minister at the end of the twentieth century could find himself going to war more often than we could have imagined, how the banks imploded, and how a princess could still be turned into a fairy tale in an unbelieving age. They take us into the sunny days that we like to remember, and the shadows too. This is no history, only an album of snapshots of people caught on the run. But together they make up a flickering home movie that is an authentic picture of six decades.

When BBC Radio 4 decided to try to assemble a gallery of New Elizabethans – in sixty portraits, to match the span of the Queen's reign – it was obvious that they could not be a definitive list of the best and brightest who might be listed in some longer version of the Order of Merit. This would be a selection to represent the contours of the age. They would be from academe and business, politics and science, high culture and entertainment. They had to represent the torrents and the calm of these years, some of the surprises as well as the established achievements. Radio 4 listeners responded to the challenge in their customary spirit, nominating about a thousand individuals in all – many with massive support – and the sifting began.

A panel was brought together with the aim of focusing shafts of light on the list from different perspectives. Tony Hall (Lord Hall of Birkenhead), chief executive of the Royal Opera House and chairman of the Cultural Olympiad 2012, supervised its proceedings with admirable calm. The members were, in alphabetical order: Sally Alexander, Professor of Modern History, Goldsmiths, University of London; Dr Jon Agar, Senior Lecturer in Science and Technology Studies, University College London; Bamber Gascoigne, writer and broadcaster, creator of the Timesearch website, and polymath; Sir Max Hastings, historian and former editor of the *Daily Telegraph* and London *Evening Standard*; Dr Anna-Maria Misra, Lecturer in Modern History, Keble College, Oxford; Dominic Sandbrook, historian.

Theirs were labours of Hercules. They were asked to find people on the list who collectively caught the spirit of the age, and to try to ensure that the sweep of the years was represented. Politics shouldn't dominate, and nor should any other single area of life. They should catch the mainstream, but the awkward currents as well. It was important to reflect popular culture, and not simply award another gong on behalf of Radio 4 to a predictable list of the great and good. And although simple notoriety would not be enough to make you a New Elizabethan, it was important that the list did not consist simply of the sixty people thought to be the most admirable in our time. That meant that there were bound to be some surprising omissions, and inclusions. I attended one of the panel's meetings – with no formal role – and was aware of the difficulty they faced in being fair and interesting at the same time, trying to represent some of the best and giving a flavour of everything else that we have lived through.

3

When I began to write these portraits I realized how cleverly they had drawn a line through the years. Like everyone else, I had my favourites who failed to make it round the last bend – that was true of each member of the panel, too – and found some of the names surprising. But together they soon took on the air of a gang of contemporary Canterbury pilgrims, each with a story to tell and throwing light on one another. For example, Enoch Powell, Jayaben Desai, Stuart Hall and Doreen Lawrence cast different shafts of light on the story of immigration and race in our time. And around them clustered the other people who might have been on the journey too, who could be brought in to play their part in the drama. Collectively they made it possible to find an interesting path across the landscape, stopping here and there for reflection, sometimes disappearing into a labyrinth of politics or public controversy, then having a laugh, then discovering the background to a scientific discovery that had been a mystery to me, or uncovering a character of whom I knew little.

The portraits in this collection are reproduced here almost exactly as they were broadcast on BBC Radio 4 through the summer of 2012. Writing for a listener is rather different from writing for someone who will read the words on a page, so there is some informal grammar and sentence structure here that is geared more to the style of a radio talk than a written essay. It seemed sensible, however, to retain their flavour as conversation pieces in this collection. That is how I conceived them, and how they were heard. In nearly every case the archive material added to the scripts for transmission has not been reproduced here, and these are the portraits as they were first drawn.

They are, of course, idiosyncratic. I have tried to be fair, although it is simply not possible to do justice to some remarkable characters in scripts that took only about twelve minutes to read on air, to be comprehensive in explaining their particular achievements. They are personal pictures, and not biographical entries for a journal of record. I hope these are more interesting for having a personal flavour. The series produced lively argument about who was in and who was out, about whether one Prime Minister deserved preference over another, whether just the one footballer deserved the sporting palm, about why there are particular novelists or comedians or musicians who don't appear in these pages. Good. If our New Elizabethans had been a bore, they would have been a pointless bunch.

I record my deep gratitude to my BBC colleagues in the Acknowledgements, because this was a collective and energetic expedition that proved exhilarating at every turn. I found myself taken back to my youth – listening to Tony Hancock, missing a Beatles concert, learning of the 'rivers of blood' speech – and then to the politics that I covered as a young journalist – the first devolution arguments, the rise of Margaret Thatcher – and also discovering characters of whom I knew little, like Vladimir Raitz and his package holidays, or Talaiasi Labalaba, the SAS soldier of whom I hadn't heard but whose statue is one of his regiment's proudest memorials. I lived through the Northern Ireland Troubles again, and tried to explain what it was that made Billy Connolly a star.

When it was over, and I was writing about the Queen for the last portrait, I was reinforced in my view that continuity has been as important as change in an era which can be too conveniently defined by decline, crisis and alarm. It is easier to think of the unsolved problems and coming threats than to remember the scientists or artists who startled the world, or the community heroes who fought for human values against a hostile tide. The useful excuse of a Diamond Jubilee, placing our age in a frame, is a chance to try to give the picture its proper proportions, and to see the light and the dark at the same time. It is neither escapist nor nostalgic, just the natural recollection of a journey through the years.

The picture has many layers, and beguiling perspectives. It is both mirror and lamp, reflecting and illuminating, and these are the characters who have drawn it. They tell our story for us.

JN, September 2012

Edmund Hillary

EDMUND HILLARY WAS THE FIRST HERO of the second Elizabethan age. His adventure was organized to make it turn out that way, and to this end the Coronation in 1953 had a piece of news attached that would both announce a new frontier and confirm that the days of unimaginable exploits in far-off places had not gone.

The timing required luck as well as skill and brawn, but it was Hillary's good fortune to carry with him for the rest of his life the impression that maybe it was because of his dignified bearing and natural modesty that everything had happened just as the expedition, and Fate, had jointly planned: so that there had never been any doubt that when he and Sherpa Tenzing set off for the last push from the South Col they would make it to the summit of Everest.

The truth at the time was different. The winds had been high and the weather bad. The two climbers who had been selected to make the first assault had been beaten back on the last, lonely ridge and at base camp no one could be sure that Hillary and Tenzing would do any better. They spent the last night less than 2,000 ft from the summit, but awoke in the dark just before dawn on 29 May to a calm that brought a surge of relief. The wind had dropped: they had a chance.

Then Hillary saw that his boots had frozen solid in the night and were like lumps of black iron. The first two hours of that day were spent thawing the boots over a flickering stove so that he could get them on. They couldn't be sure that their oxygen would last; that the weather wouldn't close in; that they'd have the energy for the last slow slog to the top.

Picture them at the stove: the tall New Zealander and the short, wiry Sherpa, who had been high up the mountain seven times, but never so close to the summit. They had no navigation system, none of the clothing and equipment that would make the next generation of climbers look like quite different animals, not even a radio. Hillary had a little camera tucked under his clothes to stop it freezing up. Their small tent, and the gear they laid out for the last day's work, would have seemed familiar to the adventurers of a generation earlier, and antique to those who had taken the same route when they had become old men.

The two men preparing for the final trudge to the top were fit and strong, and had the streak of imagination that drives the best climbers to the highest places, where others can't go. But the expedition – with 362 porters and 20 Sherpa guides – had something of an air of majestic amateurism, connecting it to the memory of wildly optimistic outings when men in hairy socks and polished leather boots forged through the snow or set sail for unknown places. There was nothing ramshackle about the Everest expedition of 1953, planned to the last detail, but the spirit did hark back: to a time when there was no oxygen, patchy maps, and an ever-present feeling of the unknown.

This story had two irresistible elements: ice and suspense. The coldest places on earth had seemed, for more than a generation, to invite the greatest effort of imagination. One of the reasons was the obsession of Captain Robert Falcon Scott. His journeys were the first truly dazzling exploits of the twentieth century as far as any British schoolchild was concerned, and the fact that his fame was sealed by a failure (to beat Amundsen to the South Pole) only proved what a stalwart he was.

Knowing that he was doomed, Scott wrote his Message to the Public: 'Had we lived, I should have had a tale to tell of the hardihood, endurance and courage of my companions which would have stirred the heart of every Englishman.'

As a youngster in New Zealand, on his two-hour journey to school, Hillary read the stories of such men. Their names cascaded down the years and inspired the expedition put together by John Hunt to conquer the unconquerable mountain, which they all saw as part of an old story – daring and sad. Where Mallory and Irvine were assumed to have failed in 1924, died and lost near the summit without having reached it, there was still a game to be played, and won.

In 1953, time and distance meant that such drama was spun out: no pictures from the scene, no breathless commentary day by day, but weeks of silence. The result, the benefit you might say, was that when good news came, of unexpected progress, or triumph, it came out of a clear blue sky like a roll of thunder. And the Everest expedition had another ingredient that infused the suspense with poetry.

James Morris of *The Times* was 26 when he was told over lunch at the Garrick Club in London that he could, if he wanted, become Special Correspondent to cover the Everest expedition. The paper had put up some money, and as a result had secured the rights to all the dispatches sent home by Hunt and his men. And in Morris they had found their man, a storyteller of brilliance and effervescent panache whose travels and portraits of people and places would make him one of the most celebrated writers of his age, both as James, and later as Jan, after he decided to become the woman who'd always been inside him.

Morris trekked to base camp with the expedition, though he had no experience of real mountains, and began to plan how he might break the great news, if it came. The problem was that Fleet Street was not going to accept for a moment the deal that *The Times* had done with Hunt, and dispatched reporters to Kathmandu with instructions to do whatever was necessary to get the story first. You can imagine the *Mail* and the *Telegraph* and the *Express* working on Sherpa guides to make sure that the news would reach them first, perhaps carried on cleft sticks from the slopes of Everest, in an icy echo of Evelyn Waugh's *Scoop*.

Morris was up to the task. He described the expedition's progress to base camp, at 22,000 ft, with elegant verve, and he wasn't going to let the story slip away. So he devised a code that would confuse any of his competitors who might see the telegram that would be flashed to the British Embassy in Kathmandu: he had no doubt that they would. And with the rest of the expedition, the only reporter in the camp, he waited.

They had no means of knowing that Hillary and Tenzing were on the way, only the knowledge that the wind might have dropped. But they were, carrying heavy backpacks and worried about their oxygen. Hillary wrote of the climb up the last ridge: 'My solar plexus was tight with fear as I ploughed on. Halfway up I stopped, exhausted. I could look down 10,000 feet between my legs and I have never felt more insecure. Anxiously, I waved Tenzing up to me.'

And they were there, alone. Afterwards, to put an end to the argument about who got there first, they issued a joint statement, saying it was done together. But later Tenzing said straightforwardly that Hillary's foot was the first on the summit – after, in his words, 'a few, very weary steps' – then they joined hands and stood together, never thinking there might be an argument over who got there first.

It was half past eleven in the morning on 29 May 1953 when they unfurled four little flags on a string tied to Tenzing's ice axe – the Union Flag, and alongside it the flags of Nepal, India and the United Nations, just seven years old. Only Hillary took photographs for a quarter of an hour – so there are none of him at the summit – and they started down.

Tenzing, the Nepalese Sherpa, had climbed the sacred mountain, which had defeated everyone else. He said that in the villages they asked him if he had seen the gods above the clouds. Lord Shiva, perhaps, for that was where he lived. No, said Tenzing, but he had felt a calm that inspired him, and did for the rest of his life.

They took their news down. Morris described seeing Hillary in the half light: 'Huge and cheerful, his movement not so much graceful as unshakably assured, his energy almost demonic. He had a tremendous, bursting, elemental, infectious, glorious vitality about him, like some burly, bright diesel express bounding across America.'

And then the telegram. 'Snow condition bad,' he wrote, which meant 'Everest climbed.' In the rest of the message, which said the assault had been abandoned until the weather cleared, he used the code words agreed for Hillary and Tenzing. The rest of Fleet Street, squatting in Kathmandu, swallowed it. *The Times* had its scoop and on the morning of the Coronation it broke the news. The bells rang out for them.

An answering telegram reached the expedition that day, addressed to Sir Edmund Hillary, the new Queen's first Knight.

He was a hero for the rest of his life. There were expeditions to both the poles, up the Ganges, back to the Himalayas, but above all for Hillary there was a commitment to the Nepalese people whom he'd come to know on the great climb. The Trust he established built two dozen schools; hospitals, bridges, airfields. He was celebrated as a humanitarian, and never lost the straightforwardness of the man who said he had always hated the 'danger part' of climbing and thought that the greatest of all feats was the comradeship that built up in the lonely places. 'The giving of everything you've got,' he said, 'is really a very pleasant sensation.'

Edmund Hillary, adventurer, scientist and beekeeper, died in 2008, aged 88.

He once said that in honouring explorers from the past people should remember that it was 'still not hard to find a man who adventures for the sake of a dream … or one who will search, for the pleasure of searching. Not for what he may find.' That was the spirit Hillary tried to bring to his time.

Elizabeth David

WHEN ELIZABETH DAVID began to write her first book for
the British on the food of the Mediterranean, her readers
were still disentangling themselves from wartime rationing. Olive
oil was something you bought at the chemist, with a warning on
the little bottle: 'For external use only.' She was going to raise
their sights, even though she must have known that very few of
the home cooks to whom she was addressing herself would have
the inclination, let alone the appetite, to follow her instructions
for stuffing a whole sheep. Yet that is what they might have done
on the Greek island where, as a young woman, she had decamped
at the end of the thirties with her married, older lover and where
she consummated a life-long affair with food.

Not food as part of a dull household routine, but food as a
creative force. More than that, food as the emblem of people's
lives: the thing that told you everything about them. When David
published *French Provincial Cooking* in 1960 she told her readers
of how she'd found a tattered book of recipes at the Sunday
market in the cathedral square of Toulouse which exuded 'a
certain atmosphere of provincial life which appears orderly and
calm whatever ferocious dramas may be seething below the
surface'. And those hidden dramas were as interesting to her as
the calm. Delving into the cuisine of the south of France, she gave

her readers a sharp nudge: 'It does not do to regard Provence simply as Keats's tranquil land of song and mirth. The melancholy and the savagery are part of its spell.'

For those brought up with the homely straightforwardness of Mrs Beeton and successive generations of advisers on fruit cakes and steak and kidney pie, wholesome broth and sticky puddings, savage melancholy was probably new in the kitchen. But by the end of the fifties David had brought a new spirit to the table. She soon cast a spell on imitators and disciples enough to ensure that she become the first of the modern British cooks. Without her, it's probably safe to say, there would have been no Delia Smith, no Jamie Oliver, none of the excitements of the cooking that became a celebrity industry and one of the most unexpected social changes of our time. She made it possible to speak of a culture of food without seeming pretentious or odd, though if she'd thought that spiky boys would one day be queuing up when they left school in the hope of becoming chefs, she would have been mightily surprised.

Her natural milieu was a privileged one. She came from money and whizzed around Europe with an abandon that only her class could afford. Yet by the time she'd got to know France and Italy and Greece, say by the time she was in her mid-thirties after the war, she had conceived a zeal that turned her into a kind of evangelist for something better for everyone; something that the English table as she'd known it had lost. She had lived with a family in Paris and Normandy whom she realized were 'exceptionally greedy and exceptionally well-fed' but learned the family cuisine of France at their table, as spectacular in its own way as haute cuisine of the Escoffier sort, and she'd also breathed in the smell of fresh lemons in the south, understood the sensuality of food, and realized – as she said – that there was nothing more alluring than the sight of a nearly ripe fig waiting to be pulled from its tree at dawn.

To readers reared on boiled beef and carrots (both overcooked, of course), she was a revelation. On Mediterranean food in 1950:

'The ever recurring elements in the food throughout these countries are the oil, the saffron, the garlic, the pungent local wines; the aromatic perfume of rosemary, wild marjoram and basil drying in the kitchens; the brilliance of the market stalls piled high with pimentos, aubergines, tomatoes, olives, melons, figs and limes; the great heaps of shiny fish ... the butchers' stalls are festooned with every imaginable portion of the inside of every edible animal (anyone who has lived for long in Greece will be familiar with the sound of air gruesomely whistling through sheep's lungs frying in oil).'

To many readers an aubergine was a strange, foreign thing – was it a fruit or a vegetable? ... perhaps neither – and David was talking to a generation that knew little of pasta, let alone the spices and the food of the East. But there was actually nothing at all foreign about eggplant: it had just somehow been forgotten in Britain. Although she was an explorer who brought news of the exotic from distant places, her real passion – and maybe her legacy – was the cooking of home. For she wanted nothing so much as the rediscovery of what had been lost, and to remind anyone who wanted to cook well that there was a history and a heritage in the gardens and fields of her native land that deserved to have life brought back to it.

So when she published *Summer Cooking* in 1955 she started with regret about the 'hypnotic power' of the deep freeze and a plea for the rhythm of the seasons to be understood and respected. She had seen people in her local greengrocer's crowding round the freezer to pay four shilling for a few strawberries in a cardboard box when they could have had seven perfectly ripe, sweet oranges for a quarter of that. And she wrote, with a knowing sigh: 'As soon as strawberries and raspberries are in season they will be clamouring for frozen pineapple and cartons of orange juice.' That could have been written half a century later, because the battle goes on, with the same forces still trying to abolish the natural calendar of the table.

Some of the recipes in that book are hymns to simplicity, a few sentences only. Yet David's purée of sorrel, or mint chutney or *polpette* of mutton, or crab mousse, come out perfectly, and cooks have found them as pleasing to read as to eat. Chefs like Simon Hopkinson have talked about going to bed with the books to bring on the happiest of slumbers. She passes on classic recipes without alteration – one begins 'skin, behead and wash some small eels' – with careful attribution, and there is never any compromise. Just as when she refused to allow the shop she founded to sell garlic presses on the grounds not just that they were ridiculous but – worse than that – pathetic, she is emphatic at every turn. 'As I understand it,' she started her introduction to the book, 'summer cooking means the extraction of maximum enjoyment out of the produce which grows in the summer season and is appropriate to it.' She could have stopped right there, the point made.

You never had to wait long for an opinion. The journalist Katherine Whitehorn once asked her how she felt about those who might not have time to bake all their own bread, as she said they should. What, for example, about women who were at work all day? 'That's their problem,' was the reply. David's independent spirit was fiery. That first affair in the thirties, the flirtation with artistic Paris and some wild and bohemian corners of Europe, were the clue to someone who was going to go her own way, especially if she was told not to. Maybe it was always likely that she'd suffer in turn, and she did, much later being left by a long-time companion for another woman, and falling out with those who ran her shops and continued trading under her name after she'd severed all ties. Her last years – she died in 1992 – had their difficulties. Life was always a swirl of action and passion.

David was born in 1913 and her great escape began in her teens, after the unexpected death of her father, a Conservative MP. Her mother wanted to encourage her interest in painting and she was sent to the Sorbonne, then to Germany just before Hitler came to power, before coming back and going through the rituals that had always been expected of her: the debutante balls and a formal introduction into society. But she had already tasted something else, and was in Greece almost before anyone noticed. When she came home, the war was over, but food was still rationed. And maybe it was the austerity itself that egged her on. 'With whatever I could find, I cooked like one possessed.'

The consequence was books that made a case for food as a pillar of civilization, without which everything might shrivel and die. At the start of *French Provincial Cooking* David said that any man or woman capable of cooking a good English roast was a good enough cook to produce something more imaginative. 'If a dish does not turn out to be quite as it was at the remembered auberge in Normandy, or at the restaurant on the banks of the Loire, is this a matter for despair? Because it is different, as by force of circumstance it must be, it is not necessarily worse.'

And so she tried to lift everyone up. There were other cooks of her time who played big parts too: Marguerite Patten maybe prime among them, who'd emerged from the Ministry of Food in the war to try to crack the problem of the rationed kitchen and inspired many cooks. The first television equivalent was Fanny Cradock, with her ubiquitous and put-upon husband Johnnie, who rushed from oven to table and back again, turning the kitchen into a place of well-meaning frenzy. But the real legacy of Elizabeth David came later, when Delia Smith decided that it was time to write a book for another lost generation, went on television, and sold millions of copies of her *Complete Cookery Course*.

There was none of David's tales of savage Provence, or whole-sheep-stuffing from the Greek islands, and Delia was a classless cook to Elizabeth's grande dame. But they were at the same game: reminding people, encouraged to turn bland by fashion and advertising and the marketing of the unimaginative, that there was pleasure to be had in the kitchen. When David was made OBE at Buckingham Palace in 1976, she reported afterwards that when she said she wrote cookery books, the monarch replied simply, 'How useful.' Nothing about savage melancholy, nor the passion of a fig, nor the joys of a long day at the pot. But, through it all, Elizabeth David did want to be useful too.

Graham Greene

GRAHAM GREENE'S GAME WAS DANGER. As a novelist he played with characters who were always throwing the dice and gambling with their moral fate. He was a spy, he said he'd played Russian roulette with a loaded gun (though hardly anyone knew whether to believe him), he was fascinated by treachery and claimed kinship with the betrayers, he toyed with women and religion.

But, through it all, the spine of his life was a high seriousness about writing. When he started to call some of his books 'entertainments' he was having fun with people again, for stories like *Our Man in Havana* didn't abandon that interest in loyalty and deceit, guilt and shame. This was his territory, a place he made his own, where anxious people dealt with a world beyond their understanding, grappling for handholds and never finding it easy. W.H. Auden spoke of things being Graham Greenish and everyone knew what colour that was. Dark, menacing, strangely inviting. From the thirties on, his output had been growing – novels, film criticism, essays, film scripts – and his lugubrious, rangy, world-weary figure, wreathed in smoke, seemed to beckon his readers to a place that might be dangerous and treacherous, but was somehow familiar.

By the time he published *The End of the Affair* in 1951 Greene was established at the top of the tree. Three characters, above all, had put him there: Pinkie the teenage gangster in *Brighton Rock*, the whisky priest in *The Power and the Glory* and Scobie in *The Heart of the Matter*, who were all in some way caught between their instincts and their obligations, and tortured as a result. He could produce moral terror in the blink of an eye, and by the fifties it seemed that he was the contemporary novelist who had the most sensitive, fingertip feel for the confusions and the alarms of the time.

'Greene-land' – a label that irritated him – was a place where people were alone, bewildered by the dilemmas forced on them by the world and haunted by their inability to reconcile that pain with their sense of something beyond: the divine, or at least the unchanging. Greene always preferred to be called a novelist who was a Catholic rather than a Catholic novelist, but his conversion in the twenties was the event that shaped him as a writer. He called himself an intellectual but not an emotional Catholic, and you don't have to read much of his fiction to start to understand the tension.

By the end of his life he was calling himself a 'Catholic atheist', and left even his friends to wonder where his journey had taken him. They did know that by the fifties he had staked out territory that he controlled, in which the lies and betrayals of daily life – about love, or country, or personal pride – were played out on a wider, dark stage, where you could never be sure what was waiting in the wings.

Naturally this irritated some people. When George Orwell reviewed *The End of the Affair* (based on one of Greene's own liaisons) he expressed the frustration of someone who found the possible intervention of divine judgment a distraction from the much more important business of human decency. He wrote in the *New Yorker*: 'He appears to share the idea, which has been floating around ever since Baudelaire, that there is something rather distingué in being damned; Hell is a sort of high-class nightclub, entry to which is reserved for Catholics only.'

It definitely had a dark allure for Greene, whose characters so often flirted with whatever went on in that nightclub or were drawn to it by some urge that they couldn't understand. The main character in his first book, *The Man Within*, is a hunted man, and right through to his later fiction – think of the spy novel *The Human Factor*, published in the late seventies – he was preoccupied with the figure pursued across the landscape by demons, some of them invisible and some of them deep inside and all too familiar.

There was another reason for his popularity, of course. He knew how to tell a story, how to play with tension – above all, how to hook a reader. The first sentence of *Brighton Rock* ensures that you're bound to read on: 'Hale knew, before he had been in Brighton for three hours, that they meant to murder him.' His screenplay for Orson Welles in *The Third Man* showed that he understood exactly how film too could tell a story: every piece falls into place, the rhythm never falters. It's classic Greene: a man seeks justice for a friend, killed in the dark streets of post-war Vienna, only to discover that he has faked his death to escape from the consequences of his own crimes.

For Greene the fifties began with *The End of the Affair* and ended with *Our Man in Havana* and *A Burnt-out Case*. All three were about weakness and deceit. And in between came one of his greatest novels, *The Quiet American*. He'd worked in Indo-China as a journalist, and the story of Pyle, the American of the title, foreshadowed all the arguments that would traumatize America over Vietnam a decade later. Pyle is idealistic and at the same time ruthless in his belief about what can and should be done to the Communists, and Greene wove a moral tale which got him targeted by the Washington authorities as anti-American, in an age when in their eyes the distinction between good and evil was rather clearer than it could ever be in a Greene story.

And readers knew that there was something going on at home too. The novel was published in 1955, the year before the débâcle of the Suez invasion. That decision by Anthony Eden's government to deceive Washington and collude with France and Israel in attacking Egypt was the foreign policy catastrophe of the age, dividing the country, shaking the political class. It was this event, more than any other, that a few years later led a former American secretary of state to coin a famous aphorism which hurt with its stinging truth. 'Britain has lost an empire and not yet found a role,' said Dean Acheson.

Greene, in *The Quiet American*, told a story that caught the wind that was blowing in south-east Asia and would bring trouble along. It also picked up, at home, the nervousness of an age in which the deep freeze of the Cold War did not stop people from realizing that everything was on the move. The post-war world was being reordered, and no one yet understood the consequences. Greene was a storyteller who was also a poet of the moment, picking up whispers from the street and tremblings of the political web.

He'd also done it as a professional spy. We know only the sketchiest outline of what he did for the Secret Intelligence Service, MI6. But he was there and enjoyed saying that he had an identification number in the service which he subsequently attached to the controller of the hapless agent Wormold in *Our Man in Havana*. Wormold finds himself recruited by British intelligence and tempted to enhance his persona as a spy, first by some fairly harmless exaggeration and then by spectacular invention. But he survives. After a fashion.

Greene worked in MI6, formally, for three years or so during the Second World War and was alongside Kim Philby, Moscow's master spy. It was not until the late sixties that the story of Philby's career and eventual defection was told to the public, after *Sunday Times* journalists penetrated the layers of desperate obfuscation that had kept it hidden.

But much earlier, following the electrifying defection of Guy Burgess and Donald Maclean from the Foreign Office to Moscow in 1952, Greene will have known the story from his friends: that enough people in Whitehall were convinced of Philby's treachery to heave him out and let him moulder away in Beirut, half journalist and half old spook, until he went to Moscow. Greene's own connections at that time, when he was a celebrated writer, have always been mysterious, not least because he liked it that way.

It does seem clear that, certainly in the fifties and perhaps for much longer, he was in touch with old friends from his service, bringing back titbits from his travels, casting a wary eye on anything that stirred his interest. In Indo-China in the fifties he certainly acted as a trusted observer and informant. His biographer Norman Sherry said that he was, in the end, 'the perfect spy … an intensely secretive man'. This is the truth of it. Evelyn Waugh, fellow novelist, fellow Catholic convert, lent support when Greene would get into trouble for some outburst, as he did in 1960 when he was criticized for defending the Soviet Union. Waugh said in a letter to a friend that Greene was 'a secret agent on our side and all his buttering up of the Russians is cover …'. Who knows? That's the thing about secretive men.

Greene's output was immense – the novels, reviews, essays, plays – and his era spanned the thirties to the eighties. In that time he became a lodestar for many writers as the master craftsman. William Golding said that he was great because he was 'the ultimate chronicler of twentieth-century man's consciousness and anxiety'.

By the fifties that judgement had become indelible. Although Greene continued to write for more than three decades after *The Quiet American* (and thought that *The Honorary Consul*, from the seventies, was his best book), his early work had established his voice as unmistakable, demanding and perpetually unsettling. There was always a question lying underneath, gnawing away.

That feeling never left him. His last words, in hospital in Switzerland in April 1991, when he knew he was dying, were, 'Why must it take so long to come?'

Michael Young

SOCIOLOGISTS SELDOM GET A GOOD PRESS, except where they don't need it.

Michael Young was a great exception. He was an innovating intellectual whose brain was happy to put theory and practicality in the same compartment, and many thousands of people who had never heard of his fifties book *The Rise of the Meritocracy* will know of the Consumers' Association and the Open University, and perhaps be thankful for them, but not attach his name to either body. Yet without him they might not have existed. He was a public figure who liked not to be very public; a force for change who achieved much more than most of the ministers and mandarins to whom he often had to sell an idea and whose most precious possession has always been to say yea and nay.

Lord Young of Dartington, as he became in 1978, was a thinker who never tucked himself away. When Cambridge University asked him to set up its sociology course, having come late to the notion, he thought the dons too rigid in their thinking and backed out quickly. He preferred to be free of confining institutions, a feeling that probably gripped him for life when as a teenager he came under the influence of Leonard and Dorothy Elmhirst. The couple had set up Dartington Hall in Devon as a radical school, intended unashamedly for a select band of children of free think-

24

ers in the intelligentsia who would be given their heads and encouraged to contemplate utopia. It was an inspiration. Thanks to Dorothy Elmhirst, Young found himself having dinner with Franklin Roosevelt in the White House and being encouraged to argue. It was his fifth school, his parents having broken up, and it became his own utopia. The urge to think differently never left him.

Politically, Young was one of the most important people in post-war Britain, though from a back room. Excused military service because of chronic asthma, he worked in an early think-tank – it had the austere name Political and Economic Planning – which gave him his first experience of bringing together people of ideas and policymakers. This experience produced a document that, by any standards, was of huge importance. At the age of 29 he wrote – more or less single-handedly – the Labour Party manifesto for the 1945 general election. After Clement Atlee's victory it became the template for a government that had a chance to be radical in the post-war era, transforming the economic model of the country, establishing the National Health Service, and outlining a social consensus that held sway across the parties for the next generation.

However, Young didn't take to front-line politics at that stage, for by the start of the fifties he had already decided that the Labour Party he helped to bring to power had run out of ideas. He left his job, went to the London School of Economics, and made a decision that would shape the rest of his life. He moved to Bethnal Green in the East End of London, an area battered by the blitz and racked with poverty, a world that despite his interest in public policy he had never seen. Politicians, he thought, had lost touch with these people: 'The local councillors heard the complaints,' he said, 'but did nothing about them because they'd been captured by officials.'

Characteristically, his first reaction was to think. He set up what he called the Institute of Community Studies. Working with Peter Willmott, he began to study the East End and write about

the people, trying to get a feel for the barriers that were preventing them from having better lives, and pondering the social
changes that might be needed. One of his first books, *Family and
Kinship in East London*, published in 1957, made a shattering
noise. It argued against the planners' lust for sweeping urban
redevelopment and tried to bring the values of family and shared
experience to bear on social policy. Over the next few years his
ideas excited, irritated and disturbed policymakers and he became
a voice of social reform in the manner of some of the Victorians
he greatly admired, like the philanthropic reformers Joseph
Rowntree and Charles Booth. This didn't sit well with some
fellow academics in his field, who found his faith in that kind of
individual action a little quaint, but he couldn't have cared less.
There was a streak of romanticism in him. He was the kind of
man who never said 'why?', but usually 'why not?'

Throughout the fifties he challenged conventional thinking
which he thought had let people down, and pursued his own
form of egalitarianism. Even many of those who wouldn't go all
the way with him – on comprehensive education, for example –
found his ideas inspiring. *The Rise of the Meritocracy*, written
with Willmott, brought a new word into the language, sold half
a million copies and was, he hoped, a warning against what might
happen to a society that was too careful in favouring the strong
over the weak.

But in the year before his death, 2001, Young confessed that he
had been sadly disappointed by the book – not because of any of
its ideas, but because people had long forgotten that it was a
satire, a caution. Instead, he was forced to lament the fact that the
Prime Minister, Tony Blair, was now using the word 'meritocracy'
with approval, as a benign object of policy. 'I do wish he wouldn't,'
he said. He recalled that the book – which he assumed Tony Blair
had never read – was a warning about what might have happened
seventy-five years on if society insisted on dividing people into
sheep and goats. He wrote, 'My imaginary author, an ardent
apostle of meritocracy, said shortly before the revolution, that

"No longer is it so necessary to debase standards by attempting to extend a higher civilisation to the children of the lower classes."'

The fire still burned into the new century, when the Young Foundation for social research, successor to his first think-tank, was still based in the East End. But there was more to Young than the ideas that he'd developed after the war. He also became a man of action.

Looking back, it may seem extraordinary that the notion of consumer power was so slow to develop. Mass marketing had grown fast, and American techniques were revolutionizing advertising, which from the mid-twentieth century had had television to give it more power. Where was the individual going to turn for help when it was needed? Young knew that something was required, and explained in one famous lecture how public clocks had been replaced by watches, ice factories by fridges, cinema by television, and how the car had become a powerful individual weapon. You didn't have to be a sociologist to work out that people who bought things – consumers, they were starting to be called – needed help, not just in making informed choices when they were being tempted by the burgeoning advertising industry, but to cope with dodgy goods and the many fake claims made about them. The power was all on one side and the balance had to be redressed. The difference Young made wasn't just that he spotted that danger: he did something about it.

The result was the Consumers' Association, founded in 1956. The idea was that members, who paid a subscription, would pool their knowledge and their energy to fight for information about goods and services, and about the choices they could make. It would give them power. As Young once put it, 'Class based on production is giving way to status based on consumption as the centre for social gravity.' He'd got the idea from the American Consumers' Union set up in the thirties during the Great Depression, and he decided that the time had come in Britain.

Along with the Consumers' Association came its magazine, *Which?*, still published today. The first edition road-tested aspirins and kettles: there was apparently a rather large number of dangerous kettles on the market and people needed to be warned against them. Around the Consumers' Association Young set up a network of all kinds of advisory bodies and services. These included advice on funerals, a helpline that was the forerunner of NHS Direct, even a language line to provide help for professionals dealing with people for whom English was a second language, an idea well ahead of its day. The political philosopher Noel Annan said he reminded him of the Greek hero Cadmus, whose deeds were the object of wonder: 'Whatever field Michael Young tilled, he sowed dragons' teeth and armed men seemed to spring from the soil to form an organization and correct the abuses or stimulate the virtues he had discovered.'

The Consumers' Association grew more quickly than anyone had imagined. It thought it might get 3,000 subscribers to *Which?* in the first year (the magazine was published from a converted garage in Bethnal Green) but within four months there were 100,000 and the organization continued to grow. Young's argument was that people wanted to make rational choices, so why not help them? In its way it was a revolution. For the first time in an age of mass marketing when people were being told 'You've never had it so good' because of what they could buy, the argument was made that individuals had to be championed, given redress when they were wronged, and encouraged to resist the road-roller of ever-bigger manufacturers using the power of advertising to have their way. He saw it as a culture war.

Much of this zeal he attributed to the energy that had flowed from the Festival of Britain – the cultural opening of the fifties and the event intended to mark the transition from wartime austerity to something different and more hopeful. The Festival championed new architecture and invention, artistic endeavour and innovation of all kinds, and designers, especially, had felt the beginning of a new era. Young epitomized the spirit of those who were terrified at the prospect of a stuffy, unchanging society which – in his view – tolerated the sore of urban poverty and resisted fresh ways of thinking.

His story is remarkable because he managed to keep up the pace, moving on, experimenting. He never tired of poking fun at an establishment, and, abandoning his old Labour loyalty, in the early eighties he became a founder of the SDP. At the same time – such a rare gift of commitment in an innovator – he stuck with the ideas that had worked and lent them all the support he could.

But it was in the sixties that he made what became maybe his lasting contribution, the one that Harold Wilson, three times Prime Minister, said was the proudest thing he had done in power: the Open University. Young couldn't see why, with the ever-present TV set, students couldn't work and study from home. There were sceptics – even Iain Macleod, the formidable and far-sighted Conservative, described it as 'blithering nonsense'. But within a few years, after a shaky start on a quagmire of a campus at Milton Keynes, the Open University was turning out thousands of graduates every year and has since become the world's leading online university, its teaching standards in many disciplines rated more highly than those in some quadrangled, much older seats of learning. Two generations of graduates have done what otherwise might have been impossible for them.

Maybe that is Young's legacy, but there is more. He was imaginative enough in the eighties, for example, to propose, after President Reagan announced his 'star wars' defence programme, the establishment of a Martian colony that he hoped would eventually declare independence from earth. He was going to simulate conditions on Mars in the building on London's South Bank that would become Tate Modern, and persuade thirty people to be filmed in a kind of serious embryonic *Big Brother*. It never happened, but he always wondered what it would have been like.

The fifties are often lazily caricatured as the dull, do-nothing decade. Michael Young's career belies it, and the evidence is still there.

Vladimir Raitz

THE SUMMER OF 1954 WAS DULL AND WET, the coolest around the British coast for nearly fifty years. June was unseasonably rainy. There was some good news in July: the wartime hangover of food rationing came to an end. But the weather stayed bad right through the summer. Holidaymakers in Southend, Bournemouth, Colwyn Bay, Scarborough and Largs were well wrapped up. The weather wouldn't have been a surprise. And, as ever, they got exactly what they paid for. They knew on the Lancashire coast that Reginald Dixon was playing the mighty organ next to 'the biggest one-ring circus in the world', that the old chip shop would be on the same corner, the same bony donkeys ambling across the sand. There would be saucy comedy: Benny Hill was television personality of the year, one of the first, and you could rely on him. A young comic called Ken Dodd appeared for the first time in Blackpool, and he'd still be playing there more than half a century later. The heyday of variety hadn't yet passed.

The old resorts with their Victorian piers, Punch and Judy shows and funfairs were doing good business. Spoilsports intervened that summer to use the Obscene Publications Act to prosecute Donald McGill, the postcard artist, for producing two cartoons that were thought to have gone too far. Weymouth

Pavilion and the pier at Great Yarmouth, which had survived wartime bombing, burned down. Otherwise you might have thought it was an unchanging world, as predictable as the next Blackpool tram clanking and squeaking up the north promenade in the rain. The weather might be determined to be changeable but the rituals of the seaside seemed, by contrast, reassuringly permanent.

That was an illusion. Something else was happening. A small party of British tourists was enjoying a new experience. That summer they could smile at the thought of their friends sheltering behind the windbreaks at home. They were gaudy explorers in sun hats and sandals, on their way to the Costa Brava. The invasion of Spain had begun.

The man who was leading it was a Russian Londoner. Vladimir Raitz was born in Moscow into a White Russian family not long after the revolution, so it was always likely that he'd have to get out of the Soviet Union. His grandparents left first, for Berlin, and later, in 1928, when he was 6, he and his mother followed them. His father stayed behind and Vladimir never saw him again. After Hitler took power in Germany in 1933 his grandparents were off again, and like so many Jewish émigrés who had to take flight they headed for London, where Vladimir joined them, a clever young man who spoke, as yet, no English at all. But there was something remarkable about this boy: at the end of his first term at Mill Hill School in north London he was top of his English class. This was the man who would revolutionize the British summer, by taking people away.

He spent the latter years of the war working for Reuters news agency as a young translator, listening to broadcasts from overseas, and when it was all over he began to wonder how he might make a success of life. He looked around for an idea – anything – and began to wonder what was going to happen to the cargo planes that had been used in the war, a little battered and travel-weary but still capable of flight. And then, with the death of his grandfather, he had a stroke of luck: an inheritance of £3,000, a goodly sum then. It was not until the early fifties that the average annual wage in Britain passed £500.

So Vladimir Raitz left Reuters and moved along Fleet Street, where he rented an office and started his own small company. It was a holiday business, and he wondered what to call it. He'd be taking people, he hoped, to places most of them had never seen and knew little about it; somewhere beyond. He had his name: Horizon Holidays.

In 1950 the number of people who took foreign holidays was much smaller than the number who stayed at home. The trades' holidays, at fixed points of the year, were the signal for a dash to the seaside: in the last two weeks of July, for example, Blackpool would become a Scottish colony, thanks to the Glasgow Fair, when the whole workforce took its break. Going abroad was expensive, and tended to be the preserve of those who had time and money. Thomas Cook had started his travel business around 100 years earlier, in 1845, when he took a party from the English Midlands to Scotland, though it was the business that he got from the Great Exhibition in 1851 that made him. But in 1950s Britain Thomas Cook hadn't yet turned its mind to mass marketing: it was still the agent for travellers with sturdy leather cases and time to kill. Visiting a branch to buy tickets was like visiting your bank, the clerks conducting their business with proper formality behind wooden desks.

Raitz wanted something different. First of all, he had his eyes on some of those old planes. The problem was that British European Airways, then in public ownership, wanted to stop him. It didn't like the idea of a freebooter offering flights to places which it already served, for a hefty fare. Raitz had a fight with the Ministry of Aviation and finally persuaded them that he was doing something different. But he was allowed to make his first trip only if he agreed to certain conditions. He could only carry people who could prove that they were teachers, or students connected with them. In other words, Horizon Holidays had to demonstrate that it was more interested in self-improvement than fun. It was fine to go to Blackpool to hear Max Miller telling dirty jokes in the autumn of his career, or listen to Sandy MacPherson on the giant Wurlitzer, but if you were going to go anywhere near the Mediterranean you'd better demonstrate that you had some higher purpose in mind.

Raitz's own purpose, of course, was simply to establish a good business – but it was an idea infused with his belief that many more people deserved the chance to travel. He had arrived in London speaking Russian, Polish, German and French, and had been turned into an internationalist. Like so many political refugees from the thirties, he brought with him an instinct and a conviction about culture: that broadening the mind, encountering other peoples, was good in itself and something that everyone should have the chance to do.

When his first chartered Dakota 3 took off from Gatwick airport in the summer of 1950, he hoped it was going to be the start of a business that would grow quickly, but it was a modest beginning. There were eleven paying passengers and twenty-one students on the plane. They weren't travelling luxuriously, or even comfortably. The plane refuelled at Lyon, then completed its six-hour flight to Corsica, landing on an airstrip at Calvi that had been laid out during the war and still bore the scars of that time. There was no airport building; nothing. Raitz remembered later that they sheltered from the sun under the wings until buses came to take them away, to a campsite where they would spend their fortnight's holiday: two beds to a tent, rudimentary bathroom facilities and washrooms. But for their all-in price of £32 10/- they got something more. At the camp there were a bar and a dance floor. The teachers and students, whatever the Ministry of Aviation thought about it, were going to do more than visit the twelfth-century citadel, look for Roman remains or the birthplace of Christopher Columbus, or try to identify the place where Admiral Lord Nelson lost his right eye while leading the siege of the city.

Their food and wine was included, although they must have been interested to learn on their arrival that a bottle of

Corsican wine was selling for 9d. In other words, if they had needed to they could have clubbed together, bought twenty-five bottles, and still have had change left over from £1. But the holiday was all-in. They were pioneers, the first package tourists. The vanguard.

Raitz was up and running. Calvi was on his map, and in the next year or two other resorts followed. And, in that grey British summer of 1954, he took the big step into Spain. Tossa del Mar, on the Catalonian coast not far from Barcelona, was a fishing village with no banks and only one or two hotels, but it was the landfall for an invasion force that would colonize that coast, then discover and conquer the Costa del Sol stretching out from Málaga in the south, and spread in vast numbers to the Balearic Islands, starting with Majorca. Spain hadn't seen anything like it since the Middle Ages: five years after Raitz's first party arrived on the Costa Brava, 77,000 holidaymakers from Britain took a package to Spain, and in the early sixties fishing villages like Torremolinos started to transform themselves into places that would tempt more and more people to come. They did. By the end of the decade the number of people taking foreign holidays had doubled, to 5 million. That number had doubled again by 1979, and by 1990 21 million Britons were going abroad on holiday.

In later life Raitz regretted some of the consequences. He didn't like Benidorm – 'it looks bloody awful,' he said – which had mutated from a fishing village into a concrete emporium of fun and noise. One estimate gives it the highest number of high-rise buildings per capita in the world. Raitz did cling to some of the hopes he'd had for his enterprise when he was battling to launch it with that first Corsican expedition. He said that the package holiday had been a social revolution. 'The man in the street acquired a taste for wine, for foreign food, started to learn French, Spanish or Italian, made friends in the foreign lands he'd visited, in fact become more cosmopolitan, with all that that entailed.'

On the other side of the ledger, in the sixties he had a deeply unhappy experience with the creation of Club 18–30, which tried to get younger people to buy packages. He couldn't make it work and sold it to Thomas Cook, where it later became a byword for unbuttoned, booze-fuelled binges dressed up as holidays. The price war in the market he'd created was becoming vicious and destructive. Business was big, but dangerous. Horizon itself was in trouble and he decided that it was time to cash in. In the early seventies he sold it to Clarkson's for a good price and was therefore protected from a collapse that would have been very painful. Within three years of the sale the company had gone bust. The business was changing as fast as it always had.

Raitz, however, remained the pioneer who had changed everything. He was the model for Freddie Laker, whose cut-price Skytrain shuttle from London to the United States took off with a fanfare in the late seventies and cocked a snook at the big airlines. Laker saw himself as the people's friend, a kind of Butlins Redcoat at the controls of a jumbo jet. It folded in the end, but paved the way for the cut-price airlines that, by the end of the century, were establishing new and unlikely routes across Europe and carrying stag parties to unlikely places like Riga and Ljubljana with exactly the kind of chutzpah with which Vladimir Raitz had once ferried his first package tourists to Corsica and Spain.

Behind, Raitz left seaside resorts that often struggled, Victorian piers that started to corrode and topple into the sea. Holiday towns had to use all their imagination to survive, and some faded to shadows. Blackpool went up and down like one of its big dippers, but was claiming, fifty years after he first tempted its holidaymakers away, that it was expanding again by providing new kinds of fun, remembering that the trick was to give people what they wanted, at a price they could afford.

If Raitz has a monument, maybe it's in the destination board at every airport, now that people think nothing of a fortnight in the Gambia or the Maldives in the summer. Maybe in October there'll be a quick one-nighter to Blackpool, sou'wester safely packed, to see the illuminations, the cleverest trick ever pulled for extending the summer season. But who knows, in an unwitting salute to Vladimir Raitz, they might be wondering about a city break in Moscow.

Francis Crick

EVEN ALLOWING FOR THE TOLERANCE of some pubs in Cambridge, where you might not be surprised if on a chill Monday evening someone threw open the door and shouted the news that Shakespeare's plays had been written by a mysterious woman whose identity was now going to be revealed for the first time (before subsiding into exhausted silence), a few people must surely have turned their heads on 28 February 1953, when two scientists tumbled into the Eagle in Bene't Street and announced that they had 'discovered the secret of life' and had the proof in their lab.

They were Crick and Watson, Francis and Jim, and the scene is worth remembering because hindsight often lends work like theirs a formal aura as if everything happened in an orderly fashion, properly, in sequence, as if planned. They had worked for years on what we would later come to know as genetic biology, but the circumstances of their great discovery were quite chaotic, and controversial too. Moreover, it was little noticed at the time that they had given a shape to the building blocks of life, and suggested how they might fit together. Not many people, after all, knew about deoxyribonucleic acid. We all know it now as DNA.

Their first scientific paper on the subject was published in the journal *Nature* in April 1953 – Crick was the principal author –

and, looking back from an age where the science of genetics has become a rolling public debate, and often the stuff of headlines, it's startling to note that it caused no public excitement at all. The only newspaper to pick it up was the *News Chronicle*, long defunct; there was no broadcast news of it, and the university paper *Varsity* could hardly claim that its short report was going to shake the world. Yet it was a story that *would*: a step into the unknown, the invention of a new branch of science, the first serious claim to understand the working of our genes. By whatever name it is known, it was a revolution.

In that first paper Crick wrote the following sentence, which is one of the masterpieces of understatement of our time, with a whiff of self-satisfaction that was characteristic: 'It has not escaped our notice that the specific pairing that we have postulated immediately suggests a possible copying mechanism for the genetic material.' In other words, how genetic messages are passed on and how we perpetuate ourselves. Not perhaps who we are, but a clue about how we come still to be here.

The 'specific pairing' was revealed by the model Crick and Watson had built in Cambridge University's Cavendish Laboratory: the double helix that would become the emblem of their discovery, and a Rosetta stone for modern science. At the top of the structure, two threads are intertwined and then, below, they flow outwards like two locks of hair freed from a perfectly pleated pigtail. As it was once described: 'The two strands of the double helix separate, and a daughter strand is laid down alongside each with a constitution determined by the base sequence of its parent strand.' They had established how messages might be carried by DNA, the memory system in our genes, and Crick postulated that there were molecular tags that could interpret the make-up of a gene – as if reading a codeword – and then deliver the right amino acid to the right living cell: the machine inside us all, that shapes everything we do.

Nine years later this was the discovery that brought Crick and Watson (with Maurice Wilkins) the Nobel Prize for Medicine, although that simple fact conceals a story of rivalry that sits uncomfortably and sometimes painfully alongside the fact of their success.

In the two years or so before the first paper on DNA, and the construction of the double helix, there was quite a race going on among those who were using X-ray crystallography to try to peer into the inner workings of our biology. Crick was at the centre of it all, and even before the younger zoologist James Watson arrived from the United States in 1951 he was cooperating with a scientist at King's College London called Maurice Wilkins, whose experiments were making progress. Fortunately, but awkwardly, Wilkins had a colleague at King's without whom the story of DNA can't be told. She was Rosalind Franklin.

It was her work that gave Crick and Watson a leg-up. On one visit to London to see some of her experiments, Watson realized that she might have provided the key. Back in Cambridge he and Crick worked on a model. They invited their rivals from King's to come and see it, describing it as 'a clever thing'. Rosalind Franklin took one look at it and realized that they had taken her results, applied them to their own, but made a serious mistake. They had built a 'triple helix', and she told them where they had gone wrong.

The background was like the setting of a C.P. Snow novel about skulduggery in the senior common room of the kind that he was just settling down to write. At King's, Wilkins did not get on with Franklin at all. And to complicate matters, the head of the Cavendish Laboratory, William Bragg, was sensitive to the feelings of the King's scientists, who didn't want their work to be copied. He is said to have suggested to Crick and Watson that they stop working on DNA altogether. Wilkins confessed his despair at the whole business to Crick in a letter, and the atmosphere is well summed up in Crick's reply, which came to light only a couple of years ago. He wrote to Wilkins: '... so cheer up and take it from us that even if we kicked you in the pants it was between friends. We hope our burglary will at least produce a united front in your group.' The word 'burglary' was presumably meant as a mild joke.

In Cambridge they seemed happy, in London miserable. Wilkins wrote to Crick about Franklin, who was about to leave King's, and used a poisonous tone: 'Let's have some talks afterwards when the air is a little clearer. I hope the smell of witchcraft will soon be getting out of our eyes.'

Crick and Watson carried on. The triple helix was transformed into the double helix, their own mistake corrected, and gradually – after a second article in *Nature* later in the year – the significance of the discovery began to be appreciated in a wider circle. And the names of Crick and Watson were bolted onto the double helix as if they were part of its origin, though many others had had a part in putting it together. Rosalind Franklin died of cancer in 1958, aged only 38.

Francis Crick was born in Northampton, son of a shoe factory owner, and studied physics in London. In the Second World War he worked on weapons in the Admiralty, designing mines. Afterwards he decided he was more interested in biology. That abrupt change of direction was quite typical of a man who had a reputation for the unexpected gesture and a tendency towards utter certainty. When Watson wrote an account of their discovery in 1968, he produced an opening sentence about his friend and colleague that summed up their over-the-top and maybe brash style, separately and together. 'I have never seen Francis Crick in a modest mood,' said Watson. Neither saw any reason to be diplomatic, even about each other.

It was not that their friendship was falling apart – it lasted until Crick's death in 2004; Watson still survives him – but that they were a pair of swashbuckling scientists, whose meticulous work often seemed to take second place to their love of the instinctive thrust, the imaginative spring. The year after the double helix was built, Watson wrote to Crick: 'The important thing is to ignore data, which complicates life.'

The style was formidable. After Crick became celebrated he had a postcard printed for his secretary for use as a reply to enquirers. It was headed 'Dr F.H.C. Crick thanks you for your letter but regrets that he is unable to accept your kind invitation to: ...' There followed a list of requests of the kind he was used to receiving: send an autograph, be interviewed, speak after dinner, deliver a lecture, read a manuscript, even 'cure your disease'. His secretary had instructions to tick the appropriate category and send the postcard. It repelled all boarders.

So Crick was a character, irascible on subjects like religion, which, like most philosophy, he abhorred. (He resigned from Churchill, a new Cambridge college, when he discovered they were building a chapel.) And those close to Rosalind Franklin, particularly, long held a grudge at what they believed was a betrayal of her originality and the contribution she'd made to genetic research.

But it would be quite wrong to picture Crick as a scientist who happened to break the mould very early – he was 36 when the double helix paper was published – and spent the rest of his life being famous for it. The truth is that much of his pioneering work was done *after* that first discovery. He never left the territory he had staked out, and long after he was one of the three men who got the Nobel Prize in 1962 he was breaking new ground.

The initial proposition had been that there was some kind of linear genetic message that could be passed on. They had discovered how genes could copy themselves and human life could replicate. We had a glimpse of how the essentials of human life were managed. But then what? It was a beginning, not an end. Crick set about working on the question of how genes coped with the instructions they'd been sent, and it was thirteen years after the first *Nature* paper before he felt able to declare that he might have an answer.

The occasion was the annual meeting of molecular biologists at Cold Spring Harbor in the United States, where he was now working. They were scientists whose field of study had more or less been created by Crick and Watson and whose successors, a generation later, would find themselves in maybe the most exciting, ever-changing field of science, mapping the genome, inspiring medical research with possibilities, opening up territory for doctors as well as scientists that not long ago had been an impenetrable misty landscape with no signposts.

Crick began that 1966 speech with the words: 'This is an historic occasion. There have been many meetings about the genetic code during the past ten or twelve years but this is the first important one to be held since the code became known.' A typically emphatic description. He went on to announce that he could now present to the world the genetic code in its entirety. It was this map that would become a guide for everyone working in molecular biology, and in medical laboratories everywhere the step-by-step unravelling of the genetic puzzle changed everything. Crick himself led the way, and it will be his name that is attached to the institute that will open in 2015 in London to bring together some of the world's finest minds in biomedicine.

It is worth remembering Watson's reminder to Crick about data complicating life: go for the big idea. When they marched into the Eagle in Cambridge in 1953 convinced they had 'got it' they weren't talking about a vast tome that they'd been writing in secret. Their article in *Nature* was only fourteen paragraphs long, and attached to it was a single diagram: the skeletal and beautiful picture of the double helix itself; the strange, sparse outline of the most intimate thing in the world.

Doris Lessing

SOME NOVELISTS TAKE YEARS to get into their stride, but it is true of Doris Lessing that if you want to understand her, and feel the full power of her imagination, you have to read her first book, which was published in 1950. *The Grass is Singing* is a story set in Africa, where she grew up, where she experienced unhappiness and political radicalization, and where she decided to be writer. More than half a century later Lessing had become a Nobel Laureate with dozens of books behind her, even an opera with Philip Glass.

The Grass is Singing takes you to the kind of rolling landscape and bush where her father farmed in Southern Rhodesia, a generation before it became Zimbabwe, and where she developed a passionate desire to see an end to colonialism. The novel is an uncompromising journey into a world of fear and racial segregation where violence is as familiar as the wind that makes the grass sing. It's a story of murder – committed by a black houseboy on the white woman to whom he is in effect a slave, but who is so fascinated and drawn to him that it nearly becomes an obsession – and a sharp-edged picture of the world, which she knew, that made the tragedy almost inevitable. Moses, the murderer, and Mary Turner, his victim, are both destroyed by the way in which they have to live. The book trembles with passion, like this: 'When a white man in Africa by accident looks into the eyes of a native and sees the human being (which it is his chief preoccupation to avoid), his sense of guilt, which he denies, fumes up in resentment, and he brings down the whip.'

Lessing had lived in Africa from 1925, when her father bought 1,000 acres in the bush and took his family from Persia, now Iran, where Doris had been born six years earlier. She experienced a childhood which she has often described as unhappy, and one of its main components was solitude. From an early age her life involved rejection, first of a community in which she watched people being demeaned and then of the Marxist solution which she thought, for a while, might be the answer. 'What fools we were!' she said long afterwards about her ten years or so in the Communist Party.

Her first marriage ended and she left her husband and two children for Gottfried Lessing, whom she'd met at a Communist book club. They had a son together but were divorced in 1949 when she decided to move to London to pursue her writing career, taking her son with her. The government of Southern Rhodesia would later accuse her of 'subversive activities' for arguing that the black population was being exploited, and she was labelled a prohibited immigrant. A phase of her life was over. It had begun in the shadow of the First World War, in which her father lost a leg: she saw him as representative of a whole generation who had been ruined by war. Africa also saddened her and made her angry. London was to be a new start.

As a writer, however, she continued to refuse to be confined, and that has been her spirit from the beginning. In *The Golden Notebook*, published in 1962, she wrote about a woman undergoing a breakdown – in a world that seems to be breaking from its moorings – and presented an unforgettable picture of her efforts to compartmentalize her life to deal with its disintegration. The novelist Margaret Drabble, one of the British writers from the sixties influenced strongly by feminist ideas, has said of the book: 'Here was a writer who said the unsayable, thought the unthinkable, and fearlessly put it down there, in all its raw emotional and intellectual chaos. She managed to make sense of her material, but at enormous risk.' The unsayable, among other things, was to talk about menstruation in the way that James Joyce had talked of masturbation and shaken Ireland, and also to subject to meticulous scrutiny the pressures and desires, and the trade-offs they demanded, experienced by women of the early sixties. All that, and around them a world in which leftist progressives were having to cope with the Russians' own revelations and denunciation of Stalinist terror. Bleakness unconfined.

Drabble pointed out that in *The Golden Notebook* Lessing was simultaneously progressive and conservative. When Anna, the main character, who is a writer, is discussing orgasm and the rights and wrongs of sex with a man whom she doesn't love, her Jungian analyst promotes a view that is traditionalist about sexual loyalty rather than radically modern and free-thinking. The book's power lies in its relentless, page-by-page denunciation of simplistic thinking. No doubt that is why it unsettled so many people who recognized it for the radical text that it was and then found it unexpectedly disturbing.

When Lessing wrote *The Golden Notebook* this novel was controversial, not least among women critics, for some of whom, in the course of a few years, it would become something of an inspiration and almost a fictional textbook for feminism. Just as she had refused to be confined by the effective apartheid of her upbringing, and then by too rigid a political reaction to it, she was not going to be turned into an icon, or even a heroine, by anyone.

Much later, in the nineties, she spoke in an interview about her regular arguments with feminists for whom she was an inspiration on the page but an irritation in the flesh. She caused a furore at the Edinburgh book festival in 2001 by suggesting that too many men were being given a hard time by women, and that they deserved less bashing: 'I have nothing in common with feminists because of their inflexibility. They never seem to think that one might like men, or enjoy them.' She came to believe that what she called 'the rubbishing of men' had become part of contemporary culture and she was having none of it.

Her refusal ever to be dragooned into a cause, or stuck in a rut, meant that she has never felt pressured to say 'the right thing'. She was asked by *Time* magazine about Robert Mugabe's Zimbabwe and said she would never go back because he was 'a monstrous little terror ... who had created a caste, a layer of people just like himself who are corrupt and crooked'. And then, for good measure, explaining how she believed the country had been ruined, she said: 'Under the whites it was an extremely efficient country. It could grow absolutely everything. We had railways and post offices and roads and water that worked. You can't just put that back overnight.'

So the young woman whose first writing had revealed her horror was willing to reflect on the experience in a way that few others, radicalized in colonial Africa, would find it easy to do. Lessing's mark has always been a refusal to follow a predictable line of argument, and not to care very much what others are making of it.

Just as she rejected the politics that first attracted her in forties Africa, where she thought everything hopeless under a status quo that couldn't last, so she would not go down the road with some of those who used *The Golden Notebook* as an inspiration, as she once put it to the *New York Times* in a way that was semi-religious: 'They want me to bear witness,' she said. 'What they would really like me to say is "Ha, sisters, I stand with you side by side in your struggle towards the golden dawn where all those beastly men are no more." Do they really want people to make oversimplified statements about men and women? In fact, they do. I've come with great regret to this conclusion.'

Although her antennae have retained a sensitive feeling for injustice – she has written of the uphill struggle of women in Pakistan and Afghanistan, for example – she preferred, after the sixties, to shift her focus to a place that was mystical rather than part of the world. In *The Golden Notebook*, Anna, in the course of trying to sort herself out, expresses interest in mysticism, and it was a clue to the path that Lessing herself would follow. She became interested in the mystic Islamic practice of Sufism. More than 1,000 years ago it was practised as a way of counteracting what was seen even then – though not in these words – as a preoccupation with the material world, the here and now. So many of Lessing's themes, in books set in different places, in different times, have concerned a means of escape (or self-realization) that it was, in retrospect, quite a natural thing, although surprising at the time. And few of those who were moved and inspired by *The Golden Notebook* would have expected its author, within ten years, to turn her attention to science fiction. That is what she did.

For twenty years she was writing books which touched on mystical ways of thinking, and in the middle of that period she published a five-book sequence – *Canopus in Argos: Archives* – set in a fictional galactic empire. In it she explored the idea which so attracted her: that individuals can find satisfaction and succour in working for a universal rather an individual good.

Lessing's place in the novelists' hall of fame – she was awarded the Nobel Prize for Literature in 2007 – came about in part because of that ability to inhabit different fictional worlds with a surefootedness that seemed unique. She was capable of travelling back from the galaxy of Canopus in 1985, for example, to write *The Good Terrorist*, which explored the ambiguities of a middle-class woman, converted to terrorism. It was a book ahead of its time, dealing with subjects that would become near-obsessions of writers of fiction two decades later. That easy breadth, the ability to move from the mystical to the horribly rational, has always been her special power: in her eighties she was writing novels about a love of cats, in *The Old Age of El Magnifico*, and about the grown-up years of Ben, the social misfit, whom she had introduced in a book twenty years before.

Running through it all has been a commitment to the business of literature that has given Lessing a special status among other writers. She began to write in the forties, published first in the fifties, and has been moving and startling her readers ever since. It's a trade she cares about. In the 1980s she wrote two books under a pseudonym – Jane Somers – to show how difficult it is to be published, and for unknown writers to start to do what she had done. They not only had difficulty being published, but didn't sell well.

It's maybe the mark of Doris Lessing that where other writers might have been embarrassed or irritated by that, she was pleased. In her nineties, after a lifetime's work at it, she is still determined to resist group thinking, being drawn along. She remains her own woman, and has made her point.

Alan Sainsbury

WHEN ALAN SAINSBURY walked into one of the first self-service shops opened by his family in Croydon, south London, at the start of the 1950s, a shopper, on being told who he was, threw a new wire basket at him in a fury. Not everyone wanted cheese wrapped up instead of being cut by a wire, nor their vegetables pre-packed. But Sainsbury knew that many did and that soon they would be the majority.

He'd been convinced in the United States. In 1949 he went there to look at the experience of shoppers in the lengthening chains of stores that were criss-crossing the country. Even before the war, 40 per cent of American shopping was self-service, the supermarkets having mushroomed through the Depression, giving people value for money and cutting out the frills, except for those sturdy brown paper bags that many of them are still reluctant to throw away. Sainsbury – 'Mr Alan' to the company board, which was still dominated by the family – argued that it was the future in Britain. There was scepticism. But he was given a chance to try.

Sainsbury's had been started in 1869 as a dairy in Drury Lane in central London and had built up a big business with shops in many parts of the country. In the twenties it expanded into general groceries (and watched with interest when another company set up shop in 1929: Tesco). So the network existed. What hadn't happened in Britain was the change to self-service. Customers still expected personal service from a person in a white coat, if it was a grocer's, and perhaps a conversation about the apples, or an investigation into the age of a cheese.

Who owned the shop was less important. After all, about a quarter of shopping in the years immediately before the war was done in co-operatives, and another quarter in shops that were part of a chain. Small, independent retailers were cherished on every high street, but they were not the whole story. The big retailers were spreading their influence, and Sainsbury came back from America convinced that it was time for revolution: self-service shopping would take off. At that early shop in Croydon he was proved right. Despite having had to dodge the flying wire basket, he saw a shop that attracted customers like bees to a honeypot. Mr Alan had got it right, and he became the architect of the changing high street, and the retail parks that were still some way off but would change the landscape. He was the father of the British supermarket.

Sainsbury started serving as an apprentice in the family store in Bournemouth, at the Boscombe branch, keeping his name a secret. He did time in the dairy department, working for Uncle Arthur and Uncle Alfred, when it was still the rule that only members of the family could order the eggs and milk. Having known the founders – he was born in 1902, only thirty-three years after the first shop opened – he had an attachment to the firm as a family concern but made a connection between that inheritance and what would now be called social responsibility. He'd worked in a charity mission in the East End of London and in the thirties his politics were not conventional for a rising figure in a rich business family. He'd thought of committing himself to some kind of social work but eventually did the inevitable, saying his mother told him it would break his father's heart if he didn't.

He campaigned for the Republican side in the Spanish Civil War, making common cause with Conservatives and Communists in the process, and became a committed member of the Liberal Party (he would join Labour in 1945 and be a founding member of the SDP in the eighties). During the Second World War he represented the grocers to the Ministry of Food when decisions were being taken on rationing, arguing strongly for a points system, which he thought would be fair, though frugal. Everyone would be entitled to something.

That was characteristic of the opinionated zeal that Sainsbury brought to his business. There was no contradiction between producing good balance sheets for the firm and providing what he considered to be a kind of public service: decent provisions at a good price. There was always an idea around the corner that could make it happen, which is why he was so excited when he came back from the United States with his vision of aisles of deep freezers.

In 1950 the change hadn't started. Marks & Spencer had done a trial of self-service a couple of years earlier, but was still very cautious. Shoppers, constrained by the surviving bits of the rationing regime, still preferred a butcher's shop with sawdust and gleaming tiles, grocers who smelt of rennet and built pyramids of home-made butter on a wooden counter. Sainsbury, however, had seen the future and within a year he knew he was right.

There were about fifty self-service shops in business by the end of that year, and they spread like mushrooms – nearly 600 by the end of the decade, when Sainsbury's had started to use the new medium of television advertising, choosing as its star product that strange new beast, the frozen chicken.

The transition had involved some risks. It was expensive to build new premises, and there was some resistance among shoppers who already started to fret about the loss of the special atmosphere in old-style stores, which they could see threatened. Perhaps there was an element of regret for the withering away of a deferential relationship between shop staff and customers, at a time when the growth in personal consumption – of greater choice – was equated with modernization and the new. Washing machines were in most homes, fridges in many kitchens, and habits had changed. In the late forties *The Grocer* magazine had said portentously: 'The people of this country have long been accustomed to counter service and it is doubtful whether they would be content to wander a store hunting for goods.' Well, now they were. Indeed, it seemed rather smart – a new way of doing things.

Looking back from a time when the wheel has turned, and supermarkets are often painted as the villains who despoil landscapes and homogenize the high street, it's intriguing to remember how fresh and exciting the supermarket revolution once seemed. Fruit and vegetables began to appear all the year round, you could fill a freezer and live off it for weeks, like a camel and its hump. And for the supermarkets there was a bonus: not only shoppers with more money to spend, and a higher turnover in shops that could eventually sell anything, but fewer staff. They could make more money.

Alan Sainsbury was at the heart of one of the changes that made this even easier for the supermarkets. In the last of the Conservatives' thirteen years in power, 1964, Edward Heath, as Lord Privy Seal in the government of Sir Alec Douglas-Home, pushed through a measure that split his party and had caused almost as much trouble for Douglas-Home's predecessor, Harold Macmillan, as the Profumo scandal which is so closely associated with his departure from Downing Street on health grounds in autumn 1963. That issue was the abolition of resale price maintenance, or RPM. Many Conservatives hated this decision.

RPM was a form of price fixing which meant that producers could set a price with the shops that couldn't be undercut. Their income was guaranteed and small shopkeepers, without any of the advantages of economies of scale, could compete on level terms with the supermarkets that were now opening in every town. Ted Heath argued that competition was better and eventually got his way, in spite of the biggest backbench rebellion a Tory government had seen since the last days of Neville Chamberlain's government in 1940. The wounds were raw, and didn't help the party in trying to prevent the election of Labour under Harold Wilson, who squeaked in with a majority of four in October 1964.

For the supermarkets it was a godsend. They had the strength to sell more cheaply, introduce the era of the 'special offer', and watch the long, slow decline of the small family business that had to rely on the loyalty of customers who were willing to pay more for the privilege or convenience of walking round the corner, holding a conversation with a shop assistant and never having to join a queue of trolleys.

Within five years of the abolition of RPM, the number of supermarkets in Britain had reached 3,700 and the age of the battle between giants had begun. When Sainsbury retired as chairman in 1967, his business was established as the market leader. Tesco opened its first superstore in 1968 in Sussex, a harbinger of the future. It was nearly thirty years before it overtook its old rival, in 1995, and went on to claim a market share of more than 31 per cent. By 2006 it was able to use the extraordinary statistic that in that year Tesco's tills swallowed up fully an eighth of all consumer spending in the whole country.

The supermarkets' dominance had come about by the exploitation in the seventies and eighties of relaxed planning laws, which gave birth to the retail parks, and marketing techniques that allowed supermarkets to be sure that the bigger they got the more vigorously they could apply their power to keep producers' prices down, give shoppers ever-better offers, and fill their stores with anything and everything. By the end of the century that power became controversial because it sometimes seemed to be untrammelled, sweeping away everything in its path, even infiltrating high streets with their own versions of 'local' stores to make life even more difficult, or impossible, for little shops without their power to sell in bulk, and cheaply. Planners, local authorities, family businesses, farmers all struggled with a balance that seemed to tilt decisively towards the big battalions. The story of the fightback on the high street would be another chapter, but the world that Sainsbury left behind when he died in 1998 aged 92 was one in which the supermarket was king.

He remembered a family firm started with capital of £100 that became the first of the giant supermarkets in Britain, and had seen a way of life transformed. He was proud of saying that part of him remained an outsider – he was the businessman who joined the Labour Party in 1945 and was never a Conservative – and he retained a strong belief that social responsibility should come with wealth. His family has continued that tradition with a notable commitment to arts and charities of all kinds. He always wanted to run a certain kind of shop. That often showed through. At the same time as he was campaigning for an end to RPM, knowing how much power it would give the supermarkets, he was fighting the introduction of trading stamps to lure customers into stores. In the early sixties he told a newspaper interviewer that Sainsbury's wouldn't use them. He told her, 'You must go elsewhere for your temptation.'

Yet temptation had always been his business. More food, better quality, lower prices, and supermarkets everywhere – on every high street and in every open space that Sainsbury's and its rivals could find, where they'd continue their endless battle for supremacy: a battle in which Mr Alan had been the first general on the field. He relished the fight, and, in his time, he won.

Alfred Hitchcock

ALFRED HITCHCOCK WAS THE FAT MAN who wanted to make our flesh creep. Like Dickens's fat boy, he could think of nothing better to do. Indeed, he devoted a lifetime to it and seemed never happier than when he was managing disturbance and alarm. That happiness, however, was never revealed: the bulbous, jowly, black-suited master of suspense never let the mask slip, and didn't smile. The compact had to be secure: I scare you, *because you want to be scared*. And when I look for fear, I promise you that I will find it.

Whereas the Hammer horror films of the fifties and sixties camped up the gore and the cobwebbed coffin lids, and gave us a keyboard of vampire incisors, they hardly bothered with genuine terror. That was Hitchcock's business, and obsession: a prairie cornfield with no hiding place from the buzzing aeroplane, a window that couldn't keep out the prying spy, a murderer's eyes that never blinked, the shower stall that promised relief behind the curtain.

Digging away at his past, people have found a solitary East London boy, born in the last year of the nineteenth century, who often felt alone, had an awestruck relationship with his mother, a father who once sent him to be locked up in the local police cell so that he would realize what it would be like if he strayed, and lots of Catholic guilt filtered through a Jesuit education. That is tempting material, of course. But remember the power of the early cinema, the movie business, which dragged him in like a magnet and gave him energy. By the time he was 21, having trained as a draughtsman, he had volunteered to work on silent movies in north London studios, and he was allowed to direct his first film within four years. Then he was off, working in Germany and absorbing expressionism, seeing the first directors working on sound stages, casting an eye over what the Russians were up to. He had grasped what film offered, and by 1929 he was directing the first British talkie, *Blackmail*. What else could the first Hitchcock film be called?

And so, by the last thirty years of his life – he was knighted in 1980, the year he died – he was inseparable from the idea of suspense. You might have thought that he'd invented the idea, because the portrayal of lonely terror seemed to come naturally. Take two of his last, best films, *The Birds*, released in 1963, and *Psycho* from 1960.

For a whole generation of cinema-goers, the jagged rhythms of Bernard Herrman's score for *Psycho* take them back to the moment when they first saw the film – and, at Hitchcock's insistence, had been there when the drapes were pulled back from the screen, because no one was allowed to come in after it had started. For it was then that they began the journey into a netherworld of fears, with the camera meandering and finally forcing its way from the sky towards a window for the first scene, and the set-up for tragedy. With Hitchcock there was never any doubt that the veneer of normality was a fake or a delusion: the interest from the first long, probing and inquisitive camera shot – some of them were astonishingly long – was in what it *hadn't* revealed and what lay behind. He was naturally attracted to the idea that much of life was a deception. The excitement always lay in stripping away the layers, one by one, to show what lurked underneath. You knew before you started that the revelation was going to be troubling, and familiar.

He was attracted to Daphne du Maurier's short story *The Birds* because he remembered a story of a bird invasion in California, and knew she shared his understanding of fear. Her novel *Rebecca*, replete with menace and lust in the shadow of Manderley, its encroaching gardens and the greedy sea, had brought him his only Oscar for Best Picture in 1940 (with Laurence Olivier and Joan Fontaine). He got the writer Evan Hunter to write the screenplay for *The Birds* – in another guise he was the sublime American crime writer Ed McBain – and together they created a picture of horror. From the moment the first gull settles on a fencepost, through the relentless gathering of wings in the sky, to the desperate struggle against the coming disaster, Hitchcock spins out the panic, refusing to let it become overwhelming and resolve itself too soon. There's always hope, which is the worst thing of all.

These films came after a few years in which he'd released, among others, *Dial M for Murder*, *Rear Window*, the remake of *The Man Who Knew Too Much*, *Vertigo* and *North by Northwest*. They all played with his knowledge that you could find fear in an open space as easily as in a locked room, and terror was never far away. For *Rear Window* he had thirty-one apartments built, into which Jimmy Stewart could spy from the wheelchair in which he was marooned. And before those, at the very start of the fifties, had come *Strangers on a Train*, where he'd explored guilt and responsibility between the two men who are drawn into a murder plot, an unconsummated homoerotic dalliance and an exchange of terrible intimacies. Who's guilty? Hitchcock seldom says. He had Patricia Highsmith to thank for the idea, from her dark novella, and he repaid the compliment.

In the history of British film-making he commands a lofty niche. He was making celebrated thrillers in the thirties – *The Lady Vanishes*, *The Thirty-Nine Steps* – and certainly into the sixties (*Marnie* was released in 1964) he still cast his spell. You can't imagine cinema in that period without him. Quite apart from his happy and very lucrative years introducing spine-chilling stories on American television, in which he revelled in the persona of the seedy purveyor of gloom, he had become for film-goers the guarantee of menace. As he well knew, people sometimes needed it. Although he had taken US citizenship in 1955, and had lived there since the thirties, he still had the echo of the streets of London in that gravelly voice, with a distinctive plummy cockney roll, and it spoke of an understanding of the dark side. He played on it, with the deadpan relish that he used when he did his silent walk-on parts, lasting only a few seconds, in most of the films.

He was one of the earliest heroes of the British film industry. In the post-war era there were many others. David Lean, too, began in black and white and made the dazzling transition to colour and the big screen with epics that became some of the most celebrated films of the age. The home-based industry repeatedly produced directors who belied the weary arguments over the lack of money and the draining effect on creativity. Mike Leigh and Ken Loach have carved out distinctive arcs; a host of other craftsmen drew on the European tradition to try to resist Hollywood. And others, to great acclaim, joined in with Tinseltown and quite often beat it at its own game: the Merchant Ivory school and the social comedies of the nineties had massive success that, whatever anyone said afterwards, wasn't expected when they started out.

Hitchcock's story takes us back to an earlier era. He learned his craft at a time when, to our eyes, the films were jerky and the cutting crude. Yet his daring mobility with the camera – a lens seeming to probe into every corner in search of the *real* story – was a technique that would remain an indelible part of his director's personality a generation later, like his love of the sharp, edgy contours of a black and white set, straight from an expressionist drawing. That lasting quality also came from his belief, quite a rigid one, in how you scared an audience. He never wavered.

That made him difficult for some actors and writers to work with. Tippi Hedren played the female leads in *The Birds* and *Marnie* a year later, and she found it hard. Hitchcock, married contentedly to Alma Reville for thirty years, seemed to have a fascination with cool blondes as vulnerable characters: their accounts suggest that it puzzled them because it was never explained, not least because it wasn't the prelude to the sexual invitations that were associated with some directors, and which they might have expected from anyone else. In an interview with the French film-maker François Truffaut, who probed this sensitive area, Hitchcock said that he was celibate and wondered aloud whether the simmering sexual tension in many of his films was how he allowed the frustration a way out.

The trouble was that cruelty was his business. In his meticulous shooting scripts – improvisation on set was never his style – he was setting scenes that would reveal vulnerability, expose emotional double dealing, and bring out moral ambiguity like some restless motif deep in the double basses of an orchestra that works its way through the woodwind until it reaches the first violins and becomes the dominant theme.

He'd ask his audiences: who is really guilty? The nightmare in *Psycho* is one that Anthony Perkins as Norman Bates couldn't escape from, even if he wanted to. It's beyond him. Solitude, in madness or in terrible sanity, is often inevitable. Hitchcock had no interest in indulging in discussions about how his Catholicism kept him wedded to the theme of fallen human beings who were forced to struggle for a path to redemption. But it's hard to look at his heroes and villains, and their companions along the way, and not see something of that acceptance in their predicament: that it is not their fault that they are walking through a vale of tears. There is nothing else for us.

The moral Hitchcock? It's easier to think of him as the man who said there was no terror in a bomb going off, only in knowing that the explosion was going to come. He understood that watching a man stepping closer to the edge is only terrifying if you can see into the chasm and he can't; and, above all, that disaster usually springs from innocence. Think of the chase on the Statue of Liberty in *Saboteur* (with the camera seemingly caught up in it), Cary Grant on the stone faces of the presidents on

Mount Rushmore in *North by Northwest*, the first glimpse of the Bates motel in *Psycho*. They never pall or fade away. Each time there's a tiny spasm of recognition: that is fear, that's what danger means.

For all the technique, the tricks of the trade, his own psychological preoccupations, his love of the business, that what was made him great. We understood, always, that he *knew*.

Laurence Olivier

Towards the end of his career Laurence Olivier made a confession about why he had become an actor. The thing he had been searching for all his life was the opportunity to amaze. 'I can't disguise myself any more,' he told an interviewer, as if that lust for the stage had been a secret. The truth is that it never was: one of the reasons why Peter Hall, for example, thought he might have been the greatest man of theatre we'd ever known was surely that everyone understood that his characters sprang from a passion for creation. It burned inside him.

When Archie Rice, in John Osborne's *The Entertainer*, says, 'I'm dead behind these eyes,' he's talking about a talent to amuse that has dried up, having never flowed very strongly in the first place. The feet still try to find the tap-dance routines, but they've gone. Olivier played him, first in 1957, with an understanding of that longing. With Archie it was talent unfulfilled; with Olivier himself it was talent that could never quite be satisfied. Whatever he did, he always wanted more.

That was because he knew he was gifted. Ellen Terry, an actress who had enthralled Edwardian theatre-goers, watched a performance of *Julius Caesar* at the Church of England primary school he attended and wrote in her diary: 'The small boy who played Brutus is already a great actor.' Olivier was 10. That was in 1917.

By the time he was in his early twenties he had reached Hollywood, like a moth drawn to the flame, and he was duly singed. He was going to be Greta Garbo's leading man in *Queen Christina*, and was dumped; and when he started filming *Wuthering Heights* the producer Sam Goldwyn thought it would be a disaster. Fortunately the director, William Wyler, kept faith and his Heathcliff was a success, leading straight on the next year, 1940, to *Rebecca*, in which his haunting inability to deal with sexual obsession confirmed that when you were looking for a brooding hero, with *life* behind those eyes, Olivier was your man.

The brilliant stroke that turned that success into something deeper was *Henry V*, the Shakespearean king who touched him with heroism. He directed the film in 1944 (after Wyler and Carol Reed both pulled out), the year of the D-Day landings in occupied Europe, and William Walton produced a score that was the soundtrack of victory. The war in Europe would – everyone believed – soon be over, and against the backdrop of family trag-edies and the devastation visited on so many cities, especially London, it was time for sights to be raised. The Ministry of Information had decided that the battle of Agincourt ~~what~~ was just what was required to remind people of the glory that was war. A *Henry V* bursting with patriotic fervour seemed just right, and Olivier gave him that voice. He made himself inseparable from a victory that people persuaded themselves had been inevitable.

Still in his mid-thirties, he was already a Shakespearean actor of breadth and panache. He'd been seen in London as Hamlet, Macbeth, Coriolanus and Iago, and came to film with a technique and a confidence – what the director Tyrone Guthrie called a 'muscularity' – that already seemed fully formed. He was flying. His first Shakespeare had been a decade before in *Romeo and Juliet* at the invitation of John Gielgud (with whom he swapped the roles of Romeo and Mercutio back and forth through the run), with Peggy Ashcroft as Juliet, but within a year or two he was leading the Old Vic company on his own.

He played Hamlet for the first time in 1937 for Guthrie and you get a sense of what a puzzle he was from the comments of James Agate, who was the incisive critic of the *Sunday Times* and therefore feared. Mr Olivier, he said, didn't speak poetry badly; the thing was that he didn't speak it at all. But he added this: that there was a pulsating vitality and excitement about his performance. J.C. Trewin, another of the critical giants of the time, said that his Coriolanus the following year was 'a pillar of fire on a plinth of marble'.

It meant that after the success of the film of *Henry V* – which got him his first Oscar – he was ready to exploit that experience for a wider audience, for whom Hollywood had turned him into the feral lover of *Wuthering Heights*, then the mysterious obsessive of *Rebecca* caught between innocence and guilt and the boy king with a warrior's spirit. The years that followed saw him propelled ever upwards. In the seasons at the Old Vic immediately after the war he played more Shakespeare – entrancing a teenage Peter Hall, whom he inspired with a love of the stage that would change his life – and in 1947 he became the youngest actor to be knighted. Everything was at his feet – which didn't stop him making a film of *Hamlet* in 1948 that cut great swaths of the text and drained his performance of some of the zest people had experienced in the theatre. That didn't prevent Hollywood giving the film four Oscars: they had decided Olivier was theirs, and loved him.

There was never any danger that he would stop playing himself in a way that the public wanted. And then there was his love life. He met Vivienne Leigh when he was filming *Fire over England* and, like Elizabeth Taylor and Richard Burton a generation later, they conducted a public affair that seemed to consume them, which is why their public loved it. Leigh left her lawyer husband behind in London to pursue Olivier to Los Angeles, seemingly incapable of being away from him, and then turned it into a fairy tale by winning the part of Scarlett O'Hara in 1940 in *Gone With the Wind* (although Victor Fleming decided she would have to put up with Clark Gable as her leading man, Rhett Butler, and not Olivier). But even before the film was released he had divorced, and so had she, so that they could marry. It was as if they were making a statement that they were going to have a fiery time together, throwing themselves together with abandon into the flames, and they did.

Celebrity gossip-mongers watched every twist and turn, and the story was all the better for Olivier's response: far from being weakened by the picture of a reckless love, he thrived on it. When his Oedipus confronted the fact that he had killed his father and married his mother, Kenneth Tynan – always ready to charge over the top – said that Olivier's scream contained '3,000 years of confrontation with the fates, the gods, with himself'. The actor said that he had perfected the noise by reading the account of how ermine are trapped for their fur: they lick salt scattered in the snow and, finding it stuck to their tongue, scream. He imagined what it must be like.

That was a typical piece of Olivier's debunking of the idea that he might have an irresistible force in him that just found its way out: he was always keen to talk about how he worked at the artifice of the theatre, with the stage his laboratory. On one hand he was celebrated for his vesuvial passion, which seemed to pour out from the depths, and on the other he liked to speak of the tricks of the trade. A stream of stories has him sniffing at actors who used 'the method', trying to think themselves into the emotions of the character instead of creating the performance piece by piece. A famous victim was said to be Dustin Hoffman, although he insisted that he looked rough on the set of *Marathon Man* only because he had been partying, and not from spending a sleepless night in order to replicate the feelings of a tortured man. There's no argument about Olivier's advice to him, however: 'Try acting, my dear boy. It's much easier.'

As he was reaching the top of his own theatrical career, in the late forties, that ability to take on a new persona with apparently little effort had become dazzling. The Oedipal scream that chilled

Kenneth Tynan's blood in 1945 came on a night in which Oliver starred in a double bill: Oedipus in one half, and in the other Mr Puff, the frothy fop in Sheridan's *The Critic* who'd be incapable of saying boo to a goose, let alone killing his father and sleeping with his mother.

The Old Vic seasons after the war confirmed Olivier's place as the leading man of the English-speaking stage, and they produced something else in him that left a legacy maybe as important as those performances. He found that he enjoyed leading a company. A seed had been planted. In 1948, at a time of vigour in the post-war cultural debate, the first moves were made to establish a National Theatre. Might Olivier like to make his company the foundation stone? He certainly would. But by the time he returned from a tour of Australia and New Zealand the first of many disappointments had come along. The scheme was in ruins, not for the last time. He and Ralph Richardson were dropped by the Old Vic as actor-directors because the theatre had gone cold on the idea of a National Theatre. There was jealousy in the air. Everything ground to a halt.

It was one of the reasons that the early fifties were a gloomy time for Olivier, and by the time the British theatre was being given a hefty kick by John Osborne with *Look Back in Anger* in 1956 he was, in the words of his biographer Anthony Holden, 'going mad and desperately searching for something suddenly fresh and thrillingly exciting'. The marriage to Leigh was taking its inevitable course towards a bitter break-up, he'd had a terrible time directing Marilyn Monroe in *The Prince and the Showgirl* in 1957, and then came Osborne's second play, *The Entertainer*, at the Royal Court Theatre in London.

Olivier was a picture of despair on stage, revealing Archie Rice as a broken, empty vessel brought face to face with his all-consuming failure. So by the sixties he was taking on new roles, full of energy, still capable of dominating in Shakespeare but turning to Tom Stoppard too, in *Rosencrantz and Guildenstern Are Dead*.

And the National Theatre was back. The Old Vic would house the company until a new theatre was built, but, even without a proper home, it would exist. Olivier was in charge and throughout the sixties, as the Royal Shakespeare Company, founded in 1960, was beginning to develop a personality and style, he was powering ahead in parallel, leading a company that seemed to *deserve* a home. By the time it was built, on the South Bank in London in the early seventies, the board had decided that it shouldn't be Olivier who would lead it in its new home, but Peter Hall, who'd built up the RSC. Time had moved on. But the biggest theatre at the National would be the Olivier, which it still is.

By the time it opened, Olivier's career was past its zenith. He took on too many second-rate films for the money, and in the seventies became, quite quickly, an actor who stirred great memories rather than gave fine performances. With Joan Plowright, his third wife, he represented a kind of aristocracy of the theatre that was losing its power, and gradually he slipped from view. As he put it in a interview with *Newsweek* in 1979, perhaps half disingenuous and half self-pitying: 'I can't disguise myself any more. I'm afraid the audience know me too well. They know every shade of the voice, every trick, every goddam movement I can make.'

But when he died, in 1989 at the age of 82 after a long, wasting illness that sapped his strength, the memories came pouring back, etched for ever in the minds of those who had enjoyed him on stage and shared his story. His actor friend Anthony Quayle, when he heard of Olivier's death, said that it marked 'the closing of a very great book'.

Benjamin Britten

BENJAMIN BRITTEN WAS A MUSICIAN who was English in every way – in social habit and in manner, by religion and upbringing, in his sensibilities and outlook – who spoke to the whole world as an *outsider*, with a voice that was his alone. The Russian giant Dmitri Shostakovich, the most celebrated symphonist of the twentieth century, once said to him: 'You great composer; I little composer.'

He was original in chamber music and opera, in choral arrangement and song, in orchestral works of every kind. He had a gift for writing for children's voices that was unique, and he was a pianist of brilliance, producing what was once described as the shimmer of sound like the shudder of electricity. He was the complete musician, whose character was stamped on his work and gleamed through every note. But Leonard Bernstein noted that his power came from being 'at odds with the world', and Britten himself said of music: 'It has the beauty of loneliness, of pain; of strength and freedom; the beauty of disappointment and never-satisfied love.'

As a description of himself, it is a good start; like his confession that two of the things he cherished most were night and silence. Behind the confidence of a musician of all the talents lay a vulnerability that never left him. Music had always offered him thrilling excitement, but solace too. In the sixties he recalled from school-days 'the vocal and energetic surprise with which the other small boys caught me reading orchestral scores in bed'. His emotions were released by music, and soothed by it, from an early age. He wrote a symphony when he was 12 and at 14 started taking lessons from the composer Frank Bridge; by the time he graduated from the Royal College of Music he was writing for the orchestra and the musical stage with astonishing verve. In his twenties he was commissioned to cooperate with the poet W.H. Auden on a Post Office film. The result was *Night Mail*, and Auden told him that he was 'the white hope of music'.

Soon afterwards came war, and the experience caused Britten to walk through fire and, more than any other event, shaped the musician who would be the unquestioned master of the era that followed, to the day of his death in December 1976, at the age of 63. If he had suspected as a boy that he was destined to be an outsider, the war confirmed it. He couldn't put aside his pacifist convictions, and decided to remain in the United States, where he'd travelled with his friend Peter Pears and joined the circle dominated by Auden and Christopher Isherwood. Though he was still in his twenties, he said: 'The whole of my life has been devoted to creation, and I cannot take part in acts of destruction.' For two and a half years of the war he stayed away from home, and by the time he came back his life had taken another decisive turn: his relationship with Pears had solidified and they would be companions for the rest of his life, proudly and defiantly (in a country where homosexuality remained illegal until Britten was in his fifties). He was excused military service because of his contribution to cultural life and threw himself into work.

Those years marked the start of his transformation into a master composer. On the Swedish freighter that carried him and Pears back across the Atlantic he wrote his plangent unaccompanied *Hymn to St Cecilia* (he was born on St Cecilia's Day) and when he landed in Liverpool he set about having a libretto written for an opera that was taking shape in his mind, inspired by reading while in America George Crabbe's poem 'The Village', which took him back to his childhood on the Suffolk coast. The result was *Peter Grimes*, for many people the greatest opera written in English in the twentieth century.

The picture of dark loneliness in the fisherman Grimes is unforgettable, picturing a solitude that is impenetrable and shivering with violence, confronted as he is by the claustrophobic power that a community can summon up when in the grip of fear. The opera had its first night at Sadler's Wells in London a month after the end of the war in Europe in 1945, and although Britten spent the whole three hours stalking around the back of the stalls in agitation it was an immediate success. There's a famous story of a conductor on a Number 38 bus shouting to passengers as it turned into Rosebery Avenue: 'Any more for Peter Grimes, the sadistic fisherman?'

It was the opera that lifted Britten to a new level, and over the next fifteen years he produced a string of them that would be performed around the world – *Billy Budd*, *The Turn of the Screw* and *A Midsummer Night's Dream* the most celebrated – and then in 1962 came another landmark, a commission that brought together his feeling for the voice and some of his deepest passions. He was asked to write a requiem to be performed at the rededication of Coventry Cathedral, bombed in the Second World War. He had the idea of bringing together the Latin mass and the poetry of Wilfred Owen, who had died in the Great War, and the result was a *War Requiem* that spoke with a directness that much contemporary classical music of the time was avoiding, as if it might somehow compromise the art. The recording of that first performance sold 200,000 copies in that year, and Britten's juxtaposition of private grief and suffering with the public business of war made an indelible mark. The German baritone Dietrich Fischer-Dieskau, who sang in the première, said of it: 'I was completely undone. I did not know where to hide my face. Dead friends and past suffering arose in my mind.' The poet Edith Sitwell, a friend of Britten, said she felt as if her tears were turning to blood.

The recording was issued just after the Cuban missile crisis, during which the British were asked to contemplate the possibility of a nuclear holocaust in a confrontation over which they had no control, and for Britten the public appetite for serious music was an affirmation of what he had always believed. Popular culture was about to change, with the liberating torrent of rock and pop about to be unleashed, but he was able to believe that his place as the inheritor of the classical tradition, which he turned to his own purposes, was secure.

By now he and Pears were settled at the Red House at Aldeburgh, on a lonely stretch of the Suffolk shore, a place of pebbled beaches and reed beds, flat farmland and sturdy Norman churches. There they had founded in the forties the Aldeburgh Festival, which became a lodestar for composers and performers from around the world. Visitors came to the Red House as to a shrine: Shostakovich and Bernstein, the world's great singers and instrumentalists, the conductors who were the guardians of the European tradition. Britten would play with them, and write for them. It was there in the early seventies that he welcomed Mstislav Rostropovich, the Russian cello master who had been given 'disapproved' status by the Soviet authorities and, finally, had to leave his homeland, penniless and emotionally broken. Britten welcomed and championed him, and his musical relationship with Rostropovich was one of the most satisfying for him.

The vigour in that musical relationship reveals Britten's zest for life. He was a ragbag of nerves before any performance, and capable of reticence that tipped easily into rudeness and even cruelty to friends. The stories of people finding themselves excluded from the inner circle, cherished then dropped like a stone, are still the folk tales of Aldeburgh. But he also liked fast cars and fun, would start the day with a cold bath to jerk himself into action, and could relax with a party-goer's enthusiasm.

That energy produced his work for children, which is one of his legacies. He particularly loved the sound of boys' unbroken voices – his devotion to the Church of England's choral tradition was a pillar of his life – and in songs, orchestral arrangements and pieces for voice and orchestra like *Noye's Fludde* he was able to do something that few composers of his weight could manage: produce music of great power in a style that meant it could be played or sung by young musicians. Such pieces were introductions to the language of music and its subterranean excitements.

In *Noye's Fludde* he produced an orchestral sound that involves everybody, with some parts written in perfect simplicity, to be played on open strings, for example. It is a masterpiece of construction. Because of Britten's sexuality, which he never tried to conceal despite the social (not to say legal) pressures to do so, there was from time to time prurient speculation about his interest in children. No one has ever been able to contradict what seems the truth: that he was energized innocently by them because inside he felt that he had never really grown up. And, like all his commitments, it never wavered.

He could seem a forbidding figure from outside – a deeply furrowed brow and anxious eyes – but for those who knew him and watched him perform he was a benign magician. Pears said: 'You could watch Ben holding his hands over the piano preparatory to playing a slow movement, a soft, soft chord – and you could see his fingers alert, alive, really sometimes even quivering with intensity. It was amazing what colours he could get: he thought a colour and he could do it.'

As a composer he had no doubt where he stood. He was as English as Elgar, his harmonies evoking a sighing reed bed on his native coast or a stormy sea that springs to life from the page, and a composer who rose above narrow classification. Original, brave, stubborn, with an imagination of genius, he towered above his contemporaries. And from start to finish he lived his life without compromise in exactly the way he wanted, carving a place for himself that would always be his alone.

He refused a knighthood but was a member of the Order of Merit and accepted a life peerage in the year he died. His death was the lead item on the BBC News and his obituaries celebrated a life that had been gilded and, above all, different. That quality was marked in the letter of condolence delivered to Aldeburgh from Buckingham Palace, in a fashion that would have been unthinkable a few years before. The Queen expressed her sadness directly to his lover, Peter Pears. Outsiders no more.

Dorothy Hodgkin

WHEN DOROTHY HODGKIN went up to Oxford University to read chemistry in 1928 she was in a band of pioneers. Not until 1920 had women been admitted as students with the same status as men, and she was one of the early trailblazers. That liberation produced a career in science that took her to the top: to the Royal Society's most celebrated award, to a Nobel Prize, and allowed her to make discoveries that shaped our time.

She cracked the secrets of insulin, penicillin and many proteins in a way that allowed scientists to leap forward. It produced medical advance, research in hitherto closed areas of chemistry, and consequently established whole new areas of study in biology. It was she who showed that understanding how molecules were built could unlock the mysteries of their biological functions. In deciphering the structure of molecules she drew a map: for many scientists it was possible for the first time to see where they were going. One of her admiring colleagues who watched her work over many decades said: 'She was one of these masters whose method of work is as exciting and beautiful to follow as the results that flow from it.' Hodgkin herself summed it up like this: 'I was captured for life by chemistry and by crystals.'

She was also the tutor who introduced the student Margaret Roberts to the chemistry lab and who, forty years on, would argue with that former student, now Margaret Thatcher – politely but resolutely – about her view of the world. With her privileged access to the only British Prime Minister to have a science degree, Hodgkin thought that she could make a rational case for better relations across the Iron Curtain, which was always one of her fervent hopes. She believed that Western scientists should help their Russian and Chinese counterparts, cut off from so much for so long, and never regretted that in the tumult of the sixties she had chosen, as a scientist, to campaign for nuclear disarmament.

Mrs Thatcher told her how much she valued her advice – though politically they were of vividly different political stripes – and she hung a portrait of Hodgkin in her study at Number 10, a striking acknowledgement of her encounter with a formidable intellect. Some in Oxford noticed that on her groundbreaking visit to see Mikhail Gorbachev in Moscow in 1987 the Prime Minister included in her itinerary the Institute of Crystallography, where Hodgkin was a valued friend.

Hodgkin's impact on science can be traced back to the work she started in a small basement room in the corner of the university library in Oxford in the mid-thirties. After graduation as Dorothy Crowfoot – men outnumbered women students in the faculty by twelve to one – she'd gone to Cambridge for her doctorate and returned to a fellowship at Somerville College, with which she would be associated for the rest of her life. She set up X-ray equipment in that small shared laboratory, and published her first serious paper, under her name alone, in 1935. It had the simple and startling title 'X-ray single photographs of insulin': a lifetime of discovery in crystallography had begun. In the next decade her work on the structure of penicillin was published under her married name. She had met her husband, Thomas, in the thirties and – a little reluctantly, it seems – accepted the social convention that from then on she'd be the chemist Hodgkin.

Her method was X-ray crystallography, which allowed you to take a picture of how the atoms fitted together in the molecule.

Her work on penicillin was a revelation because it had proved impervious to that kind of examination in the past: to put it simply, no one knew exactly how penicillin worked. Once you had a picture of it, you knew. The most important discoveries were made during the war and kept secret. Afterwards manufacturers had an interest in maintaining that secrecy for commercial advantage, so it was only in 1949 that, with others, Hodgkin could finally publish her research. It was a time of great excitement because the potential power of the computer was beginning to be understood, and the possibilities of her work were being transformed. By the mid-fifties she had unravelled the complexities of a molecule of vitamin B_{12}, which had long baffled her peers. For a chemist, one of her admiring colleagues said, it was like breaking the sound barrier.

Hodgkin was a woman of striking appearance. She had fair hair and blue eyes and was fond of wearing handmade clothes, in defiance of any fashion that might be around, cutting a notable figure in Oxford. And politically she was fiery. Early on in the thirties, encouraged by her mother to lean to the left, she developed political commitments that she never abandoned. When she was reaching the most productive phase of her life as a chemist, during the fifties, this caused her considerable difficulty. She was a socialist; her husband Thomas was closely associated with the Communist Party and in those days that was a taint that was hard to erase. The State Department in Washington declared her 'statutorily inadmissible' to the United States in 1953, citing her membership of Science for Peace, a body it regarded as little more than a Communist front. At that time, with Senator Joseph McCarthy whipping up alarm about the influence of Communists in American institutions of all kinds, it was very hard for her to overcome the obstacle: academic distinction was not enough. It took her four years – and McCarthy's disgrace and fall from influence – to have that ban waived, but throughout her life she still had to seek special permission each time she visited the United States on academic business.

At home, her alarm about nuclear weapons led her to become one of the most influential scientists attached to the Campaign for Nuclear Disarmament. CND came about as a consequence of an article in the *New Statesman* in 1957 by the writer J.B. Priestley, and by the following Easter it had enough support to organize a four-day march to the nuclear research establishment at Aldermaston. The protest was led by a colourful assortment of public figures, among them the philosopher Bertrand Russell, Canon John Collins of St Paul's Cathedral, the writer and Labour figure Michael Foot and the historian A.J.P. Taylor. Hodgkin was one of CND's first supporters and one of those who, because of her scientific credentials, lent the movement a weight that it would not otherwise have had.

Into the early sixties, the Aldermaston marches at Easter were public events of considerable significance and captured a great deal of attention – although CND had undergone internal splits and Canon Collins resigned the chairmanship – and even after its influence waned quite fast Hodgkin continued throughout that decade to support political campaigns – for example, against American military involvement in Vietnam. She also went on visiting the Soviet Union and China, at a time when contacts were much more difficult than scientists of a later generation could imagine. The fact that one of the reasons she was welcomed so warmly was because of her criticism of the West didn't bother her at all: she wanted to talk to fellow chemists. Until the darkness of Mao Zedong's Cultural Revolution descended and China was cut off from the outside world for years, she was one of the scientists who travelled there regularly from the West, and she was able to report on the progress made by Chinese researchers into insulin, in parallel with her own research. In the last year of her life, 1993, although frail she defied her doctors to attend one last conference in Beijing.

She was criticized for allowing her convictions about scientific cooperation to cause her to ignore the suppression of individual freedom – in the Soviet Union, for example – but she remained

DOROTHY HODGKIN

determined to pursue her contacts however often she might be accused of being politically naïve. In 1987, in old age, she was awarded the Lenin Peace Prize, in the last days of the Soviet Union – and regretted none of her political activity.

All through the sixties she had pushed back the barriers in her chosen field of rescarch. Work in Cambridge demonstrated that protein molecules could indeed be subject to X-ray crystallography and she and her group continued to work on insulin, the subject of her first investigations in the thirties. By 1969 she was able to bring that work to a triumphant conclusion and reveal insulin's whole molecular structure.

The accounts of the climax of that research catch something of the excitement that seemed to well up in every lab where Hodgkin worked. She and her colleagues spent a weekend building a model of the molecule. Suffering from severe rheumatoid arthritis, she was wearing slippers because of her swollen ankles, but like the rest she laboured through the night to complete the model. When it was unveiled a few weeks later it was the product of half a lifetime's work. She put it like this: 'I used to say that the evening I developed the first X-ray photograph I took of insulin in 1935 was the most exciting moment of my life. But the Saturday afternoon in late July 1969, when we realized that the insulin electron density map was interpretable, runs that moment very close.'

From accounts by her colleagues a picture emerges of a passionate and warm woman – her students knew her as 'Dorothy' and nothing else – who was able to inspire them with the excitements of science. Despite the pain she often suffered she had great dexterity in the lab and she loved the practical business of devising experiments and seeing them through, each one a journey of discovery. Her work on vitamin B12 brought her the Nobel Prize for chemistry in 1964 – she was the first woman scientist to have won it since Marie Curie in 1911 – and in the seventies the Royal Society honoured her with its most important award, the Copley Medal. Although she told friends that honours didn't interest her she did accept membership of the Order of Merit in 1965 (on the

77

same day as Benjamin Britten), the first woman to be celebrated in this way since Florence Nightingale.

In her later years Hodgkin had the satisfaction of watching rapid medical advances that owed a great deal to her work in unlocking the structure of molecules, giving biologists the information they needed to understand much that had been impenetrable. And she never lost her appetite for discovery. She once said that 'there are two moments that are important. There's the moment when you know that you can find out the answer and that's the period you are sleepless before you know what it is. When you've got it and know what it is, *then* you can rest easy.'

She had an intriguing hobby. She was born in Cairo (in 1910) and her parents later moved to Sudan. So it was maybe not surprising that she developed an early interest in ancient artefacts and archaeology – as a student she combined archaeology and chemistry until she decided to specialize. And all her life she retained and interest in ancient mosaics in particular – as if they were human creations that matched in their beauty some of the miracles of nature that fascinated her all her days.

Harold Pinter

HAROLD PINTER'S LITERARY CAREER might have finished before it had begun. It was saved by one review of a play which didn't appear until after the play had closed because everyone else thought it was so bad. He kept framed on his wall at home a record of the box-office takings at the Lyric Theatre, Hammersmith, which started at £140 on Monday – the first night of *The Birthday Party* in 1958 – and had dropped to £2 9/- by the Thursday matinée, when only six people came. The reviews suggested that they were brave souls.

Fortunately for Pinter, Harold Hobson of the *Sunday Times* had joined the tiny audience on the Wednesday, and although his notice appeared after the management had decided to cut their losses and close the doors as soon as they could, it did say that he had experienced the most original, arresting and disturbing talent in theatrical London. Pinter had a lifeline, and clung to it. From deep discouragement, he crawled back, kept at it, and within a couple of years that 'arresting' talent was the talk of the town. Later he would not only see that play become one everyone wished they had been at, but also have the mixed pleasure of receiving the Nobel Prize for Literature and having his name pass into the language. For 'Pinteresque' became the label for any silence on the stage that seemed, mysteriously, to be more important than the words that surrounded it.

His understandable despair at that caricature was only one of a host of irritations that risked turning him into a public misanthrope. But that was misleading. If he was on a protest march – especially against some new twist in American foreign policy which he thought devilish – he would appear unbendingly sour and strident, but if he was at Lord's watching a test match he would be a picture of gentleness, soothed by warm beer and conversation about some century of yesteryear or the art of leg spin. His passions were entwined, and not at all simple. Simplicity was something he seemed not to believe in; and his best characters all feared it. They knew that too much clarity in life was dangerous.

He was once asked why he thought so many of his audiences were drawn to the conversations in his plays: why were they so effective? He said: 'I think it's possibly because people fall back on anything they can lay their hands on, verbally, to keep away from the danger of knowing, and of being known.' That struggle to survive by spinning a yarn, or going on the attack, or playing games is one that fascinated him and gave most of his plays their energy. In *No Man's Land*, which is where the two principal characters find themselves, they never explain what they have escaped from or precisely what they fear – except that in circling each other, hinting at darkness, then telling a joke, probing a little, then closing up, they paint for an audience a perfectly comprehensible account of what no man's land is, though you can't be sure of how they got there, how much they want to get out of it, and what their chances are. Worlds of the here and now and of the imagination collide, and we're never sure what the end result will be.

His experience with *The Birthday Party*, which nearly put him off playwriting, occurred when he was in his late twenties. In the following decade he wrote radio plays and revues, film scripts, and two plays in particular that filled West End theatres: *The*

Caretaker and *The Homecoming*. He was also directing and acting, for which he'd trained. He was making money, had a fashionable following, and above all had found a voice. It chimed with the puzzled excitement of the era, because it was questing but unsatisfied, restless and persistent. He'd made the break with the past that he wanted.

Although *The Birthday Party* was quite conventional in form, he was indeed telling his audiences, even then, that they were going to get something more than they were used to. Much later he said: 'I couldn't any longer stay in the room with this bunch of people who opened doors and came in and went out.' So onto the stage came people who didn't obey the rules of theatrical naturalism, sometimes hardly seemed to move, but instead conducted conversations (and held pauses) that were games of hide and seek in which they tried each other out, ran for cover, and were often driven by obsessions and fears that remained mysterious in every way except in their power to disturb and isolate those who felt them.

In *The Caretaker* he examines the relationship between a man who has had mental upheavals and the tramp he befriends. We're not sure who's really in charge. In *The Homecoming* the family around which the play revolves has unresolved misunderstandings and fears that condemn each of its members to a different kind of limbo. Two of his films with Joseph Losey, *The Servant* in 1963 and *Accident* in 1967, poke away at a British class system that gave Pinter, the son of London Jewish parents, a great deal of entertainment but also plenty of anger. Who is controlling whom, and how does it work? This was a question that could never fully be answered, one of the most common feelings for a Pinter audience, whom he was always challenging.

His dramatic grip on audiences in the sixties was produced by the penumbra of mystery that seemed to surround every text, and by his meticulous language, pared down to its skeletal minimum. Conversation was tight, controlled like a fugue, so that patterns repeated themselves and new ideas always changed the shape of the whole. And then there were the pauses. It was obvious that Pinter would become the butt of many jokes about silence, because no one used it quite like he did, and he turned it into a fingerprint on any script. His biographer Michael Billington tells the story of a conversation with the actor Michael Hordern in which Pinter, as director, was giving his notes to the cast after a rehearsal: points he wanted them to note, changes he wanted made. He explained to Hordern how he saw the silent beats in one line, and said: 'I wrote dot, dot, dot and you gave me dot, dot.' The point of the story, Billington says, is that Hordern, as an actor who had understood Shakespearean rhythms all his life, knew immediately the difference between a short pause and the long pause that Pinter was trying to capture.

In struggling for survival, which is what so many of his characters are doing, language is both the battleground and the place of safety. There are weapons to be forged, deceptions to be practised: in his play *Old Times* in 1971 we're never told which of the three characters is telling the truth about the past (if any is). None of this would matter if Pinter was writing in an abstract way about deep feelings that are never properly revealed: there would be no drama, and not even six people at the Thursday matinée. But the reason that he cast a spell on so many audiences was that he understood the nature of dramatic tension: that there is not much fun in not knowing something, unless you suspect that it is sufficiently menacing or dangerous to matter. You have to care.

By the end of the sixties Pinter was the leading English dramatist to make the final break with the cosy past that John Osborne had first confronted with *Look Back in Anger* in the fifties, and had created a language which was his own. In a later play like *Betrayal*, in 1978, he caught perfectly the struggle of two upper-middle-class people to cope with the fallout of an affair and to try to settle who is the greater betrayer. The play, inspired by his own seven-year affair with Joan Bakewell, distils the excitements and the nightmare of the consequences into conversation in which everything that is said points to a much deeper argument that is kept out of the room but is always knocking at the door.

It wasn't surprising that Pinter should use this affair to make drama, because his own life had become increasingly public. He didn't like it, but acknowledged that in a way he was asking for it. Of his failed marriage to the actress Vivien Merchant – they wed in 1956 and she died of alcoholism in 1982 – he said: 'While she was alive, if you think about it, so much of my work was about unhappy frozen married relationships.' He got out of his own by falling in love, in 1975, with Lady Antonia Fraser, writer, daughter of the eccentric Labour peer Lord Longford, member of a famous Catholic family, and wife of a right-wing Conservative MP.

They fell for each other in a trice, married in 1980, and until his death in 2008 they were inseparable. When she wrote a memoir of their time together she called it 'Must You Go?', which she says he said to her at the end of a lunch party at which they hadn't been properly introduced. She stayed, and really never left. They were a gift to the gossip columns, and hardly a week went by without a peashooter being aimed at them, though sometimes it fired a poisoned dart: he was the champagne socialist who protested about human rights abroad but lived in luxury at home; she was the Lady Bountiful of every fashionable cause you could think of that wouldn't be approved of by the papers who attacked them. In short, they had set themselves up as perfect targets.

Romance was in the Pinter mix. On the day they moved in together, Antonia Fraser remembers, the house was filled with flowers, with Pinter, nervous, emotional, bubbling with fun. Under the stern exterior, which got even darker in his last years as he threw himself into protests over war and human rights, was an almost schoolboyish appetite for fun. It seems as unlikely as the fact that he trained as a young actor in Donald Wolfit's Shakespeare touring company, famous for the over-the-top histrionics of its actor-manager. Yet Pinter said that Wolfit's Lear was the best he ever saw.

That's a clue to the passions that ran close to the surface. Pinter once said that it was language that kept him alive – its possibilities and power – and in his last years, when he was afflicted by one illness after another, he never lost his appetite for words. His final stage performance was in Samuel Beckett's *Krapp's Last Tape* at the Royal Court Theatre in 2006, an agonizing exploration of his past by a man listening to taped recollections, which Pinter, weakened by illness, played in a motorized wheelchair. When he talks at the end about 'the fire in me now' it is the cue for the tolling of a funereal bell.

The fire did burn to the end. He died in 2008 a Nobel Laureate, author of more than thirty dramas, twenty-five screenplays, poetry and criticism, and he'd been an actor and director who, if he'd never written a word, would still have left his mark. He sent a power surge through the theatre and loved doing it – with apparently only one regret. He said in 1989: 'I made a terrible mistake when I was young, I think, from which I've never really recovered. I wrote the word "pause" into my first play.'

Richard Doll

IN THE EARLY FIFTIES around four out of five adults in Britain smoked. Advertisements told you that it was smart – the rich and the famous were always opening a packet, or slipping a cigarette out of a silver case – and even when you went to the doctor, perhaps with a cough, you'd be quite likely to catch a whiff of tobacco in the surgery. In the cinema, smoking and sex went hand in hand on the screen. On every park bench, in every bus, someone was lighting a cigarette or pipe. No one questioned it; wherever you were, smoke got in your eyes. The man who changed everything was Richard Doll.

He was the first doctor who established beyond doubt the link between smoking and lung cancer. It was a startling assertion, challenging a vast, profitable industry to defend itself against the charge that it damaged public health; and it posed a dilemma for successive governments, which slowly but inexorably were forced to confront the question of how far it was proper in a free society to try to restrict access to a legal substance that had been shown to be one of the main causes of premature death.

After the Second World War the Medical Research Council embarked on a project to find out why deaths from lung cancer were rising. Doll had joined the MRC in 1946 after serving with the Royal Army Medical Corps and in 1950 he published the first report – another came two years later – which made a connection between smoking and lung cancer. It was not widely publicized or discussed, partly because cancer in those days was still the unmentionable disease – generally not given a name, and the subject of behind-the-hand whispers. Nowadays it seems remarkable that the first time the *Daily Mail*, for example, decided to break a taboo and print the word 'cancer' was in 1965 after the announcement by Richard Dimbleby's family that the reason for the absence from the screen of the television star, who had been a household name ever since becoming the first broadcast war correspondent, was that he was suffering from the disease. In the fifties such matters had been private.

Doll's research, however, could not be ignored and it was he who engineered one of the most startling social changes of his time. He lived to the age of 92, having witnessed a steep drop in the number of people smoking – the proportion in Britain had fallen by nearly three-quarters since his first research was published – and not long after his death in 2005 governments in Britain and across Europe began to legislate to ban smoking in public places. Yet when he started his investigations, in partnership with another doctor, Austin Bradford Hill, smoking was not the target they had in their sights.

The Medical Research Council was puzzled in the late forties by the rise in deaths from lung cancer. In particular, the disproportionate increase in male mortality from the disease seemed strange. If the figures were rising because doctors were getting better at diagnosis – as some people thought – and the cause of death was being more accurately recorded, wouldn't you expect the rates of premature death among men and women to be the same? They weren't. Why not?

When Doll and Hill began work they suspected that the answer might lie in the coal smoke that hung heavily over most cities and produced choking smogs in the winter fog. The Clean Air Act was still a decade away. Doll also wondered about the roads, because the tarmac that was being used to upgrade them was known to contain carcinogens. They discovered something else.

Doll made a preliminary observation after interviews with thousands of people who had been diagnosed with lung cancer: 'I found in cases where a cancer diagnosis was wrong, the patient always turned out to be a non-smoker. But when the diagnosis turned out to be correct, the patient was always revealed to be a smoker.' From there, he powered on. He and Hill published their first paper in the *British Medical Journal* in 1950 under the tentative title 'Smoking and Carcinoma of the Lung: Preliminary Report'. The reaction in the medical establishment was really a long yawn, and the paper attracted little public attention. Cigarette sales were still rising. But by coincidence four American studies were being done in the same year that made the same link, and Doll and Hill set about producing enough evidence to nail the conclusion that, privately, they had already reached.

Where better to start than with doctors themselves? They began the next phase of their work in 1951 and persuaded 40,000 British doctors to take part in the research. They asked them whether they smoked, and how much, and then monitored their health. To put it bluntly, they wanted to find out when they would die. By 1954 they were able to report in the *BMJ* that, among the doctors, lung cancer rates were higher among those who smoked, and moreover that the incidence of the disease increased among the heavy smokers. And in the course of their research they were able to broaden their hypothesis: in 1957 they reported a link between smoking and increased rates of heart disease and lung and chest conditions apart from cancer. The evidence was overwhelming, and as a consequence the scepticism that had greeted their first paper began, slowly, to dissipate.

In 1957 the British government became the first to accept formally, though reluctantly, that smoking was a cause of lung cancer. The tobacco companies, which were big employers, were still sufficiently powerful to be confident that no legislation would follow, but the long struggle between the manufacturers and the government had begun. It was almost half a century later that legislation banned smoking in public places in the United Kingdom, in a deliberate effort to cut smoking rates.

Doll was already fighting on another front when he published the research on smoking. He studied the health of workers for Turner Brothers Asbestos in Yorkshire, with the cooperation of the company, and came to a dramatic conclusion: heavily exposed workers had a much greater chance of developing lung cancer, by a factor of up to ten. Against the company's protests – it argued that asbestos was militarily important, and then that its employees' health records were its private property – Doll and Hill published their findings, which were the foundation for further research into the hazards of working with asbestos. Eventually the dangers were understood and quantified.

By the sixties Doll was in the forefront of the research that was changing the attitude to public health. Having acknowledged the link he had established, governments of both parties in Britain began to grapple with the implications, and with the tobacco industry, which was well aware of the threat. A report from the Surgeon General in the United States in 1964 corroborated the association with lung cancer, and by coincidence Doll and Hill published in the same year the results of their ten-year study into doctors' health. It produced a remarkable headline statistic: about half of the doctors who smoked had given up the habit in that decade, and compared with the rate among those who continued to smoke, the incidence of lung cancer among them had dropped dramatically. Government was in doubt about the effect of smoking on health, but how far should it go to try to change people's habits? The first step in Britain came in 1965 with a ban on tobacco advertising on television, in a voluntary agreement with the Independent Broadcasting Authority. Six years later the first government health warnings appeared on cigarette packets.

The man who had started all this had always been someone with a campaigner's zeal. Richard Doll was born in Middlesex in 1912 to a medical family – his father was a surgeon – and even by the time he became a student at St Thomas's Hospital in 1931 he was developing a sharp social conscience. The plight of the First World War generation was unhappy: their lot was far too often unemployment, miserable social conditions and poor health. During his training he was profoundly affected by the living standards he found in south London, where he was required to deliver babies in the slums.

He was politically radicalized, believing that the need for social change was urgent. He joined the Communist Party in the early thirties and volunteered his services as a doctor to the Jarrow marchers who walked to London from Tyneside in 1936 in their historic protest against unemployment. Unsurprisingly, he helped to raise funds for the Republican side in the Spanish Civil War, which began in that year and was a magnet for the idealism of the young left. When the Second World War itself started, he travelled with the Royal Army Medical Corps to the Mediterranean and Middle East, being repatriated in 1944 after he developed renal tuberculosis.

When peace returned, Doll, with his future wife, Joan, was one of the many doctors who campaigned for the establishment of a National Health Service, which came into being just as he was beginning his research on the effects of smoking. Later in the fifties his political allegiance shifted – the couple abandoned the Communist Party after the Soviet Union's invasion of Hungary in 1956 – but his commitment to government action in the cause of public health remained.

Those years after the war shaped the rest of his life as a doctor. He worked with a celebrated gastroenterologist, Francis Avery Jones, at the Central Middlesex Hospital and conducted what may well have been the first factorial randomized clinical trial. He then went to study with Austin Bradford Hill, whose work in epidemiology – the study of the incidence and the patterns of disease in the population – fitted perfectly with his desire to harness medicine for the social good. That partnership was the foundation for Doll's work on cancer.

His eminence in his field – he was knighted in 1971 and become a Companion of Honour in 1996 – was guaranteed by his longevity. He lived to see the publication of the results of the fiftieth-anniversary report of the survey into doctors and smoking which he had started. It concluded that between a half and two-thirds of heavy smokers would die from the consequences of the habit.

Doll was noted among his colleagues for a clarity of mind and straightforwardness, even when it was uncomfortable. In 2001 he horrified some of them when he said that, despite a lifetime of work on cancer, he lost no sleep over the effects of passive smoking. 'The effect of other people's smoking in my presence is so small it doesn't worry me,' he said. But it was he, more than anyone else, who had changed the public's view of smoking. In the year of his death the Scottish government passed legislation to ban smoking in public places – it was implemented in 2006 – and England and Wales followed a year later. Governments had agonized for decades about the extent to which it was justified to use the law to restrict a personal habit, and tangled with the tobacco industry, relentless in its opposition to restrictive legislation.

Doll lived through a revolution in which he had played a major role. In the course of two generations everything had changed. He would recall in old age, as the arguments continued about appropriate legislation, the first government press conference in 1957 to discuss the 'worrying findings' of one of his reports. 'The minister who announced it,' he said, 'was smoking a cigarette at the same time.'

Tony Hancock

FOR MOST OF THE FIFTIES and into the sixties, 23 Railway Cuttings, East Cheam, was the epicentre of the little man's struggle against the world. The address had an air of melancholy frustration and injured dignity, but was also a place of dreams. They came, and they went. You knew that if you walked through the door you would probably see on the hall-stand a heavy over-coat with an astrakhan collar and a black Homburg, and that somewhere inside, pursuing a new scheme or reflecting on another failure, would be the proprietor of that suburban homestead, Anthony Aloysius St John Hancock.

Tony Hancock was the first comedy actor to become a star on British television. When his radio series transferred to the screen in 1956 he was able to ride the tide of that first television age – every home was getting one – and for the next few years his travails and battles with officialdom, and his gloomy reflections on the injustices visited on him, were in every living room. There was no one who didn't care or at least know about him.

In an age of variety, with its song-and-dance men and patter merchants, Hancock produced a different kind of laughter. Situation comedy was still in an embryonic state, and he was an actor who seemed to do it all by himself: he was the centre of his world, alone, always struggling against something, quite often himself. As a result his persona came to represent everyone who felt they had missed the boat or sensed that the glories of the world were eluding them. Hancock painted a picture of decline and wounded pride, and took everyone with him. For he was uproariously funny.

By the time *Hancock's Half Hour* was first heard on BBC Radio in 1954, he had been at it for more than ten years, building up a character capable of flights of surreal fantasy, and it was as tutor to the ventriloquist's dummy in *Educating Archie* that he revealed a special talent – significantly perhaps in that he had to forge a relationship with a wooden doll. He appeared frustrated, uncertain, vulnerable, and soon the character was unleashed to take off on its own.

The radio series ran until 1959, three years after the television version began. Looking back from a time when comedians pour out of the stand-up clubs and pop up on television in bewildering numbers, it's easy to forget how dominating a personality like Hancock's could become in a simpler, less cluttered age. His originality could shine.

He had the good fortune to have stumbled across the best comic writers in the first days of television, Ray Galton and Alan Simpson, who were able to write for his natural style, almost as if he were engaged in a half-hour exercise in stream of consciousness. There was no improvisation at all, but a meticulous attention to the script, which he infused with feelings that communicated themselves to his audience because they seemed natural: real. Hancock was indeed the sad clown. He first fell out with one of his sidekicks, the master of camp *double entendre* Kenneth Williams, and wouldn't keep him on the show. And much later he made the catastrophic decision to dump Sid James, whose gurgling laugh and spivvy antics as Hancock's lodger on both radio and television had been the perfect foil to his precious effort to keep up a dignified front. The story was that he was jealous of James's success in films – Hancock's own *The Rebel* and *The Punch and Judy Man* hadn't done nearly as well as he'd hoped –

and he did his last TV series for the BBC, in 1961, without Sid. He was already succumbing to feelings of betrayal and jealousy.

It didn't stop him, in that series, from producing at least two of his great sketches: 'The Radio Ham' and 'The Blood Donor'. No one who watched the first can forget his encounter with a lost sailor on a distant sea, veering from excited fellow-feeling with a soul in trouble when he heard 'Mayday' to prickly self-importance and bungling stupidity. And from 'The Blood Donor' came a line that everyone knew and which would always bring his bloodhound features to mind, and his fear of what he'd hoped was going to be a little pinprick: 'A pint! That's very nearly an armful!'

Everyone could remember a Hancock sketch that would cheer them up when the sky darkened: the spoof of Henry Fonda in the jury room of *Twelve Angry Men* when he praised Magna Carta as 'that brave Hungarian peasant girl', or the thriller borrowed from the library with the last page, and the name of the murderer, ripped out, or the time they all got stuck in a lift. He was always being done down, and always wondered why, though he knew it would soon happen again.

He was always 'Hancock', never 'Tony', and the trick was that the mask never slipped: he was gullible and obviously lonely, but fatalistic and unsurprised by his lot. Those heavy eyebrows gave his big eyes a cartoonist's picture of weariness with the world, and the hangdog look would always settle back into place after a burst of hope or excitement that never lasted long. Even before his career began to head for the rocks, which it did at breakneck speed, he had established such a powerful, lugubrious presence that everyone suspected it told the truth: you couldn't imagine for a moment that off screen he was a happy-go-lucky fellow.

And that was true. Kenneth Williams left a harsh, waspish entry in his diary: 'The man was incredibly destructive all his life – never did anyone waste people and opportunities as he did.' There was some truth in that too. After the last BBC series he parted company with Galton and Simpson. The decline was irreversible. Galton and Simpson just carried on, and the following year created the sitcom that would blaze a trail for everything that followed. The first appearance of *Steptoe and Son* was in the Comedy Playhouse slot in January 1962, a series followed immediately, and within a year the rag-and-bone yard in Shepherd's Bush was a comedy Shangri-La for the whole country. The audiences topped 20 million, and just before the general election in October 1964 the BBC agreed that the episode due to be shown early on election evening should be moved because it might reduce turnout.

Meanwhile Hancock was sliding down the slope. He was drinking very heavily, unsettled in his personal life, lost. The most startling insight into his darkening world came in a series that became one of the television landmarks of the time, because it presented interviews with public figures of a kind that no one had ever seen before. In *Face to Face* the interviewer was John Freeman, former editor of the *New Statesman*, and for the first time cameras recorded his subjects responding to intimate questioning which stripped away many of their protective layers or pretensions. Evelyn Waugh's irascibility and coldness were displayed to the full, the television star Gilbert Harding wept in talking about the death of his mother, and Hancock spoke about unhappiness, with obvious discomfort. He told Freeman: 'the only happiness I could achieve would be to perfect the talent that I have, whatever it may be, however small it may be. That is the whole purpose of it and that is the whole purpose of what I do.'

He still had that last series in him, but the revelation of his turmoil was a signal of what lay ahead. There was a thought in *Hancock's Half Hour*, regularly repeated in various forms, that spoke not just about the character on the screen, but the real man: 'Nobody will ever know I existed. Nothing to leave behind me. Nothing to pass on. Nobody to mourn me. That's the bitterest blow of all.' Asked by Freeman about comedy, Hancock said this: 'I think you expose your own pomposity and other people's and get probably to the real truth of the way you live.' That truth was exceptionally painful.

The *Face to Face* interview, which troubled the BBC because it revealed the vulnerability of one of its biggest stars, affected Hancock a great deal. His brother, Roger, said that it was his biggest mistake because it was the start of a self-examination that was disastrous. 'Self-analysis,' he said. 'That was his killer.' The drink helped too. Having been in the fifties a meticulous performer who worked hard with his scriptwriters and producers, Hancock let it all slip and in his last series needed prompt cards where he had once been able to do a 'take' of a half-hour show with what was close to dramatic perfection (the early radio shows had all been live). A fellow comedian, Spike Milligan, who knew all about despair, said in an interview with *Rolling Stone*: 'I thought – he'd got rid of everybody else, he's going to get rid of himself.'

These years were miserable. The film *The Rebel* in 1960, in which a clerk goes to Paris to become an artist, did have a brief popular success (it was written by Galton and Simpson) but *The Punch and Judy Man*, three years later, did not. It was the story of a failed seaside entertainer called Wally, unhappily married, and written by Hancock himself. Wally's trials were uncomfortably close to the truth: the decline was unstoppable.

Hancock was already a figure from the past. Comedy was heading for new territory. In 1960 Peter Cook, Jonathan Miller, Alan Bennett and Dudley Moore took the Edinburgh Festival by storm with *Beyond the Fringe* and a new generation of satirists was born. The following year a group of anarchic public schoolboys founded *Private Eye* and in 1962 *That Was the Week That Was* announced to television viewers that the age of deference had gone (and invented David Frost). There was no stopping that crowd, and the hilarious, touching Hancock stories were slipping from view. A devoted following would remember him, and celebrate the sixty-three television *Half Hours* (of which only thirty-seven are thought to have survived), but his day had gone.

As his brother Roger had realized, there was no way back. Hancock went to Australia in the hope of a revival with exactly the kind of flimsy dream that his on-screen character had so often clung to, and the result was the same. He knew it was over. His first series wasn't a success, and even though his producers had decided – maybe even on the day that he had died – to risk commissioning another, he never knew it. On 25 June 1968 his body was found in his apartment in Sydney, where he had taken his own life. He was 44.

In a suicide note he left a few words that had exactly that mixture of puzzlement and fatalism that had always been the mainspring of his brilliance as a comic actor, and they became his epitaph: 'Things seemed to go wrong too many times.'

Philip Larkin

WITH A POET, START WITH THE POEMS. You can get to know Philip Larkin by reading 'The Whitsun Weddings'. He travels to London, which he didn't much like, and casts a knowing and roving eye on the parties joining the train on a day that was traditional for weddings. He's intrigued, rather than moved, by the women who 'shared the secret, like a happy funeral'. And as he approaches the city – past standing Pullmans and walls of blackened moss – he finds a sadness stealing in. With the tightening brakes,

there swelled
A sense of falling, like an arrow shower
Sent out of sight, somewhere becoming rain.

The melancholy certainty of rain, the way the fields and hedges, the canals of the countryside, turn into a place with 'postal districts packed like squares of wheat'; and the bubbling excitement of the newlyweds – the certainty they may have found – is set against his own falling spirits. He can understand their happiness, but not fully share it.

There was no other poet of his time in this country who exhibited a weariness quite like Larkin's. Ted Hughes's agonies when he was Poet Laureate were muscular, John Betjeman – his predecessor – was drawn again and again to his enthusiasms like a benign pixie; Larkin was always aware of the skull beneath the skin. His lines were chiselled, sometimes bare, and sharp.

The era in which his best poetry was written was a time when the social furniture was being rearranged. By the early sixties people were challenging the assumptions of deference that were thought part of a well-ordered society: everyone knowing their place and behaving accordingly. Satirists were on the loose, for the first time there was music available that was a means of separating the young from their parents, class stereotypes were being challenged. Larkin was absorbing the feeling of change, and responding to it with poetry that was mostly rooted in the language of every day, written with a feeling for ordinary speech, yet crafted carefully to produce a gleam from within. As a result it was immediately comprehensible, then enticing. He once said: 'I think a poem should be understood at first reading – line by line – but not exhausted at first reading.'

His first influence, when he was a student at Oxford in the early forties, was W.H. Auden, and he was prolific, getting a poem published in the BBC weekly *The Listener* when he was still in his first year. And by the time he graduated – the shy boy from Coventry with a stammer that he couldn't conquer until he was in his thirties – he was part of a group that would eventually be known as the Movement, young writers who were developing their own literary patois. They included Kingsley Amis, who would be a lifelong friend, Iris Murdoch and the novelist John Wain. When he was looking for work in the early fifties Larkin was already committed to the business of writing and it was not at all surprising that, apparently by accident, he became a librarian, first of all in Shropshire, then – via Leicester University and Queen's, Belfast – at the University of Hull, where he arrived in 1955. He lived in Hull until he died in December 1985.

In his first year there he published a volume of poems, *The Less Deceived*, that *The Times* and *The Spectator* singled out as one of the books of the year. The days of student toying with Auden pastiche, and half-finished semi-pornographic novels, were over. From the United States came a magisterial blessing from one of the giants of the time, Robert Lowell: 'No post-war poetry has so caught the moment, and caught it without straining after its ephemera. It's a hesitant groping mumble, resolutely experienced, resolutely perfect in its artistic methods.'

Lowell understood that already Larkin wasn't picking up the flimsy, outward signs of changing times and playing with them: he was getting to the heart of it all. Through the poems in that collection – like 'Church Going' – the figure of Larkin starts to take shape, ruminating about the world, wondering where he fits:

Bored, uninformed, knowing the ghostly silt
Dispersed, yet tending to this cross of ground
Through suburb scrub because it held unspilt
So long and equably what since is found
Only in separation – marriage and birth,
And death, and thoughts of these – for which was built
This special shell?
For, though I've no idea
What this accoutred frowsty barn is worth,
It pleases me to stand in silence here.

Over the next ten years or so, until the collection *The Whitsun Weddings* in 1964, Larkin was writing with confidence, though in his letters – he was always writing to friends and family – he constantly worries away at his craft, questioning a line, dismissing a piece of emotion as cheap. Underneath, though, there was no doubt of his seriousness and his belief in his poetry. He was writing about people and a country that was being transformed from a self-confident hub of empire to a place where the swagger had been lost, and with it perhaps some of the romance of England, which, though he represented it in language that was never swollen, he felt deeply.

The former Poet Laureate Andrew Motion, born just as Larkin was starting to get up speed at the start of the fifties, argues in his biography that there are opposites at work: a remorseless factuality and downbeat language and imaginative daring that produces moments of transcendent beauty. From that collision, he thinks, comes the energy.

As a man, Larkin was happy in his work in Hull but led a personal life that was famously hit-and-miss. The relationship which meant most to him was with Monica Jones, who was his girlfriend – surely the right word in the circumstances – for nearly forty years, though she lived with him for only the last two. There were other affairs, but never a marriage. So the shy boy remained shy, unwilling or unable to turn these liaisons into anything that seemed permanent. The poet who announced notoriously that 'sexual intercourse began in 1963' was never at home in that territory. He once said: 'I had grown up to regard sexual recreation as a socially remote thing, like baccarat or clog-dancing, and nothing happened to alter this view.'

The picture that took shape in the fifties remained: tall, bald enough to reveal a high dome, with thick, black-rimmed glasses that made him look as if he was peering intimately at something even when he wasn't. But he was often photographed smiling – and many pictures were taken by himself with a delayed-action camera that he liked – so that he frequently appeared happier off the page than on it.

He revealed a quirky privacy about his work, for all his commitment to it: 'I can't understand these chaps who go round American universities explaining how they write poems. It's like going round explaining how you sleep with your wife.' He was never going to let himself go. Revelation would come in tightly controlled lines that often compress feeling into a few words, especially when dealing with the biggest things in life, like death.

In 'Aubade', in 1977, he wrote:

Being brave
Lets no-one off the grave
Death is no different whined at than withstood.

The individual behind those lines is a perplexing one. When Andrew Motion's biography revealed his lively interest in pornography, and his political drift rightwards became known, he turned into something of a *bête noire* for the liberal literati who labelled him a misogynist curmudgeon with unhealthy sexual appetites, all the worse for being largely unfulfilled. Yet Jean Hartley, his publisher, recalls uproarious lunches and the way that he and Kingsley Amis kept alive the 'anarchic spirit' of their students, though no doubt some of its crudity and reactionary political sentiment wouldn't have made everyone happy.

It's safer to go back to the poems than worry about how precisely these different strands in his personality were entwined. Take a quatrain written in 1982, after most of his poetic energy was spent, looking back to happier times – when he wasn't contemplating death – and using for an image his star sign, Leo:

Whatever conceived
Now fully leaved,
Abounding, ablaze –
O long lion days.

Larkin could have been Poet Laureate. It's said that he was tipped the wink at the memorial service to John Betjeman, of whom he'd been so fond. Betjeman's deceptively simple poetry had probably been surpassed by his work on conservation and his courageous and triumphant fight to save the beautiful things from our Victorian and Edwardian heritage, but he and Larkin – so different – had cared about many of the same things. Poet Laureate, however, was not for him, and anyway it was probably too late. Ted Hughes was appointed in 1984, the year before Larkin died, of oesophageal cancer, aged 63.

He'd been writing serious poetry for thirty-five years and traced his own path in the sand: dealing with suffering the death of another, the moments of joy in an everyday scene, the pain underneath, the lurking fear of inadequacy. He was also a poet of rampant enthusiasm, despite the world-weary melancholy that often seemed to surround him and was reinforced by his some-what gloomy and forbidding physical presence. In black and white pictures especially he can often wear a disapproving look, as if he's just spotted something of which you should be ashamed. Perhaps he has.

But read him on jazz, a passion. For ten years he reviewed records for the *Daily Telegraph*. Listen to him on a favourite pianist: 'Fats Waller's face … was the kind you can carve on an orange; squeeze it one way and it laughs, another and it weeps or looks puzzled.' Of John Coltrane he said he was possessed of 'an almost Scandinavian unloveliness'.

Larkin seemed to feel his own 'unloveliness' a good deal, though in his letters there are fun and frolics as well as bitter put-downs and evidence of darkness inside. But he never had any doubt of his own talent, knowing from early days that he would write, in one way or another.

He was a celebrated librarian, turning his university library into one Hull could be proud of, and a poet who sang a song of his time. He wrote of the moment, not a vanished past, and he wondered where it would take us all. Death always fascinated him, but his life wasn't spent waiting for it. Life, he said, had a practice of living you, if you didn't live it.

Maybe he did believe what he wrote at the end of his poem 'An Arundel Tomb', in *The Whitsun Weddings*:

The stone finality
They hardly meant has come to be
Their final blazon, and to prove
Our almost-instinct almost true:
What will survive of us is love.

Barbara Windsor

BARBARA WINDSOR IS THE ACTRESS who leapt out of a saucy seaside postcard, landed precariously on her size one and a half feet and, wobbling a little, gave a filthy chuckle of welcome to every busty blonde joke that greeted her, as if saying hello to an old friend. From her pedestal as the perpetual tease in *Carry On* films to pub landlady in *EastEnders* she has played the role of the good-time cockney girl for decades with a gusto that betrays the truth. The role is also her life. She has been starlet, serial celebrity companion, gangster's moll.

All this and a national treasure too. Windsor has usually been able to count on the public vote, even managing to write about her friendship with the East End godfathers, the Krays, and her first marriage, which introduced her to gangland, without sacrificing affection. Three decades after she made her last *Carry On* film she was still being stopped in the street by people who giggled at the memory of her bra being whipped off by a hidden fishing line (in *Carry On Camping*) – although of course it was filmed from behind, for reasons of decorum – and treated with familiarity by anyone she met, as a flighty and maybe wicked member of the family, but a cherished one all the same.

She encapsulates the end-of-the-pier-show naughtiness that was a happy residue of variety, and, like the camp comedians who'd get laughs from old ladies with references to sexual practices that would mystify but scandalize them in equal measure at home, she seemed to turn it all into a parlour game. The rule was that no one was allowed to be offended if she talked about the ever-present danger of her breasts breaking away from their moorings or a predatory man pinching her bulging backside, once voted by readers of some magazine or other as 'Rear of the Year'. All she has to do is giggle, and anything goes.

Appropriately her first part in a film, as an anonymous schoolgirl when she was 17, was in *The Belles of St Trinian's*, the first of the five films set in that school, a den of chaos and vice presided over by Alastair Sim in drag as the headmistress. The girls' hormones were jumping, Joyce Grenfell was the blue-stockinged hockey mistress trying to keep up standards but longing for a good man, a *galère* of wide boys played by the likes of George Cole and Sid James were bent on their latest scam, usually involving horses and a blast of sexual fantasy, and the lurking threat of authority came in the form of the man from the Ministry who was likely to arrive at any moment to shut the place down, in the interests of propriety and national order. From there it was natural that she should slip off to the set of the *Carry On* films, which, for more than thirty years, kept up one long scream of innuendo, from hospital to school to Cleopatra's Egypt, to the African jungle, Paris in the revolution, and, of course, up the Khyber.

They were the screen equivalent of pantomime: outdated and predictably clunky, but for the first generation after music hall a harmlessly crude antidote to anything serious that the sixties was offering. The regulars could be relied upon to deliver the goods: Kenneth Williams as Julius Caesar – 'Infamy, infamy – they've all got it infamy' – the mincing Charles Hawtrey, Hattie Jacques, and Sid James, with his pugilist's face and obscene laugh, who got many of the best lines. When Joan Sims said she expected him to behave like a gentleman but had sore misgivings, it was Sid who said she ought to put talcum powder on 'em.

Windsor was a member of the team from *Carry On Spying* in 1964 and, as she admitted in her autobiography, it was only a matter of time before she had an affair with Sid James: because he chortled at her body and was polite enough to open the door for her. There was a madcap other-worldliness about the whole enterprise: when the team made *Carry On Cleo* they used the sets and clothes that had been prepared for Richard Burton and Elizabeth Taylor in their 1963 epic *Cleopatra* – during which they started their hyper-powered affair – before the lovers relocated to Rome to try to make the film more spectacular. The *Carry Ons* were absurd and slapstick, and when comedy in the seventies started to become more explicit and adventurous they couldn't compete, looking hopelessly old-fashioned and trying some artificial respiration by getting dirtier. Windsor got out, aware that it couldn't last much longer, and that it was only the illusion of innocence that had made anyone laugh in the first place.

In the sixties they peddled a harmless potion of slapstick and smut which suited her perfectly: mother's milk. Had it not been for St Trinian's, though, she might have ended up elsewhere. As a youngster in the fifties – she had her first panto role when she was 15 – she'd learned her trade with Joan Littlewood at the Theatre Royal Stratford East, a stone's throw from where she was born in Shoreditch. Littlewood was one of the innovators of post-war theatre, devoted to opening the doors to audiences by means of adventure and originality. She was an artist of the left, but adept at mingling high seriousness in the theatre – her première of Bertolt Brecht's *Mother Courage and Her Children* was famous – with rich and popular productions, especially musicals. She built a theatrical hothouse.

It was a grounding that gave Windsor a good start on the stage. She got a part in Littlewood's successful version of *Fings Ain't Wot They Used T'be*, a Lionel Bart musical that could have been written for the likes of her – an affectionate tour through East End life – and it was in Littlewood's production of the satirical music drama *Oh! What a Lovely War* on Broadway that she was nominated for a Tony Award. She had reason to think of herself as a proper actor and not a typecast bimbo – she had parts in TV series, including early sitcoms like *The Rag Trade* – but *Carry On* was her passport to celebrity. In nine of the films in the series she wiggled and wobbled her way across the screen, casting off bits of clothing as she went and generating a festival of ogling.

The sixties suited her, because for the first time a little limelight was splashed on performers who seemed to live life on the edge. Celebrities began to be less remote, no longer living on planet Hollywood, and Windsor's first marriage was to an East End character called Ronnie Knight who might have been provided for her by a casting agency. He was a villain who went to prison for a bullion robbery, was later acquitted of murder, and was one of the early absconders from the law to the extradition-free territory of rogues around Marbella on the Costa del Sol – someone called it the bit of Spain that fell off the back of a lorry. At the time, gangsterland was only hinted at in the newspapers. Everyone in East London in the sixties knew of the Kray brothers, who supervised a suite of criminal enterprises and vicious protection rackets, but their names were unknown beyond the borders of their 'manor'. Windsor and her husband breathed the same air, understood the milieu of the hard men, and when Reggie Kray died in 2000 one of the first public messages of condolence was from Babs, who said she had always found him charming and polite.

In 1969 Kray had been sentenced to a minimum of thirty years in jail for the murder of Jack 'The Hat' McVitie. His twin brother Ronnie was put away for a different killing. The publicity surrounding their convictions, and the length of their sentences, meant that – along with the rival Richardson gang across the river in South London – they took on the mantle of mafia-style godfathers in popular culture, bywords for an underworld with tentacles in every pub and a watcher on every corner. But any newspaper reporter could find someone from their street who would tell stories of how kind the Kray boys were to their mother, or how they'd help poor kids to get a start in life through a boxing club or a greengrocer's stall.

There was therefore a piquancy in the casting of Barbara Windsor in 1994 as Peggy Mitchell, chatelaine of the Queen Vic, the pub in Albert Square that is the hub of *EastEnders*. She became the embodiment of family loyalty in a rough and tumble world, in which her hard-boiled sons were usually in trouble and, having denied in the early days that there was any echo of a real person, she said in an interview in 2000 that she had used Violet Kray – the gangsters' mother – and her own (whom she described as an East End snob) as inspirations for the character.

Her relationship with her own family was difficult. She'd changed her name, from Barbara Anne Deeks, in her teens, after doing very well in the 11-plus exam and being sent to a convent school in north London. In later life her sister and her father, a costermonger, gave interviews in which they revealed some bitter feelings about the star. But, for the public, Windsor remained lovable. She might talk in her autobiography about her string of affairs – her conquests included George Best, the most glamorous sixties footballer, and Maurice Gibb of the Bee Gees – even the fact that she had five abortions because she didn't want children, but she still managed to exude a cheery, girl-next-door spirit. In her fifteen years on *EastEnders*, which quickly attracted a huge and loyal audience when it was launched in the mid-eighties, she was barmaid and matriarch, mother confessor and tough old bird. Retiring in 2010 at the age of 73, she said she wanted to spend more time with her husband; a kind of settling down.

It was nearly sixty years since she had first tripped onto a stage as a 13-year-old, remembering a grandmother who was in musicals, conscious of a tradition that still resonated in the post-war East End, a part of London that, through the experience of the Blitz, was able to claim that its old ties of family and community spirit had survived and made it somehow different. Great change was on the way – the death of the docks in the seventies, slum clearance, a shifting population – but Barbara Windsor is a cockney sparrow who harks back to a different time. Maybe that's why she survived for six decades as an actor and a character.

In the most flashy, ephemeral business of all – celebrity – she exhibited the most precious commodity of all. Under the wig, behind the wobble, the tiny feet and the big everything else, there was authenticity.

Lord Denning

L ORD DENNING WAS THE BEST-KNOWN JUDGE of his era.
A liberal defender of the individual against any big battalion
trying to throw its weight around, he was also a conservative
defender of a moral code that he thought the law should protect,
so from time to time he would find himself hailed as a champion
of liberty, and the week afterwards as a crusty apologist for
outmoded social values. He preferred the description that the
public assigned to him: friend of the common man, the people's
judge.

He made that reputation in the twenty years that he was
Master of the Rolls – heading the civil division of the Court of
Appeal – from 1962 until his retirement. It was an unusually
long stint, and meant that his judgments become widely known
at a time when social attitudes were changing faster than at
any time in his life (he was born in the last year of the nineteenth century). They were also celebrated because he encapsulated in the diamond-sharp language of his decisions the
to-and-fro arguments on one of the great questions of his age:
how people should be treated by the law at a moment when
power in government, in business, in trade unions, seemed to
be increasing at the expense of the freedom of action of
individuals.

Among lawyers, his style became famous. One judgment, in 1967 in the case of *Beswick v Beswick*, a family contractual dispute, began with these words: 'Old Peter Beswick was a coal merchant in Eccles, Lancashire. He had no business premises. All he had was a lorry, scales and weights.' Again in *Lloyds Bank v Bundy* in 1974: 'Broadchalke is one of the most pleasing villages in England. Old Herbert Bundy, the defendant, was a farmer there.' Every case was a story; and people were at the heart of it. He spoke, he believed, for them and their country. He started his judgment in *Hinz v Berry* in 1970: 'It happened on April 19, 1964. It was bluebell time in Kent.'

He was not a judge, however, who is simply remembered for his turn of phrase. Denning was an innovator, challenging some of the assumptions of lawyers and the courts as assiduously as he took on the powerful interests whose responsibility to society he saw it as his duty to constrain. His career was therefore gilded with controversy, whether he was offending other Court of Appeal judges who felt he was too intent on shaping the civil law, or – late in his career – when he appeared to be holding onto attitudes that had changed in many people's minds: for example, having to apologise in 1982, the year of his retirement, for remarks about the possible unsuitability of black jurors.

Alfred Denning, always known in his family and beyond as Tom, was born in Whitchurch, Hampshire, and retained all his life – he died two months after his hundredth birthday in 1999 – the rolling burr of his home county. He read mathematics and law at Oxford, was called to the Bar in 1923, made a King's Counsel in 1938, and a judge for the first time – in the family division of the High Court – in 1944. Within five years he was a Lord Justice of Appeal, a law lord from 1957, and then Master of the Rolls at the start of the sixties. At that stage the public knew little of him, but chance gave him an unlikely starring role in the sensational story of the time.

The Prime Minister, Harold Macmillan, asked him to produce a report after the resignation of the Minister of War, John

Profumo, when he admitted lying to the House of Commons about an affair with Christine Keeler, who was also sleeping with an attaché at the Russian embassy among others. For most people there hadn't been a scandal like it (at least not one that had been so fully reported): naked swimming parties at Lord Astor's Cliveden estate, a minister consorting with prostitutes organized by a society osteopath, whispers about the Russians, and a tide of rumour that raked up all sorts of other scandals. One Cabinet minister was even forced to have his genitals examined by a doctor to confirm that they weren't the ones shown in a photograph of Margaret, Duchess of Argyll, with a man whose face had been cut off the picture. The so-called 'Headless Man' turned out not to be the minister, but a Hollywood star.

Macmillan's government appeared out of touch and weary. Denning's report, which became an overnight best-seller, blamed Profumo for his morals and his lack of truthfulness. In retrospect, when material emerged about what the security service MI5 had known, and the participants in the events began to talk more openly, Denning's report seemed thin, even simplistic. But it still stands as evidence of his approach to matters of morality, one of his most notable characteristics.

He took a strong view of the sanctity of marriage. In the fifties he'd written a Court of Appeal ruling that a deserted wife occupying the marital home had a right to stay there. The Law Lords took a different view and reversed it, but it was Denning's approach that prevailed in the Matrimonial Homes Act of 1967. Later in his career, in the seventies, he created the first framework for the division of family assets in divorce cases which hadn't previously been defined in law.

In the civil law, he took the view that judges should be more active in updating case law rather than relying too much on precedent. 'My own view is that is what it should be. Although there's a cast of thought amongst some who think it ought to be static, and they call it certain, and by making it so, never moves forward. Whereas I take fundamentally the view that the judges ought to be progressive, and ought to keep the law in touch with the needs of the time.'

He said his intention was always to make the principles of law and ordinary living 'simple for the ordinary folk'. That wasn't patronizing, but a statement of his belief that his role was to be a watchman at the gate, ready to stop an abuse of power by government or anyone else. If a judge didn't do it, what chance did the 'ordinary folk' have?

A famous example was his judgment in a case in 1976 in which a TV licence payer had applied for a new licence early before the old one expired, to avoid a £6 increase in the fee that was about to come in. The Home Office demanded that he pay the increase, the licence payer refused, and had his licence revoked. Denning was presiding when the Court of Appeal decided that the government had acted unlawfully. Bernard Levin, cheerleading for Denning's stalwart individualism, wrote his column in *The Times* under the headline 'Blow the Trumpets for Us over Them in the TV Licence War'. It was a headline that Denning must have enjoyed. His approach to the law was that it had to represent the grain in a fair society, and strive for a standard of justice that could be widely understood and accepted.

Inevitably he ran into brick walls. At one time nine of his judgments in a row were overturned by the law lords. Although he said he didn't mind being shown he was wrong, and starting again, he stuck to the task he had set himself of modernizing the law, turning it to the service of people's lives as they were lived, not as they had been whenever the relevant case law or statute had first been established. 'Modernization', however, is a difficult word because Denning found himself, particularly late in his career, being caricatured as a judge who had ceased to be in touch with the social mores that he said the law must understand.

He was emphatic about his own views on personal morality, and proud that they were unchanging, but in relation to the shifting character of public opinion he sometimes looked to have been left behind, even when he was celebrating the importance of the law in adapting to the circumstances of the time, and offering redress against new threats to personal liberty. His last year as Master of the Rolls was made deeply uncomfortable by the publication of his book *What Next in the Law*.

In this he referred to the possible unsuitability of people who had come to England from overseas for jury service, and found himself being threatened with legal action by black jurors who had served on a case in Bristol. It affected him a great deal, his wife telling the papers: 'He is very distressed. He has done more for the black people in this country than any other judge. He is very upset. He realizes that he has made a mistake.' He offered the Lord Chancellor his resignation, which was refused, but he retired later that year. The extent of sympathy for him, however, was revealed in a letter to *The Times* by Rudi Narayan, secretary of the Society of Black Lawyers, who referred to his many friends abroad, and said: 'A great judge has erred greatly in the intellectual loneliness of advanced years; while his remarks should be rejected and rebutted he is yet, in a personal way, entitled to draw on that reservoir of community regard which he has in many quarters.'

That regard, however, was often subject to challenge. Down the years Denning's judgments irritated lawyers, other judges and sections of the population who found themselves the target of some pithy rebuke. He never held back. In 1980 in an appeal by the 'Birmingham Six', who had been jailed for the IRA pub bombings in 1974 – and whose convictions were famously quashed some years later – he said that they should be stopped from pursuing their appeal. If they lost, he said, a great deal of public money would be wasted, and added: 'If they won, it would mean that the police were guilty of perjury, that they were guilty of violence and threats, that the confessions were involuntarily and improperly admitted in evidence and that the convictions were erroneous ... That is such an appalling vista that every sensible person should say – "it cannot be right that these actions should go any further."' That brought a familiar storm breaking over his head.

There was no one interested in the law, it seems, who did not find some of Denning's judgments inspiring and some infuriating.

He had a view about the law and justice which convinced him that it was the responsibility of those making judgments, in the civil or the criminal courts, to try to mould the law to protect the balance in society between the powerful and the powerless, the victim and the criminal. He encapsulated that in his crystal-clear language, and as a consequence many of his judgments have become courtroom classics. Intriguingly there were many people who had never darkened a courtroom door, or knew little about the arcane working of the law, who nonetheless got the feeling that – more often than not – Denning would be the judge who'd be on their side.

They also had in their minds the picture of a judge who was somehow *different*, and they were right. Few of his colleagues in the Court of Appeal, before or afterwards, would have started the judgment in the way he did in the case of a man who had sought an injunction to stop a village cricket club from playing because whenever someone hit a six it landed in the garden of his newly built house. In *Miller v Jackson* in 1977 Denning began like this: 'In summertime, village cricket is the delight of everyone. Nearly every village has its own cricket field where the young men play and the old men watch. In the village of Lintz in County Durham they have their own ground, where they have played these last seventy years.' The cricketers won.

Paul Foot

Paul Foot never had to learn the language of protest, and had no Damascene moment when he decided to reject authority. He was a dissenter by blood, raised in the tradition, and cherished his inheritance from a family where poetry was as important as politics and the heroes were almost always outsiders. Those whom he admired had, more often than not, come unstuck. He used to walk past a naked statue of Percy Bysshe Shelley in his Oxford college, and once asked a senior don about the inscription saying that the poet had spent only a year there. The reply itself was bare: 'Poor fellow. He was drowned.' But Foot well knew that Shelley had been sent down from the university for publishing an attack on organized religion. Already he had a hero.

Foot was drawn equally to the idealism of Shelley's poems and their spirit of rejection – of old ways and conventional thinking – illuminated by a romantic vision of escape. That was why he became a crusading journalist and why he broke with the formal politics of his family, spending his whole life on the outer fringes of the left, with no interest in a parliamentary career, happier to be a rabble-rousing pamphleteer than to sup with the establishment, although he knew its manners well. Indeed, part of his beguiling quality was that his contempt for what he called the ruling classes was wrapped up in a polite, warm and generous personality that disarmed anyone who expected to encounter at first meeting a sour and unforgiving Robespierre.

He was the most effective campaigning journalist of his time, in *Private Eye* and the *Daily Mirror*, and although he claimed to believe to the end of his life in the imminence of the socialist revolution that stubbornly refused to come, it was as a crusading writer about miscarriages of justice and public corruption that Foot flourished. For forty years from the sixties he was targeting people whom he'd spotted as crooks or charlatans – he thought they were everywhere – and retained, to the day of his death in 2004 at the age of 66, a zeal for the fight that hadn't aged. He had the same haircut as he'd worn as a young radical, still used *Private Eye* to poke the establishment where it hurt, and retained the cheery, impossible optimism of the campaigner who always believed that the day of victory was around the next corner.

He had limbered up at Shrewsbury School with Richard Ingrams, Willie Rushton and Christopher Booker, a trio who succeeded in never growing up and representing for decades a blend of anarchic humour and obsessive bloody-mindedness that they made a sixties fashion. They turned the school magazine into something scurrilous (for which they were punished by a house-master who enjoyed beating his boys in the old way, trousers down, with a belt), then Foot edited the student newspaper *Isis* at Oxford. So when Ingrams founded *Private Eye* in 1961, he was a natural member of the gang. Alongside the jokes and the school-boyish delight in mocking the fading power of the Macmillan government – and revelling in the gift of the Profumo scandal of 1963, where government incompetence and sex seemed to reach a shuddering climax – the magazine quickly became a conduit for information that had no outlet in the mainstream press, some of it scurrilous, some of it tantalizingly accurate, though it was always difficult to tell which was which.

When Foot joined full-time in 1967 he was therefore quite at home. He'd started as a journalist in Glasgow on the *Daily*

Record, where he discovered left-wing politics in the shipyards and joined the Trotskyite International Socialists, who eventually became the Socialist Workers Party. That allegiance never wavered, despite the relentless and often comic schisms and personal feuds that characterized the factional galaxy of the far left. Ingrams gave him two pages at the back of *Private Eye* which became a platform for campaigning journalism and investigations of a kind that Foot made his own. He was launched.

Over in Fleet Street, Harold Evans was turning the staid *Sunday Times* into a powerhouse of journalism, its Insight team opening up new territory with their investigations. Foot's campaigns in the *Eye* were complementary one-man crusades, and the two fed off each other, one turning an establishment newspaper into more of a thunderer and the other a column where Foot peddled the unthinkable, starting from the assumption that everyone in a position of power – in government, in a local authority, in a business – should be regarded with suspicion. He liked to quote the left-wing polemicist Claud Cockburn: believe nothing until it has been officially denied.

Foot's antecedents had prepared him for this role. His father was Hugh Foot, later Lord Caradon, and he was born in Palestine in 1937, when his father was an administrator under the British mandate. Three uncles went into politics: Dingle was Solicitor General under Harold Wilson, John became a Liberal life peer, and Michael was a left-wing campaigner and writer, cabinet minister, and eventually leader of the Labour Party, briefly and uncomfortably, from 1981. The family was of West Country liberal stock and Isaac, Paul's grandfather, was a noted bibliophile who imbued the whole family with an enthusiasm for poetry and the reformist fervour of Milton, Swift, Hazlitt and the Romantic poets. It was the kind of family where you were expected to be able to quote long passages of *Prometheus Unbound* at breakfast, and know your way around *Paradise Lost* before you were into your teens.

So Foot's work at the *Eye* sprang from that history. Some of his friends who approved of his suspicion of all authority were always puzzled, however, by his refusal to abandon the febrile world of extra-parliamentary politics or to apply his formidable talent for polemic and scorn to some of those who paddled with him in the same waters. After Foot appeared on the BBC's *Question Time*, Clive James wrote in the *Observer* that his views always showed signs of having been hatched in an upper-middle-class incubator: 'Paul is absolutely certain that outmoded institutions must be swept away. You have to be brought up in sheltered circumstances to have that absolute certainty.'

But he did have it. He and his uncle Michael were fond of each other but the nephew could never accept that parliamentary politics offered anything by way of real change. He yanked Shelley into his cause – irritatingly for those who thought his reading of the poems was crude – and railed against a corrupt world. That would have made him a bore to everyone except his comrades in the SWP if it had not been for his journalism: many who wouldn't travel far down the political road with him celebrated his campaigns.

In the late sixties he wrote blistering polemical biographies of Harold Wilson and Enoch Powell which portrayed them as the inevitable products of a hypocritical political system, and by the end of that decade he was one of the main reasons for the burgeoning circulation of *Private Eye*, which had started life as a ragged thing on thin paper, its layout patched together on sheets of cardboard in a Soho back room, proud to have been banned by W.H. Smith from all of its shops.

At the *Eye*, Foot had a sharp style that was his own, and among many revelations that caused discomfort and cast light in dark corners, he began to unravel a scandal in the early seventies that became a national *cause célèbre*. John Poulson was an architect who bribed and manipulated a network of acquaintances in public bodies to get himself contracts and was eventually jailed for corruption in 1974, bringing down with him the Conservative

Home Secretary, Reginald Maudling, who had become entangled in his affairs. In Newcastle upon Tyne the Poulson case revealed a corrupt network of contractors and local politicians, and Foot could rightly claim that he had opened the door on a hidden world. Poulson was one of his proudest victims of the *Eye*, but it was in miscarriages of justice that he found his greatest satisfaction. He spent years investigating a string of cases in which he believed that the justice system had failed, and demonstrated a tenacity that few other journalists could aspire to. In the case of the 'Bridgewater Four', jailed for killing a 13-year-old newspaper delivery boy in 1978, he spent eighteen years arguing that they had been wrongly convicted, and finally prevailed.

That case began after he had left the *Eye*. His old friend Ingrams, dismissive of all political ideologies, was uncomfortable with some of his zealotry, and Foot ceased to be a columnist in 1972. He did remain an assiduous contributor to the magazine, however, throughout a period when he devoted most of his energy to political agitation and pamphleteering. Then came a surprising offer: just after the election of Margaret Thatcher in 1979 the *Daily Mirror* gave him a column. For the next fourteen years – including a rocky time under the bullying Robert Maxwell as proprietor – Foot had a mass circulation for his campaigns, pursuing local authorities, businesses and government on behalf of people whom he believed had no power without his pen to help them. The column was emblazoned with a phone number for readers to ring and Foot thought that by the time he left the paper he had responded to 100,000 phone calls and letters. No one else did it quite like him.

And the 'absolute certainty' that drove him never faltered. One of his longest-running campaigns was to clear the name of James Hanratty, who was hanged in 1962 for what was known as the 'A6 murder'. Foot wrote books about the case, spent hundreds of hours pursuing new leads, trying to assemble the truth that he believed had remained concealed. Eventually, in 2001, Hanratty's body was exhumed and, from the DNA evidence obtained, the

Court of Appeal ruled that it was beyond reasonable doubt that he had indeed committed the crime.

Foot could not accept that he had been wrong, He said in a television programme: 'I'm a complete illiterate in relation to the science of DNA, physics and so on. I know nothing about it at all. My doubts stem solely from my very, very clear belief that this man did not commit this murder, so if the science is saying he did commit the murder I say ... there must be something wrong with the science.'

It was pretty weak: his beliefs were so strong that science couldn't get in the way. Friends knew that that was why his politics had played out in the way that they did. And when he had made up his mind – about the hypocrisy of a minister, the inadequacy of a police investigation, the impossibility of a fair society under capitalism – he was immovable. It was an inflexibility that he would mock in others, but without it in himself he would never have had the energy to pursue the campaigns that enlivened and often lifted journalism. His voice was a clarion call to many colleagues in the trade who were encouraged to make more phone calls, dig deeper, refuse to be bought off, never lose their scepticism about officialdom. In the age of spin, many who wouldn't buy his politics did buy that.

Foot stood proudly in a tradition of old English liberalism: independent, contrary, strong-willed to the point of obsession, fearless. Not so much a rebel, more a believer.

Francis Bacon

FRANCIS BACON PAINTED LONELINESS and pain, and left unforgettable images of suffering. Twisted limbs, agonized faces, open mouths ready to scream: Bacon's people are his own, instantly recognizable and the property of no one else. They made him an artist of the first rank, and left a series of pictures that each captured the sensation of a moment – for he said he didn't believe in anything else. That was no pose: his friends say that it was true.

He once said that he wanted his pictures to look 'as if a human being had passed between them, like a snail, leaving a trail of the human presence and memory trace of past events, as the snail leaves its slime'. The misanthropic image caught something of a man who hated his parents, said that life was meaningless, was haunted by the crucifixion but had no religion, yet in the old Soho where he was a famous boozer and barfly he could be convivial, gregarious when the mood took him, funny and generous, a loner who often needed company. When he died in 1992 his paintings were changing hands for tens of millions and had made him a British figurative artist who, like Lucian Freud, touched the whole world.

Bacon was born of English parents in Dublin in 1909 but lived almost continuously in London from the late twenties. Part of the reason was the distance he felt from both his mother and his father. Bacon described his father as narrow-minded and unpleasant, a horse trainer with no friends – which sounds unlikely – and his mother as someone who only established contact with him when she realized he was making money out of painting. He also specialized in self-loathing, saying he disliked his own face, and only went on painting it because there was no one else to sit for him. He said that one of the nicest things said by the artist Jean Cocteau was: 'Each day in the mirror I watch death at work.'

But of course his pictures are full of life. His people leap from the canvas, exposing a distended eye or a broken body, leering or copulating, giving a silent scream. As a painter he was recognized from the forties onwards as an artist who could turn a moment of ugliness, perhaps pain, into a lingering image that couldn't be expunged. He said that he was trying to use established techniques in painting to do something different. 'I think my sensibility is radically different,' he said, 'and if I work as closely as I can with my own sensibility there is a possibility that the image will have a greater reality.'

That sensibility was formed in part by his break with his parents – his father more or less banished him when he was in his mid-teens – and also by his homosexuality, which he discovered early and gave full rein in London, patrolling what he called 'the sexual gymnasium of the city', having limbered up in Berlin. He was attracted to the decadence of the thirties and the strange menace and darkness of the war years. His friend Daniel Farson claimed that he managed to escape being called up with a successful ruse: he hired a German shepherd from Harrods and slept beside the dog the night before his army medical to aggravate his chronic asthma.

By that stage his talent was already being recognized. His 1933 picture *The Crucifixion* was noticed, even though it had been painted by someone untrained and in their twenties. By the end of the war – he claimed he survived those years by gambling – he had established a style that was unmistakably his own. In 1945 he exhibited a triptych called *Three Studies for Figures at the Base of a Crucifixion* which seemed to depict human beings who had been subjected to some terrible, unknown act of violence: they're barely recognizable as people, more like severed limbs and a torso, set against a bright, violent-orange background. The painting caused a fuss, but with the support of artists like Graham Sutherland he was launched, making enough money to leave London for a time and play the tables in Monte Carlo.

By the early fifties, back home, he continued to develop what he called his obsessions. In a series of long interviews with the critic David Sylvester he said that as a non-believer he saw the crucifixion as an act in man's continuing behaviour to others. 'I've always been very moved by pictures about slaughterhouses and meat, and to me they belong very much to the whole thing of the crucifixion. There have been extraordinary photographs which have been done of animals just being taken before they were slaughtered, and the smell of death.'

Yet, for all his profession of insulation from any kind of religious feeling, Bacon had a strange fascination with papal images, saying that he was haunted by the painting of Innocent X by Velázquez, which he considered one of the greatest of portraits. Where Velázquez pictures the Pope on his throne giving a penetrating gaze, quizzical and maybe wise, his mouth set in a determined way, Bacon's own study from the portrait, painted in 1953, has Innocent X screaming, apparently in pain, and gripping the arms of his throne, which seems to be encased in a cage from which he can't escape. It's a picture of suffering and imprisonment. Perhaps rage.

Bacon certainly did not believe that there was an easy escape from the darkness of the world. In his Sylvester interviews he said he thought of life as meaningless: 'We create certain attitudes which give it meaning while we exist, though they themselves are meaningless, really.' That meaning, he said, was simply a way of existing from day to day, with no purpose at all.

Yet he was an artist who could talk of the enjoyment of the 'gilded squalor' of his life in London, especially in Soho. In the fifties and sixties he became a denizen of a drinking club called the Colony Room, which everyone knew as Muriel's, after its formidable proprietor, this being a time when pub opening hours were heavily restricted. Bacon is said to have earned £10 a week for introducing customers to Muriel's, where the clientele included writers and musicians, artists and drifters, and Soho oddballs of every kind. You might find yourself at the bar next to Lucian Freud or a rough young man from the East End hoping to be taken home by Bacon for the night. It was his patch, and he revelled in it.

But there was another side to Bacon. He worked hard. People who saw him lurching from a long and happy lunch in Wheeler's oyster bar to Muriel's, up a creaky stair in Dean Street, maybe didn't guess that he had probably been up very early that morning painting with intense concentration. He worked in his studio habitually from first light until noon, while the drinkers whom he'd join in the afternoon were still sleeping off the previous night's excesses. It was also said that when he waved bottles of champagne around in Muriel's and similar drinking dens, more alcohol would end up in other people's glasses or on the floor than in his own. He described himself as a drifter – from bar to bar and person to person – but he was a deeply serious artist.

The studio where he worked from the sixties onwards was moved, piece by piece, to a Dublin gallery and reconstructed. It took two years to catalogue the contents – 2,000 samples of painting materials, 1,500 photographs, hundreds of books, a hundred slashed canvases, champagne boxes, and torn-up corduroy trousers which he used to create certain textures with paint. There were also drawings: he called them his 'secret vice' because he liked to spread the idea that he couldn't draw and that painting sprang from within, like one of the beautiful canvases that he said were the stuff of his every daydream.

His studio struck visitors as cramped, as if he enjoyed confined spaces. It was inevitable that connections would be made between that and the unhappiness of his early life, his attraction to confinement and pain, and he did offer a partial explanation, though it could have been a tease. The story was that when he was a boy in Dublin his parents would leave him in the care of a maid or housekeeper, whose soldier boyfriend visited her when the coast was clear. Little Francis was locked in a cupboard for the duration of their tryst, because he had an annoying habit of interrupting them, and he says he was kept in the dark, sometimes for hours, screaming to get out. 'That cupboard was the making of me,' he said. It seems a story almost too good to be true: the boy who understands the pain of confinement becomes the painter who executes unforgettable images of loneliness, pain, suffering at the hands of unseen tormentors.

Yet the suffering did come from somewhere. Bacon's paintings, as his first admirers recognized in the forties, have a directness and weight that is sometimes bewildering, making them impossible to turn away from. Bacon spoke of painting as an act that would always be mysterious: 'I know what I want to do but I don't know how to bring it about.' For him, the untrained painter inspired by Picasso and a Velázquez painting of a Pope, it was the only way. He said: 'The cause of the difficulty of painting today is that it will only catch the mystery of reality if the painter doesn't know how to do it. And he's carried along by his passion and doesn't perhaps even know quite what those marks will make ...'

He said that when his idea for a picture had crystallized in his mind, he worked very quickly, and he returned again and again to the themes that wouldn't let him go: crucifixion, the hidden hand of fate that has dealt some wounding blow, fear and loneliness. And mouths. They dominate so many of his paintings, including the self-portraits, and most of them, he said, were screaming. 'I've always been very moved by the movements of the mouth and the shape of the mouth and the teeth ... I like, you may say, the glitter and colour that comes from the mouth.' Then he said that he would like to paint the mouth like Monet painted the sunset.

Photographs of Bacon, young or old, show a man who seemed not to change very much. A wide, rounded face with full cheeks, downturned mouth, big, questing eyes, a quiff over his brow. Usually, he looked serious, often puzzled. You have to look long and hard to find a picture of him laughing.

And maybe, in these pictures, there is longing. He once said: 'I've always wanted and never succeeded in painting the smile.'

John Lennon and Paul McCartney

LIKE MANY YOUNGSTERS OF MY AGE in the early sixties, I just missed the Beatles. In my case, because of a snowstorm. They were due to play at the public hall in our nearby small town – nothing special, a New Year dance – but their plane from Hamburg was diverted, the roads were bad, and they didn't make it. The following night, 3 January 1963, they played at the Two Red Shoes in Elgin, backed by the Alex Sutherland Sextet, the resident band. The Elgin Folk Club had booked them, and paid them £42. But it was too far and for someone of my age, not yet in my teens, still out of my league: the Two Red Shoes was a pleasure palace that would have to wait.

So they passed through, heading for the Highlands for a few more modest gigs, never to return. The local paper advertised them as 'The "Love Me Do" Boys' – that single had been released in October – just to remind people that they had fame beyond our patch. Within a few weeks the problem wasn't attracting a crowd, it was keeping people away. They recorded the album *Please Please Me* in one day in February 1963, a month after skidding through the Highland snow, and the dam broke.

By the summer the screaming hordes were following them around the country, police were on overtime to hold them back and carry off the girls overcome with hysteria, and the Beatles were the phenomenon of the age, responsible for a musical explosion that was louder than any we'd heard: the big bang in which the youth culture of the sixties was born. 'She Loves You' in August was their third number one of the year and stayed there for seven weeks. There have been hundreds of performers since who have stirred their fans to frenzy, and covered their walls in platinum discs, but this was the *first* time; no one had experienced it before, a dance of teenage ecstasy to a soundtrack by Lennon and McCartney. Two generations on, sated by music and dazzled by stars, the young must find it difficult to realize how much of a revelation they were.

The memory of missing the Beatles on stage is a reminder of the speed with which those golden days passed away. Their last public concert was at Candlestick Park, San Francisco, in August 1966, less than four years after 'Love Me Do', and by the end of the sixties their entire recording career as a band was over. No revolution in music had ever been accomplished more quickly, and completely. By the time they broke up and went off in different directions, they had shaped a world that was unrecognizable from the one in which they'd set sail from Liverpool at the start of the decade. They were innovators with a magnetic pulse, a rhythm so distinctive and confident that it became the theme for a thousand variations, a style that, by the end of the sixties, had already launched a whole generation of rock and pop musicians who could all take off in their own directions.

Paul McCartney met John Lennon in July 1957 and agreed to join his skiffle group, the Quarrymen. They were only 15 and 16 years old at the time. George Harrison joined a year later. They found a drummer, Pete Best, in 1960, in the same week that they went to Hamburg for the first time as the Beatles. Nineteen sixty-two was the year in which they failed an audition with Decca, and signed for EMI's Parlophone label, with George Martin as producer, a brilliant musician best known at that time – strange as it may seem – for the fifties novelty song 'Nellie the Elephant'.

Their path was set, and Lennon and McCartney were working on original material for the band.

They weren't the first teenage boys to break into rock 'n' roll, the world that Elvis Presley had opened up for a generation of Americans in the mid-fifties – Cliff Richard, Adam Faith, Billy Fury and others were swept up in it – but by the time Lennon and McCartney had finished writing most of the material for the third album – *A Hard Day's Night* in summer 1964 – the Beatles were established, permanently so it seemed, as the most successful performers of the new age, dressed in the collarless suits that no one else would dare imitate, with their own haircuts, and a manager, Brian Epstein, shrewd enough to realize what he'd got his hands on.

From the start Lennon and McCartney could work magic in the studio. McCartney was a natural tunesmith who could find an original melody on a keyboard or a haunting chord progression with an instinct that he'd always had. Later in life he spent a little time with a distinguished teacher of composition at one of the leading music academies who concluded that there was not much point in continuing: not because McCartney couldn't learn the formal rules of harmony and the niceties of theory, but because he had it all naturally. There was no need to clutter up a native brilliance with academic apparatus. It was infused, instead, by Lennon's fiery instinct.

Lennon was clever and even bookish at school, but restless. His Aunt Mimi, who looked after him even before his mother was killed in a road accident when he was only 16, said: 'He was a bohemian, even as a boy.' He listened to the Goons on the radio, wrote satirical poetry about his teachers, drew cruel caricatures. At Liverpool College of Art, for three years until 1960, he was said to have been an aggressive loner determined to go his own way. With McCartney, who could find a musical voice for any mood, Lennon's edginess and feeling for pain became one of the strands in their music – his voice refusing to succumb to anything too comfortable or too smooth. There was always a rough edge of regret.

In Hamburg, where they played at a club on the notorious Reeperbahn, a street of red lights, they learned the full fun of raw performance, and by mid-1962, with Ringo Starr having replaced Pete Best on drums, they had a sound. Epstein knew how to sell it, but even he didn't know what was coming. Both Lennon and McCartney cherished their inheritance from the American rock 'n' roll on which they'd grown up, and discovered, in just two years or so, that they could turn it naturally into a sound of their own. Their second album, *With the Beatles* (released on the day of President Kennedy's assassination in 1963), established them as the all-conquering band, only a year after 'Love Me Do'. A few months later more than 70 million Americans watched them on *The Ed Sullivan Show* and the roller-coaster took off.

It was powered not simply by instant fame and the first mass fan base in the history of popular music, but by innovation. The Lennon–McCartney partnership couldn't stand still. That was why it broke up in the end (before either of them was 30). It was never shaped by comfort, but energy. Songs that sounded like nothing they'd written before; albums that did things in a new way.

Their albums got better. *Revolver* in 1966 was the precursor to, a year later, an album that still stands as one of the landmark recordings of the sixties, *Sgt Pepper's Lonely Hearts Club Band*, with its cover by Peter Blake, the early flavour of flower power, and a good dose of the drug culture with which they were experimenting (legend having it that it was with Bob Dylan that Lennon started to smoke marijuana heavily, before turning to LSD). The journalist Hunter Davies had persuaded the Beatles to let him follow them around for eighteen months to write a proper account of their lives, and his description of the *Sgt Pepper* sessions in Abbey Road in the resulting biography is a picture of Lennon and McCartney at their creative peak: experimenting with new instruments, searching for new sounds, playing with words, and improvising in sessions that would last for two days at a time.

When tapes were issued years afterwards revealing some of the sessions from their later time together, they captured an echo of these years of creativity: two musicians with different personalities, different ears, but lifted by each other.

Around them, as beneficiaries of the revolution, bands were multiplying and pursuing their own paths. The Rolling Stones were often set up in opposition to the Beatles – the rougher inheritance from blues being their trademark – and it was true that John Lennon found it irritating that Mick Jagger had the street swagger and the bad-boy image that he'd always wanted, only to find himself dressed by Epstein in neat suits and presented on stage with shoes polished and every hair in place. He wanted to escape.

They all did. After *Sgt Pepper* it was less than two years until the Beatles were over. Lennon's drug-taking was increasing, he dabbled with transcendental meditation before falling out of love with it (and the Maharishi Mahesh Yogi, who'd lured them to India), and the song-writing partnership was strained. In the last three years there were two albums that seemed to suggest that inspiration could still flow between them (*The White Album* and *Abbey Road*) but the silliness of *Magical Mystery Tour* and, especially, *Yellow Submarine*, seemed to sound a death-knell.

From Epstein's death in 1967, of a drug overdose that is thought to have been accidental, they took a downhill path. *Abbey Road* was released in summer 1969, the year McCartney was finding that Lennon was more interested in spending time with Yoko Ono, the artist whom he'd married. The journalist Ray Connolly, who was close to both of them, tells of a meeting with Lennon in Canada in which Lennon said: 'I've told the other Beatles I want a divorce from them.' Then he giggled; but it was true. McCartney was upset to be named as the instigator of the break-up: 'I didn't leave the Beatles – the Beatles left the Beatles, but no one wants to be the one who says the party's over.' It was. Years of acrimony followed.

McCartney began a solo career, first with his own band, which was extraordinarily successful. He wrote pop songs, some rock 'n' roll, film scores, even a mass, was knighted, and continues to perform in his seventies, a sixties' elder statesman. Lennon was different. He lived in New York with Ono, agitating, sometimes performing, but apparently frustrated. Asked by a friend if he had retired, he said in the mid-seventies: 'Retired? Hell, I'm dead.' The end came when he was shot dead outside his apartment in the Dakota building on Central Park West in New York on 8 December 1980. He had just turned 40.

Lennon and McCartney left an indelible trail: they gave popular music a personality and a character that they invented, fomented a revolution, and captured the spirit of a generation. They weren't imitators, but trailblazers. The sixties without them can't be imagined. They had few years together, but they were golden.

Margot Fonteyn

DAME MARGOT FONTEYN was the most famous ballerina of the twentieth century, her name as recognizable to people who had only seen her glide across the stage on television as to those who crowded into theatres to watch her perform, and her story is inseparable from the history of the Royal Ballet. She was as delicate and passionate in her middle years as she had been when she hypnotized audiences as a teenager, and her life – taking her to international fame and then a solitary old age on a remote farm in Panama – was a gilded progress shot through with melo-dramatic fire.

She was anointed Prima Ballerina Assoluta by the Royal Ballet in 1979 – a title that harks back to the foundations of classical ballet in Russia – and when she danced for the last time in the eighties everyone knew that there was coming to an end an era of dominance that might not be seen again, stretching right back to the thirties and leaving a series of images of performances that were unforgettable.

Margot Fonteyn was born Margaret Hookham in 1919, of an English father and a mother who was half Irish and half Brazilian, from whom she took her looks and her olive complexion. She was known as Peggy as a girl and it was with that name that she was first seen by the woman who recognized her special artistic gifts and made her a star. She was Ninette de Valois, a half-Irish dancer, born Edris Stannus in Dublin, who became the most important figure in ballet in Britain, founding and leading the companies that set the highest standards.

In the twenties she had danced for the Ballets Russes led by the Russian impresario Sergei Diaghilev and became mentor to the young Alicia Markova, who, with Fonteyn, would come to represent ballet at its most sensuous and exciting. Then, in 1931, de Valois joined Lilian Baylis, who owned the Old Vic and Sadler's Wells in London, to set up her own company. Both were women of immense determination and each was a colourful and forceful character: at the Old Vic Baylis was putting together one of the most celebrated ensembles ever seen on the English stage – it was the domain of Laurence Olivier, John Gielgud, Ralph Richardson and Peggy Ashcroft, among others – and de Valois was trying to bring to London the magic she had seen from Diaghilev.

She had the good fortune to find two figures who could help to make it happen: the composer Constant Lambert and the choreographer Frederick Ashton. As a trio they were unstoppable. And it was in their company, the Vic-Wells Ballet, that Margot Fonteyn arrived as a student, aged 14, in 1934. Her first named role was in a ballet called *The Haunted Ballroom* in that year. She'd changed her name from Hookham to Margot Fontes, taking the Portuguese word for 'fountains' because her mother was the illegitimate daughter of a Brazilian businessman. Never again would she be called Peggy. Then she settled on Fonteyn. De Valois understood her talent immediately, and said: 'We are just in time to save her feet.'

Fonteyn herself, who had not only seen Markova dance but had taken some lessons from her teacher, was already committed to a life in classical ballet, and formed her first important artistic relationship with Ashton (with whom she later had an affair). 'I was exactly the right age to be able to develop coincidentally with the Vic-Wells Ballet,' she recalled. 'I was like a surfer riding a particularly long wave, and it was Markova's departure that launched me.' The star had decided to found her own company at the Windmill Theatre and danced for the last time with the Vic-Wells just as Fonteyn arrived.

Ashton had his eye on her. In 1935 he created the role of the fiancée in his ballet *Le Baiser de la Fée*, with music by Igor Stravinsky, and already Fonteyn was a name in the company. One critic said at the time that her nickname in the gallery was 'the glow worm' because even when the extraordinary flow of her movement stopped, and she stood perfectly still at the side of the stage, you couldn't keep your eyes off her. Yet she told her mother that she found some of Ashton's steps nearly impossible. He said of her that he was already aware of her innate musicality, her wonderful physical proportions, and her sense of line when she danced. Within a very few years her talent had matured: she danced her first Giselle in 1937.

During the Second World War, far from going into hibernation the company was busier than ever. It had been renamed the Sadler's Wells Ballet, with de Valois still dominating proceedings. They danced nightly for troops on leave and war workers, with regular matinées thrown in, touring between their London seasons, and for Fonteyn, like the other dancers, it was less a time for working patiently on technique and interpretation than of adjusting to a gruelling life of perpetual performance.

After the war Fonteyn, in her mid-twenties, was the star of the company, and everyone knew it. But de Valois had to contend with simmering rivalries offstage. In particular, she had a brilliantly attractive dancer in Moira Shearer, who felt that Fonteyn was pushing her aside. But in 1948 Shearer starred in the popular film *The Red Shoes* and became a household name. As it happened, Fonteyn tore a ligament in that same year and couldn't dance for three months. Her starring role in Ashton's new ballet, *Cinderella*, to a score by Prokofiev, was taken over by Shearer, with another famous dancer of the day, Beryl Gray, also in the cast. But before the end of the run Fonteyn was back to alternate with Shearer in the title role, and their performances were the talk of London.

Sixty thousand people saw the ballet. The company went to New York in 1949, and by the time they got back to London Fonteyn was basking in glory: her performances as Princess Aurora in Tchaikovsky's *The Sleeping Beauty* had brought the audiences at the Metropolitan Opera to their feet. It's said that the Mayor of New York, William O'Dwyer, leaned over to de Valois during one performance to give her an accolade: 'You're in, lady.' She had to ask what he meant.

In the early fifties Fonteyn was established as the dancer everyone wanted to see. Sadler's Wells became the Royal Ballet in 1956 and she was the pride of the company. The story is told of a performance at Covent Garden of *Apparitions* by Ashton, with music by Liszt, during which the general administrator of the theatre, David Webster, was in tears as she danced. Somebody asked him what the matter was. 'If you don't understand, you certainly don't deserve to be told,' he replied. They were glory years.

Then, in 1955, she married. It was a decision that, however happy it made her at first, eventually brought in its wake a great deal of pain and trouble. Her husband was a Panamanian named Roberto de Arias who was ambassador to London but was no mild diplomat: he was steeped in the volcanic politics of Central America. Papers released by the National Archives in London in 2012 revealed the story of an attempted coup in Panama for which he had tried, and he believed with some success, to get support from Fidel Castro, who seized power in Cuba in the Communist uprising of 1959. Fonteyn was caught up in the escapade, during which her husband was trying to recruit supporters to take up arms while he and his wife were pretending to take a Caribbean fishing holiday. She was briefly imprisoned in Panama in 1959 and, according to official papers, told the whole story to the British government.

In one minute, dictated at the time, the Foreign Office minister John Profumo – whose name would later become synonymous with sexual scandal – described a meeting with Fonteyn after she had been released from jail. 'I had to pinch myself several times during her visit to make sure I wasn't dreaming the comic opera story that she was unfolding,' he wrote. The British ambassador in Panama was less amused. He wrote to his superiors in London saying that her behaviour had been reprehensible and he hoped she would stay away from Panama for a long time.

Roberto de Arias was shot in an attempted assassination in 1964 and as a result spent the rest of his life in a wheelchair. Meanwhile Fonteyn was dancing, and in 1962 had formed the partnership on the stage that would define her for a new generation of ballet audiences and bring her fame far beyond the confines of any theatre.

On 16 June 1961, at Le Bourget airport in Paris, a young Russian dancer gave the slip to the KGB, who had been watching him on a tour by the Kirov Opera, suspecting that he might try to defect. He was Rudolf Nureyev. He'd only been allowed on the tour because one of the principal dancers was injured, and – frustrated and depressed by the Soviet regime and its restrictions – he took his chance. Within a week, to the consternation of the Russians, Nureyev was dancing with a French ballet company and making news around the world. It was not long before Ninette de Valois asked him to come to London. He performed at a matinée at the Royal Academy of Dance organized by Fonteyn, and de Valois said of his curtain call: 'I saw an arm raised with a noble dignity, a hand expressively extended. I could see him suddenly and clearly in one role – Albrecht in *Giselle*. There and then I decided that when he first danced for us it must be with Fonteyn in that ballet.'

He did, on 21 February 1962. No modern partnership in ballet could touch it. Nureyev's very presence brought drama, and his appearance was magnetic: chiselled features, broad shoulders on a body that tapered to a thin waist, heavy-lidded eyes. He was only 22, she twenty years older. They made magic together, dancing later that year in *Le Corsaire*, and in 1963 creating roles in *Marguerite and Armand* and dancing *La Bayadère* for the first time.

For nearly fifteen years they danced together, and filled the stage. People who had never attended a ballet knew them on television and shared the excitement of audiences who queued for hours to get a standing place at the back of the stalls at Covent Garden or squeeze into a corner in the topmost rows of the theatre. Once, in Vienna, they took eighty-nine curtain calls. They were a phenomenon of their age.

Offstage Nureyev was intemperate, famous for his violent rages and feuds with other dancers and anyone he could find, and in his last years, with his health fast waning from the effects of AIDS, he cut a sad figure during tours on which his admirers believed he should never have embarked. But the tantrums and the failing powers couldn't wipe the memory of the great days that remained.

Fonteyn, too, came to know some sadness. Her husband's incapacity was a huge financial burden and her last years, after retirement in 1979, at the end of a spectacularly long career, were spent in a remote part of Panama, in a farmhouse where she looked after him until his death in 1989. On her last visit to London a year later there was a gala for her at the Royal Opera House in which Nureyev was able to dance and Placido Domingo sang. She died in February 1991 in Panama at the age of 71. De Valois, who outlived her, said that those who had seen her dance would never forget it.

No ballerina of the modern era had achieved such fame, nor had seemed so admired for her beauty, her elegance and her style. Fonteyn lived for the theatre, to hear music and to dance, and it was maybe there, with an audience, that she was happiest. She once said: 'Life offstage has sometimes been a wilderness of unpredictables – in an unchoreographed world.'

Peter Hall

PETER HALL WAS THE SHOOTING STAR of British theatre in his twenties, and one that never burned out. He created the Royal Shakespeare Company, became the first director of the permanent National Theatre, took opera under his wing, and in his eighties is still working harder than many directors half his age. No one could recount the story of the modern English-speaking theatre without having his familiar, bearded figure somewhere close to the centre of the stage.

In a fashion that became familiar, he made his mark with a loud bang. At the age of 24 he directed the first production in English of *Waiting for Godot*. Samuel Beckett's play had opened in Paris two years earlier, 1953, and almost no one in London had heard of it. Hall said it came to dominate his life, the play that ditched literal naturalism. He says: 'Godot provided an empty stage, a tree and two figures who waited and survived. You imagined the rest ... Since Godot, the stage is the place of fantasy.'

He put it on at the tiny Arts Theatre in London, where he was earning £7 a week, and summoned up a storm. At the end of the first week it looked as if it might close; at the end of the second everyone wanted to see it. The actor Robert Morley wrote gloomily: 'I have been brooding in my bath for the last hour and have come to the conclusion that the success of *Waiting for Godot* means the end of the British theatre as we know it.' In a way he was right. A new era was announced, and Hall was leading the charge of the coming generation.

But he was no iconoclast, determined to tear everything down. The reason he was hypnotized by Beckett's play was his language, the text itself: 'I soon felt secure in Beckett's rhythms. This was real dramatic poetry, not applied but organic.' He believed it was the start of modern theatre, and the reason was its poetry. When he made the first great leap of his career, and founded a new company in Stratford-upon-Avon, it was that passion that gave him energy, an obsession with the text. As one young actor complained when Hall was telling him how to speak Shakespeare's lines: 'He's an iambic fundamentalist!' It's true.

That love of the poetry, the near-obsession with text, was instilled in him as a student at Cambridge, where he attended lectures by the fearsome F.R. Leavis, who was no man of the theatre but whose analytical criticism attracted Hall and excited him. He learned why the words mattered. He'd already decided in his teens that he wanted to work in the theatre and he became mesmerized by language, encouraged by another Cambridge don, George 'Dadie' Rylands at King's, who was the polar opposite of Leavis – he was in love with performance – and taught generations of students to love the sound of Shakespeare's verse.

Hall was restless and wanted to turn all this to a purpose, and he sensed that he had a chance. *Godot* had given him celebrity; a young writer of whom he'd never heard, Harold Pinter, sent him a new play. Tennessee Williams wanted to work with him. He directed Peggy Ashcroft in a famous production of *Cymbeline* in Stratford in 1957, and around that time began to think of how the Shakespeare festival there might be given new life and escape the rhythms of its rather tired summer seasons. On a company tour to Leningrad he made his pitch to Fordham Flower, chairman of the board of the Shakespeare Memorial Theatre, whose family had been the pillar of the festival since it began. He'd establish a company that would play Shakespeare at his best, but perform the work of other playwrights too; he'd get directors on board who understood the continental European tradition, like Peter Brook; and, most audaciously of all, he'd create a London base for the company to run alongside Stratford. It was a huge political and financial gamble. He says that Fordham Flower told him: 'You're completely mad, but I'll back you.' And he did.

In 1960 the Royal Shakespeare Company was founded and Hall began to write a chapter in the history of English-speaking theatre. The productions were unrecognizable compared with some of the creaking warhorses that had been pulled out for visitors year after year. The plays were being reworked and freshened, and Hall's regime put the poetry at the heart of it all. A rolling roster of young actors flocked to Stratford to join the new ensemble, a music department began to work with the actors in ways that hadn't been seen before, and, alongside Hall, Brook and the French director Michel Saint-Denis brought a perspective that was quite new. Take two of the productions from those early years: *The Wars of the Roses* and *Marat/Sade*.

Hall and John Barton, a Cambridge don whom he'd lured to Stratford, turned four of Shakespeare's English history plays into a sequence – *The Wars of the Roses* – that, for a generation, revealed the subtle political drama that had often been concealed. This was televised, and Stratford – with the Aldwych Theatre in London as its partner in the West End – was suddenly a powerhouse. Productions like Peter Brook's *King Lear* with Paul Scofield in 1962 and Hall's *Hamlet* with David Warner three years later were benchmarks. And, just as he'd promised, Hall was putting on other plays.

Brook's production of *Marat/Sade* in 1964 was a company landmark. Peter Weiss's play, written in German the year before, dealt with the persecution and death of Jean-Paul Marat in a French asylum at the hands of the Marquis de Sade. For the British theatre – in which censorship was still exercised by the Lord Chamberlain, and whose men sat in the stalls and reported back dutifully on unacceptable outbursts of profanity, sex and violence – *Marat/Sade* was a test case. It passed muster, triumphantly. Two years later Brook won a Tony Award for the Broadway production. The RSC was only six years old.

By the end of the sixties all the risks associated with its birth seemed to have passed away. Hall, exhausted by the pace he demanded of himself, and everyone, had handed the baton to his protégé Trevor Nunn, another product of the Cambridge school of criticism who shared Hall's reverence for text. And it was for him in 1970 that Brook's production of *A Midsummer Night's Dream* set the seal on the company's first decade.

The actors were placed in a fantastical world, performing acrobatics in a vast white box on stage. Movement and text were fused in a rhythmic dream, conceived in meticulous detail by Brook, and executed with dazzling precision. There were none of the familiar props, plenty of heightened sexual imagery, and a cast – with Alan Howard as Oberon – who so beguiled the audience that on the first night there was a standing ovation at the interval. No one had seen a *Dream* like it before; it became an international success that electrified stage production.

Hall's time in Stratford had been revolutionary. It was the same when he became director of the National Theatre in 1973. Laurence Olivier had run the company for ten years but it was Hall who was chosen to supervise the opening of its permanent home on London's South Bank in 1976. He was there for fifteen years, establishing the National, with its three auditoriums, as a home for classical theatre and new work side by side, and as a forcing house for new directors. Throughout his time he continued to battle with the Arts Council and successive governments, convinced that politicians' instincts were fundamentally philistine, and was frequently fed up to find himself an obvious target when anyone wanted to attack public funding for the arts.

He said that whoever was running the National was in a position like Nelson's column: pigeons dumped on you just because you were there. He did take some pleasure, however, from hearing that Margaret Thatcher as Prime Minister had once greeting one of her arts ministers with the words: 'When are we going to be able to stop giving money to awful people like Peter Hall?'

By that stage in his career the awful man was having a ball, despite the ceaseless running battle with those on whom the National had to depend for financial support. In the seventies he took with gusto to the opera stage, alongside his work in the straight theatre, and prospered. Productions of the three Mozart operas with librettos by da Ponte – *The Marriage of Figaro*, *Don Giovanni* and *Così fan tutte* – were among the best of their era, conducted at Glyndebourne by Bernard Haitink, and Hall's success led to a daunting invitation. In 1983 he produced the four operas of Wagner's Ring cycle at Bayreuth, the shrine to which Wagnerians progress every summer, often rather solemnly and always with critical antennae twitching.

It was the centenary of Wagner's death and at the opera house still run by his descendants the expectations were even higher than usual. The operas turned out to be one of the few genuine flops in Hall's career: critically savaged and apparently leaving audiences generally unmoved. Not a happy summer. But at home, Sir Peter, as he'd become in 1977, was still the most powerful force in theatre: the National had survived funding crises, union troubles and governmental disdain, and had put down foundations that wouldn't crumble. When he took over the National it was mounting three or four shows a year; when he left in 1988 there were about twenty.

By the end of the eighties Hall could say that he had shepherded into the world two companies – the RSC and the National – without which English-speaking theatre would have been much less bold and confident, a fragile thing without the prospect of perpetual renewal: the promise that keeps it alive. 'The theatre is always dying, always has been, because it's always changing,' he once said. 'Change looks like imminent death sometimes. But it won't ever go away because it's live and there's nothing you can compare it to because of that.'

The lure of that life has never left him. After he left the National in 1987, he formed his own company and immersed himself again in Shakespeare and Ibsen, Shaw and Pinter. With Pinter, who thought Hall's production of *The Homecoming* was a peak of his career, Hall seemed an inseparable partner, demonstrating his need for classical and contemporary theatre to be played side by side, refreshing the repertoire, discovering new ideas hidden by fashion or neglect, and always returning to the text: its rhythm and its poetry.

As he approached his eighties he was raising money for a new theatre – the Rose, in Kingston, outside London – where he remains artistic director, and planning another summer season with actors who he knew would come when he called them. 'I shall go on until I drop, I suppose,' he says.

Peter Hall can't imagine life without the theatre; and for more than half a century theatre in this country couldn't have been imagined without him.

Terence Conran

No one has had a bigger hand in designing the lives of the British in the past sixty years than Terence Conran. He invented a style in the sixties that gave practicality a flair that seemed continental, and he was the biggest influence in reshaping living rooms and kitchens in the homes of the rich and not so rich alike. He wanted to make things work, and be beautiful too. He was right when he said: 'There's a bit of William Morris in me.'

Morris and the other leaders of the Arts and Crafts movement were the designers who fused an aesthetic belief in beauty with the demands of everyday life and in doing so established a style in the late nineteenth century that became the template for a generation of architects and carpenters, jewellers and metalworkers. Conran's achievement was to recover in the 1960s some of that passion for design, and to banish the unimaginative habits that had taken a grip after the thirties and were encouraged by the austerity of the post war years. It was time to break out, and he did.

It started for him with the Festival of Britain on the South Bank in London in 1951. He had studied textile design at the Central School of Art and Design in the capital, having been inspired by teachers at Bryanston School in Dorset, which had been a lucky choice by his parents: it prized creativity in all the arts, and he found himself utterly at home there. Aged 19, he worked for the architect Dennis Lennon on the South Bank – they were designing a model of the Saunders-Roe Princess flying boat for the Festival – and within a year he was off on his own. It was the centenary of the Great Exhibition at Crystal Palace and Conran saw the site around the newly built Royal Festival Hall as 'a beacon of hope'. He said: 'It started people thinking in a different way – not just about their needs, but about their wants.' He started making furniture and selling it from a basement flat in Notting Hill. Conran and Company was launched in 1952. Four years later he founded the Conran Design Group. One of its jobs was to design the interior of a shop being opened in Knightsbridge by a young fashion designer named Mary Quant.

But the sixties hadn't yet arrived. London was still grimy, its buildings blackened, and choking pea-souper fogs were still very familiar. Clothes were dull and harked back to an earlier time. Even as the sixties began, a visitor would find the men who worked in the City all dressed in a uniform of black jackets, striped trousers, white shirts and bowler hats, as they had been for decades. The scene hadn't changed much since T.S. Eliot watched them walking from the train across London Bridge to their offices and quoted in *The Waste Land* from Dante's *Inferno*: 'I had not thought death had undone so many.'

Change was coming at last, but when Conran was building up his business in the fifties he found it difficult to reach the domestic market. His imagination was frustrated. The breakthrough came for him with a factory in Norfolk, built in 1963. He could produce more furniture with new machines, and it was from there that he dispatched the first consignment of boxes that would one day be so familiar: flat-pack furniture. Things were on the move. The first colour supplement was printed by the *Sunday Times* in 1962, picturing the allure of a stylish life, and he was perfectly placed to take advantage.

Boutiques were opening up, a youth culture was starting to bubble away, and in 1964 Conran opened a shop in Fulham

Road, west London, that he thought would attract a generation of homeowners who were looking for something different and perhaps wanted to feel a little tingle of the shock of the new. It was called Habitat. It had white walls and colourful displays, lots of space, and things that shoppers weren't used to seeing: woks and beanbags, duvets and paper lanterns, furniture with contemporary lines, and colourful wall-hangings. Mary Quant designed clothes for the staff, and Vidal Sassoon did their hair. If you went there you were participating in change, and you were helping to create a fashion.

The design owed a good deal to Conran's affection for the German Bauhaus school, which had flourished in the twenties, in which style and function were combined and then presented with modernist simplicity. Though the aesthetic form was quite different, Morris and his followers would have understood the idea. Conran's notion was that when his customers came through the door they would see that every detail in the shop had been finished with confidence and style. They wouldn't be confused by a mishmash of styles: pieces of furniture would sit happily together, there would be light and colour and a simple layout that would be reassuring. And the prices would be reasonable. When he was planning what he would make and sell, as a guide to himself, he thought of his average customer living on a teacher's salary. They would have some money to spend, but none to waste.

At the start it was a fairly small business. His wife bought all the kitchen equipment and he himself spent a great deal of time in the shop. London, however, was changing fast. It was more prosperous, there was a fashion for fashion, Carnaby Street became a byword for a new dress sense for young men and women, and everyone wanted something new. That hadn't happened before, in the immediate post-war years, and it played into Conran's hands. He didn't have to adapt to change; he had been waiting for it to come.

His vision was to bring home some of the lifestyle that he knew from the continent. He said that when he saw how the French lived in their small towns – with markets piled high with fruit and vegetables, cheese and fish and charcuterie – he wondered why it couldn't be like that back home, and took it as a guide. It was therefore inevitable that, as well as producing furniture and trying to make objects that people wanted, he would turn to food.

Conran had opened two small restaurants in the early fifties, but it was much later that he made his leap. Habitat was expanding – with four shops in London – and he was already associated with a style of domestic furnishing and décor that was part of the sixties. In 1971 he opened in London the Neal Street Restaurant, with menus designed by David Hockney. It was later run by his brother-in-law, the chef Antonio Carluccio, and Conran used it as the start of a food empire. Bibendum in the Michelin Building in Fulham Road, with a Conran Shop next door, opened in the eighties, and by the nineties he was pioneering the 'gastrodome', starting with a cluster of restaurants and food halls on Butler's Wharf, which had been lying empty on the south bank of the Thames. Here he could seat 1,000 people and sell them fresh vegetables, wine and dozens of different kinds of oils, before they rolled home.

When London began to gain a reputation, around the turn of the century, as one of the food capitals of the world, Conran could rightly claim to have been one of the innovators who brought it about. The obsession with quality and simplicity that he brought to domestic design was perfectly suited to a food revolution in which style and ambience would go hand in hand with brave and imaginative cooking. Again he was careful to aim at a mid-market clientele – though he had some restaurants that were cherished by high rollers – and for more than two decades not a year seemed to go by without a new Conran eaterie opening in London or New York, Paris or Tokyo.

His secret is that he has always believed that a taste for beautiful things, or a love of flair in life, doesn't have to be taught, just encouraged. Conran believes that it is there, a natural part of us.

The lesson that he has carried with him through the years was learned in Habitat. In the sixties, he and his designer Stafford Cliff came up with a winning formula for the stores' catalogue: glossy and full of tempting advice about how to create a stylish home, it became part of popular culture. And from this derived *The House Book*, equally eye-catching, which sold more than 2 million copies. In the high street, Conran went on to buy the Heals furniture business, establish the Storehouse Group, create Next, run British Home Stores and Mothercare, and see his design concepts become embedded in the shopping habits of ordinary families.

For nearly forty years after he made his first furniture, these shops were his passion. In 1990, however, he severed his ties with Habitat – there had been trouble behind the scenes – and he confined his retail business to the Conran Shops themselves, the brand established in 1973 on the site of the original Habitat store. He ran interior and architectural design businesses, his restaurants flourished even in recession, and – in a generous gesture of belief – the Conran Group gave many millions of pounds to the Design Museum which he had co-founded. In 2012 it was relocated from the South Bank to Kensington, where it will expand its work in celebrating original and inspiring design in everyday objects as well as in architecture and high fashion.

The Habitat story came to a rather melancholy end. The shops were sold on twice to new owners, and all but three of them closed in 2011. In their prime they had been part of a revolution that the changed the way people in Britain lived, dressed, ate. Conran says that he thinks it took his country fifty years to begin to accept modernity alongside its love of the past, but he can claim to have been one of the pioneers, a kipper-tied, flare-trousered man of the moment in the sixties and a pioneer who re-engineered the living room and the restaurant in the decades that followed.

He doesn't stop. Of his furniture business Benchmark, he says: 'I design something on a Sunday and have a finished prototype by

Friday ... My office has 400 or 500 models of furniture sitting on the shelves. It's like being in a doll's house.' The words of a man who discovered design and style as a boy, and has never forgotten the fun of it.

Enoch Powell

No POLITICAL FIGURE of the past half-century has risen to such heights of fame and influence on such a brief, fragmentary career in office as Enoch Powell. For most of his thirty-seven years in the House of Commons he was an outsider, yet he had a mesmerizing influence on prime ministers and their governments, an electric parliamentary presence, and for many years a fingertip ability to sway the public mood with a word or a glare. Some thought him a preacher of the truth and a philosopher king; others a logician at sea with the realities of politics, even a fanatic. For decades, if they heard the one word 'Enoch', people in politics would stir: something was about to happen.

He was a man who had dreamed of being Viceroy of India, and who – a little more realistically – wondered if he might one day lead the Conservative Party. The speech that made him famous put an end to that ambition. He became instead a relentless and baleful commentator on the evils of pragmatism in politics and a crusader who lost more battles than he won. Yet in old age, out of Parliament, Cassandra regretted nothing. 'I may have failed,' he said. 'That does not mean that I was wrong.' No phrase catches him better. There was right or wrong for Powell: no in-between. He had an absolutist's belief that the choice, once made, had to be carried through. This endeared him to admirers who were refreshed by his contempt for make-and-do political thinking, and often alarmed the others. His Conservative colleague Iain Macleod said: 'Poor Enoch, driven mad by the remorselessness of his own logic.'

That cast of mind was one of the reasons for his brilliance as an orator. The sentences rolled in perfect waves, with a classicist's precision in rhythm and cadence, and he had a gift for the penetrating phrase and memorable conundrum. They were the apparatus of the Tory constitutionalist, but he was a populist too. He spoke of the good sense of the people, the imagined silent sea on which he swam, and knew how to stir it up, on immigration, on Europe, on spendthrift government.

But for more than half his parliamentary career he was defined in the minds of many people by a single speech. It was made on a Saturday afternoon, on 20 April 1968, at the Midland Hotel in Birmingham. Powell had told his friend Clement Jones, of the *Wolverhampton Express and Star* (the local paper for his constituency), that it would 'cause a buzz that will last'. It did.

Immigration and race were sensitive matters in the West Midlands, where Powell had been elected for Wolverhampton South-West in 1950. There had been an ugly racially tinged campaign in the 1964 election in nearby Smethwick, so talk in the West Midlands of a threat to national culture was no academic observation: it was red-raw politics. Powell capped it with an allusion that would always be associated with him. He quoted Virgil: 'Like the Roman, I seem to see the River Tiber foaming with much blood.'

A thunderstorm broke over his head. The next day Edward Heath, leader of the Opposition, sacked him from the shadow cabinet, and the political establishment turned on him. But Powell claimed that he received more than 100,000 letters of support, and dockers from East London – trade unionists to a man – marched to Parliament Square chanting, 'We Want Enoch.' His defence was simple: that he had never believed in the superiority of one race over another. Had he not made a famous parliamentary speech in the fifties – admired in all parties – attacking the policy of his own government in relation to abuses committed on black Kenyans in the Hola camp? He had never supported discriminatory attitudes: his only purpose was to draw attention to the consequences of immigration on communities who had no say in its administration.

His opponents didn't buy that. If he was so concerned about immigration, why had he hardly spoken of it in eighteen years as an MP? And where was the evidence that he cited in his speech for the rampant fear of the white population: a letter from a woman, 'the last in her street', said to have been terrorized, with excrement pushed through her letterbox? She couldn't be found. The accusation was that he knew the effect his words would have, chose the time and place, and let rip with a populist's lust for fame.

The man who divided opinion with such zest had an iron self-control, with surging emotions underneath. As a brilliant classics scholar at Trinity College, Cambridge, he worked relentlessly – starting at dawn – did little socializing, and took all the prizes. He put away the clarinet, which he played well, because he thought it might impede his studies, and never touched it again. He was ambitious, and only 25 when appointed to the chair of Greek at Sydney University. But he had hardly arrived in Australia when he insisted on leaving. There was a war on, and his country needed him.

After serving in the intelligence corps in North Africa he was posted to Delhi. He fell in love with India and imagined a public life that might one day make him Viceroy. Then came independence, in 1947. Powell was horrified, and bewildered by the idea of an Empire with a self-governing India outside it. He agonized, and decided that it must be the end of his cherished Empire. Therefore the emerging Commonwealth, an imperial delusion, was empty. As ever with him, it was all or nothing. He prepared for a political life.

He had been seven years in the House of Commons when he was made a Treasury minister in 1957: it lasted a bare year. He resigned because of his conviction that Harold Macmillan's government was stoking inflation (Powell had become an early monetarist). He did return as Minister of Health in 1960, a post raised to Cabinet rank two years later, but the loner's life still beckoned. After Macmillan's resignation in 1963 – Powell had come to abhor him – he refused to serve under his successor, Sir Alec Douglas-Home, not on personal grounds but on principle because of the way he had been selected by what Iain Macleod called 'the magic circle', acting for the last time before the Conservative Party began to elect its leaders.

Powell took a maverick's third place in the Tory leadership election of 1965 and, after the foaming Tiber speech three years later, returned to his natural place on the back benches. There, with Michael Foot from the Labour left – who liked and admired his fellow dissenter – he raised a famous campaign to force the Wilson government to abandon House of Lords reform, arguing that the supremacy of the Commons must never be challenged by a more powerful rival chamber. This was a rehearsal for what lay ahead.

Ted Heath had one shining objective after the Conservatives' return to power in 1970: to secure the British entry to the European Common Market that had been blocked by France in 1963. Powell saw Parliament under siege from abroad, denounced his government, stirred up his party's nationalist wing, and, after Heath's success in taking Britain into Europe, plotted revenge. He made an offer to Harold Wilson, the Labour leader, who was delighted to organize a political coup. At the climax of the general election campaign of February 1974 Powell broke with his party – Labour having cleared its calendar on the day of his speech to make sure he had a clear run – and denounced Heath and all his works. Vote Labour, said the Highest Tory of them all. To a heckler's cry of 'Judas' afterwards he cried out, 'Judas was paid! I have made a sacrifice.' Both he and Heath, who nurtured a mutual loathing for the rest of their lives, believed it was the speech that tilted the election and let Labour, just, slip back to power.

Powell had forfeited his seat, but was soon taken on by the Ulster Unionists in South Down. Another lost cause, his opponents said, but, in the years when the IRA campaign against British rule was at its most relentlessly violent, he prized a constitutional platform. Not that his fellow Unionists found him at all comfortable: most of them wanted their devolved parliament back – it had been suspended, and direct rule from London imposed in 1971 because of the Troubles – but Powell never believed that Westminster could parcel out its sovereignty and still remain the Parliament he thought it was meant to be.

Margaret Thatcher's election in 1979 was something that should have brought a sparkle to his eye. They had long admired each other, and in a way he had been an architect of her victory: one of the parliamentary soldiers with comrades like Tam Dalyell on the government back benches who denied the Labour government parliaments in Scotland and Wales, fighting devolution every step of the way. Thatcher did look to him for support in the early days, when she championed monetarism (though Powell thought her version half-baked), and then especially when she danced with danger in the unexpected crisis in the Falklands in the spring of 1982, and embarked on a naval campaign in the South Atlantic put together almost overnight that throbbed with risk. Typically, he didn't offer simple, unconditional support. He challenged her.

He reminded her in the Commons chamber that she had been given the sobriquet 'the Iron Lady', and then coined a typical Powellism which he turned into a pun: the country would now discover of what metal she was made.

But he would break with Thatcher, as he had with so many before her. When she was persuaded to take the first step on the long road to accommodation with Dublin on the future of Northern Ireland, by involving the Republic in the mechanisms of the Anglo-Irish Agreement signed in 1985 – which was intended as a symbolic break with the past – Powell accused her to her face of betraying her country, just as he had Heath on Europe, and she was cut to the quick.

Powell was stern, and literally unbending: he had a soldier's ramrod stride. He dressed formally in Parliament, and with those penetrating grey-blue eyes, the deep clefts on each side of his mouth, that monotone voice with its Birmingham echo, and his devastating sharpness in debate, he was an immense figure. Even when he decided to raise a mere point of order, the learned clerks of the Commons would watch him nervously, reaching for their history books.

Behind the scenes he could be witty and warm – although never very clubbable – and he had a notably happy marriage that lasted for forty-six years, and between working on New Testament commentaries and classical texts had the unlikely hobby of DIY. But Powell's public life was not misleading: his purposes were as serious as his appearance.

He died in February 1998 at the age of 85. He was buried in his brigadier's uniform, a badge from the years when King and Empire had inspired him, and before he was gripped for good by a sense of feeling for decline and loss. They were emotions that ran deep, and he knew their power. He once said that the reason that he listened to less music as he was older was that he feared encouraging longings in himself that couldn't be fulfilled.

There was darkness there. Asked as he was about to turn 80 how he would like to be remembered, he replied: 'I should like to have been killed in the war.'

Cicely Saunders

C ICELY SAUNDERS helped a great many people to die. Her assistance was not in ending life prematurely – she was resolute that she could never countenance euthanasia – but in understanding a need that she believed everyone had: for a death that was dignified, as free of pain as possible, and recognized as the last, natural passage of life, stripped of taboos and free of fear. The hospice movement that she founded has championed these principles around the world.

Saunders lived long enough to see the idea that had forced itself upon her half a century before it had become commonplace: that it was good to think more about palliative care, that death could be discussed more openly, that people would face it calmly if they were in the right surroundings with those they knew and loved. She herself died, in 2005, in the first hospice she founded, St Christopher's in south London. By then there was a network of them across the country, and for many people, faced with terminal illness, they were providing exactly the sort of care that she had once had to fight for.

Cicely Saunders was born into a prosperous family in Hertfordshire in 1918. She said her school years were not particularly happy, and her parents didn't think much of her ambition to be a nurse. She read Philosophy, Politics and Economics at St

Anne's College, Oxford, but the war intervened before she graduated. In 1940 she took her chance to follow her instincts and began nursing training at St Thomas's Hospital in London: the first time in her life, she said, that she felt she had fitted in. She went back to Oxford to finish her degree, but was soon back at St Thomas's training as an almoner: performing a role similar to the social work departments of hospitals that would be established after the National Health Service came into being a few years later. She worked with poor families, organized convalescent care, and tried to minimize the damage to families caused by illness.

It was while she was almoner at Archway Hospital in north London that she had an experience that, in retrospect, she realized had changed her life. She met David Tasma, a young Jewish refugee from Poland who had escaped from the Warsaw ghetto. He had inoperable cancer, and in the course of his last days they often discussed the needs of the dying. The relationship was platonic but it left a mark on Saunders that never faded. It was the first of three encounters with Polish men – the last leading to marriage – that made up part of her life's pattern. In his will David left her £500, along with the message that all he had ever wanted was what was in her mind and her heart: he would be, in his words, a window in her home. For the rest of her life she quoted this as an illustration of what she meant when she said that the dying needed not only rigorous medical care, but spirituality and compassion too. 'I realized that we needed not only better pain control but better overall care. People needed the space to be themselves. I coined the term "total pain" from my understanding that dying people have physical, spiritual, psychological and social pain that must be treated. I have been working on that ever since.' David became her inspiration.

Around this time she talked to one surgeon about her interest in the end of life and he told her she must study medicine. 'It's the doctors who desert the dying,' he said. So in 1951 she began her six years of study, becoming a doctor in 1957.

In the late fifties she wrote a series of articles laying out her thinking. The first, for the *St Thomas's Hospital Gazette*, was called simply 'Dying of Cancer'. In subsequent articles in *Nursing Times* and the *Lancet* she sketched out her vision of end-of-life care, talking of a medical team that might 'work together to relieve where they cannot heal, to keep the patient's own struggle within his compass and to bring hope and consolation to the end'.

In 1960 at a hospice for the poor called St Joseph's, in Hackney, Saunders met a Catholic Pole called Antoni. She was his doctor and they developed a deep spiritual and loving relationship through his last days. She has described it as an experience that was the hardest but the most peaceful, the most inhibited but the most liberating that she ever had. Antoni asked her if it would be long, and she told him, 'Not long.' At his death she said that, although she was devastated, she felt happy too. They had had a mere month together.

At the beginning of the sixties, Saunders's thinking about death was radical. There were some charitable hospitals and homes that cared for the very ill, often run by religious institutions, but they were few and the practice was often to pretend that death wouldn't come, until it did. She was arguing for a change of heart about the end of life. She started to raise funds to set up a hospice: it would be called St Christopher's. She had plans for a place where there would be teaching and research as well as care for the patients, and from the start she hoped that the idea would spread. It was a bold piece of thinking: individuals might be sympathetic, but the medical establishment in general was conservative in its thinking.

Saunders wanted a new approach, one that might allow death to be approached in a different atmosphere. 'I didn't have any memories. You see we didn't have a past. So often in bereavement you can go back and unpick and get the good things out of the memories and forgive the things where you got cross, regretted and when you were angry with them. We didn't have any of that so I had to grow up in my bereavement which I suppose was why it turned into such a very creative thing because it was in a sense the power behind all the work that went into finding the money and building St Christopher's.'

The first patients arrived at St Christopher's in 1967. It had only fifty-four beds when it opened, but its impact was enormous. By now there was interest in the United States in her ideas and she had been on three lecture tours. The dean of the nursing school at Yale had been inspired enough by meeting Saunders and hearing her speak that she established the first American team providing care both at a hospice and in the home, in New Haven, Connecticut. Back in the UK, a number of influential doctors were beginning studies into care at the end of life, and one of them, John Hinton, Professor of Psychiatry at the Middlesex Hospital, published a book called *Dying* in 1967, the year St Christopher's opened. It was a study of the acceptance of death among patients – earlier Hinton had studied the care of cancer patients – and his work complemented Saunders's own.

More study was being done on pain relief, but progress was often slow. Two decades would pass before palliative care would be accepted as a formal part of medical training, in 1987. By that time many health professionals had been given training as a result of the founding of St Christopher's. At Saunders's own death, in 2005, 50,000 of them had passed through.

Her thesis was simple: 'You matter because you are you, and you matter until the last moment of your life. We will do all we can to help you, not only to die peacefully, but to live until you die.' Her prescription was the truth. It was important for doctors and staff to say, 'I don't know,' if that was true, and platitudes would be seen for what they were. She believed that sometimes it was important to say nothing, because perhaps what a patient wanted most was the appreciation that what was happening was hard. 'We don't want to smooth everything over and say that everyone is cheerful in a hospice but we do want to say things are real – and reality, when you come to terms with it, has an extraordinary amount of joy hidden there.'

Saunders based a good deal of her thinking on her own Christian faith. It had not been inculcated in her as a child but came later, in her thirties. Although it was firm, and became a bedrock for her, she was insistent that it should not be forced on anyone. Speaking of how she would face her own death, she often said that it was a question of making time. 'I would like to have time. I think one needs time to say thank you. One needs time to say I'm sorry and one needs time to sort out something of yourself and what really matters until perhaps you can finally reach the place and say "Well, I'm me and it's all right." And of course I would be facing death as a Christian with the belief that I will not travel that journey alone and although it isn't a mystery it is a mystery of love. But we wouldn't ever want to impose that feeling on our own patients unless they came forward and asked for it.'

Advances in medical science, including palliative care, have made the approach to death a subject which is now part of the daily discourse: an all-round approach to the care of the terminally ill is accepted not only as good medical practice, but common sense. Campaigns to help more people to fulfil their wish to die at home instead of in hospital get huge public support, end-of-life care is an important part of the training of many health professionals, and many of the taboos surrounding death have been lifted.

Saunders, who became Dame Cicely in 1980, was responsible in part for this change in thinking. On some subjects, however, her own view never changed. She was absolutely opposed to active intervention to end life, and was an important influence on the 1975 Church of England report *On Dying Well*, which made the case for everyone to have a right to reach the end of their days without pain and with dignity: to 'die well'.

She married the third Pole in her life, the artist Marian Bohusz-Szyszko, in 1980. They had first met in 1963 when he was exhibiting in London, when she bought one of his works for the walls of the hospice. He eventually became artist in residence at St Christopher's, setting up a studio there. He died at the hospice in 1995.

In her last twenty-five years Saunders travelled the world spreading her word. In the United States alone there are now more than 3,000 hospices serving over a million patients. In Britain there are 220 hospice and palliative care units and the hospice movement has been established as a model of good medical practice and humanity: exactly the combination that the young almoner Cicely Saunders had envisaged in St Thomas's Hospital during the Second World War.

When she entered St Christopher's for the last time, as a patient, she knew that she had succeeded.

Basil D'Oliveira

THE MOST IMPORTANT TEST MATCH in Basil D'Oliveira's cricket career never took place. He didn't play, and instead was dropped like a stone into a pool, sending ripples through the sporting world, ripples that became waves. The power of that tide was greatly increased by D'Oliveira's adoption of the best values in his game: calm and patience, dignity and rock-solid determination.

As a consequence he was respected not only as a formidable all-round cricketer but the South African who became British because he had to, became famous because he took everything fate could throw at him and managed it, emerging from an ugly and personally distressing political crisis in 1968 with his honour intact, and carrying a moral authority that those who tried to use him had abandoned in the process.

When he arrived to play cricket in England in 1960 he was ready for none of this. For a start, he was suffering culture shock. He had never seen a television, didn't know where he was supposed to sit in a train – might people like him be consigned to a special carriage at the back? – and was playing day to day on grassy pitches the like of which he'd only walked onto a few times in his life. The South Africa that he was leaving behind had not been good to him in any way, but adapting to what was waiting for him wouldn't be easy either: a long summer in the Central Lancashire Cricket League, watered by a good splash of northern rain.

Basil D'Oliveira was born in Cape Town, probably in 1931, although it's disputed and he may have been older, to an Indian-Portuguese family. He was therefore classified under the apartheid rules of South Africa as neither white nor black but 'coloured', and that determined his education, where he lived, his access to public facilities, how he went about his daily business and with whom he could play games. He had no choice. It was the law. The fact that he was a talented cricketer in a sports-mad country, with a natural eye and a gift for bat and ball, was neither here nor there. His path was laid out for him by the state, and he couldn't stray from it. Had his parents been white his talent might have taken him anywhere, even into the national team – but he couldn't set a foot on that ladder.

He was stuck with non-white cricket, in which he was able to prove his skills. In an unofficial Test match against the Kenyans in Nairobi he got 139, and took a couple of dozen wickets on the tour. He knew he was a good player, and was frustrated. So in the late fifties he made a decision that changed his life, and wrote to a hero, the writer and broadcaster John Arlott.

Arlott's was the voice of summer. It seemed to roll out of a Hampshire pub, as rich as the froth on a pint of the best ale, his warm burr paying homage to village greens and shady pavilions under spreading chestnut trees. Like Neville Cardus in Manchester, or C.L.R. James in Trinidad, he wrote about cricket as an explorer might describe a lost city or a climber a new route up a rock face. Arlott also held the resolute opinions of an old liberal, and apartheid was poison to him. He wrote back to D'Oliveira and offered his help.

After a couple of years there was a modest success: a place with Middleton in the Central Lancashire League; £450 for the whole season and he'd have to find his own fare from South Africa. But it was enough. He played well, his contract was extended for two years, and he was taken on an international tour to East Africa, where in Kenya he hit one century in an hour. On a winter visit home to Cape Town he found crowds lining the streets to cheer him, and in England he was on the way up. Tom Graveney, the great Worcestershire batsman, had been on the East African tour and managed to get D'Oliveira signed up, the first non-white South African in the county game. In his first match for his county he scored a century and was a fixture in the team that retained the county championship in 1965: only he and Graveney scored more than 1,500 runs in that season.

D'Oliveira became a British citizen, so a Test career for England now beckoned. He played against the West Indies in 1966 and there was a gleam in his eye: an England tour to South Africa was coming along in the winter of 1968, and he had every reason to suppose that he would be in the team, making a home-coming that would fulfil his dream. He might yet play in a Test in Cape Town.

The Australians toured England in 1968 and D'Oliveira played well in the first Test, being the only England batsman, amid a weak display, to score more than 50. He was 87 not out. And then he was dropped. The first signs of panic in the cricketing establishment were starting to show. Why wasn't he playing? The MCC gave no adequate explanation, and maybe felt some embarrassment when he had to be brought back as a late substitute in the Oval Test at the end of the series, and gratefully scored 158 to help England win and draw the series. As he passed 100, one of the umpires leaned over to him and said: 'You've put the cat among the pigeons now.'

Everyone in cricket knew why. The South African government had been making it clear for months that its apartheid laws forbade its team to play against any side that included a non-white player. There had been one hint from the hardline Prime Minister John Vorster that racially mixed teams might one day be admitted, but anyone who thought that this included D'Oliveira was whistling in the wind: the crisis was about to break.

Vorster followed the Test in Johannesburg, in the company of Tienie Oosthuizen, head of a tobacco firm that had been trying to lure D'Oliveira back to South Africa for a non-white coaching job, very well paid, that would take him out of the spotlight. The deal was that he would never choose to play against South Africa. Now Oosthuizen rang the secretary of Surrey at the Oval after D'Oliveira's batting performance. 'Tell them that if today's centurion is picked, the tour is off.'

At the end of the Oval Test, with D'Oliveira the hero of England, the MCC selection committee sat down to choose the touring side for South Africa. They spent six hours at it, finalizing the squad in the early hours of the morning. And he was omitted, the best Test average of the season not being enough to get him a place.

Some of the minutes from that meeting are missing, so we don't know who said what. But when the chairman of selectors, Doug Insole, announced afterwards that he thought they had picked rather better cricketers than D'Oliveira for the side, the *Guardian*'s editorial said that anyone who believed that would believe the sun was a currant bun. D'Oliveira's biographer, Peter Oborne, wrote years later that at least one person in the room had been acting as a South African spy, feeding information to the South Africa Cricket Association as a channel to Vorster. Those in cricket and in business – in both England and South Africa – who were desperate for the tour to continue, were determined.

But after the touring party was finalized, MCC members whipped up enough support for a meeting of members, the *News of the World* announced that it was signing D'Oliveira as a reporter to cover the tour, and in South Africa Vorster rumbled in response that 'guests who have ulterior motives ... usually find they are not invited'.

Over the next eighteen days the MCC was engulfed by the row. On one side was the cricket establishment, determined to tour South Africa and clinging to the argument that to provoke Vorster by picking D'Oliveira would be playing politics. On the other was the growing anti-apartheid movement and some prominent critics of the old guard in the game, who said that it was South Africa, not England, that had brought politics into sport. Arlott wrote that the MCC 'had never made a sadder, more dramatic or more potentially damaging selection'.

D'Oliveira kept calm in public, but Graveney saw him weep in the dressing room. He received thousands of letters of support, and the government joined in the criticism of the MCC.

In September the MCC found a way out, announcing that the bowler Tom Cartwright was injured. D'Oliveira was picked. For him, it was not a political victory: simply a chance to prove what he could do.

Vorster's government had no interest in such a thing. 'We are not prepared to receive a team thrust upon us by people whose interests are not in the game but to gain certain political objectives which they do not even attempt to hide.' He said it was the team of the anti-apartheid movement. The tour was off.

The D'Oliveira affair was a landmark in the South African story. Peter Hain, a South African still in his twenties who was then leading protests in Britain against apartheid, said afterwards that Nelson Mandela – in prison on Robben Island at the time – told him later that the episode was 'decisive' in the fight against apartheid. For South Africa, years of sporting isolation were beginning.

The place of D'Oliveira as one of the sporting giants of his time is not because of his achievements on the pitch – though they were enough to make him a first-rate cricketer and one of the great all-rounders of his day – but because of what he represented. He was no political campaigner himself, and it was that distance from street protest and raw politics that gave him extra weight. He was simply a cricketer who wanted to play in his homeland.

That the South Africans wanted to stop him was not surprising in the age of apartheid, when they saw the whole world as the enemy; that the MCC was willing to buckle under Vorster's political pressure was a shock to many in the game, though others would take years to admit that they were wrong.

D'Oliveira himself played happily for many years in county cricket, became a coach, and remained a hero in many cricketers' eyes until his death in 2011, aged 80. They knew that all he had ever wanted to do was to play the game.

George Best

THERE IS LITTLE POINT in starting an argument about where precisely George Best ranks among our greatest foot-ballers, because it would never be settled. Better simply to say that he was one of the first to be a modern celebrity, in the era when 'superstar' first became a word, and that his fame was matched by his talent. He was the ragged-haired Belfast boy who dazzled the world, and the artist-footballer who destroyed himself with drink. He will stay in the storybooks. The greatest of the sports writers, his friend Hugh McIlvanney, once said that he had feet like a pickpocket's fingers.

Best arrived at Manchester United at a time when football clubs, for all their fame and the magic their names could evoke, had none of the ostentation that the multi-millionaires of the modern game bring with them. Their owners weren't billionaires – and certainly weren't from Russia or the Gulf – and the young players were more likely to stay in digs with a club landlady than in some suburban hacienda with five garages. There was a passion for the game that wasn't glitzy or measured in gold; fans stood on the terraces; tickets were priced for ordinary families.

Best was spotted in Northern Ireland by a United scout who told the club: 'I think I've found you a genius.' He'd kick a tennis ball around the streets, learning how to hit it precisely at the centre of a door knob so that it would bounce straight back to his feet, and dribble his way to school from the Protestant Cregagh housing estate in east Belfast where he was brought up in a Free Presbyterian family, went to church at least twice on a Sunday, and joined the Orange Order as a teenager. It was a rough upbringing, learning the byways of a sectarian, divided city where vicious taunts were waiting round every corner. But escape was at hand.

When he was only 15, in the summer of 1961, he set off for a two-week trial at United. It didn't go well. Clubs at that time tended to let young players fend for themselves: he was homesick for Belfast and headed back after two days, spooked by Manchester. His father worked on him, and he went back – this time for good. The rules at that time meant he could not turn professional for two years, so he did some menial jobs on the side, until he could sign for the club in May 1963. That month the Beatles were enjoying their first number one, 'From Me to You', and for Best the youthful adventure had begun: a world opened up. He wouldn't go home again. He was selected for the first team five months later, just after the start of the new season – still a skinny slip of a boy who looked, in his own words, like a stick of rhubarb – and by the end of the year he got a place in the team that remained his.

The romance that quickly attached itself to Best was already swirling around his club. When he arrived, only three years had passed since an air crash in the fog at Munich airport after a European match had taken the lives of eight members of the team that had been built by Matt Busby, manager since 1946, and was known as the Busby Babes, swashbuckling boys with Duncan Edwards the best of them all. Bobby Charlton had been on the plane, a 20-year-old, and for him the rest of his time at United – he remains a director of the club – was tinged with the memory of what had been lost, and his awareness of his luck in surviving.

The rebuilding of the team produced a phoenix with rare and exotic plumage. Charlton, Best and Denis Law were brilliant and colourful, instinctive players with different characters on and off the pitch but each with breathtaking flair. Best had arrived at precisely the right moment. Charlton was the playmaker with an old head on young shoulders; Law – signed in 1962 after being one of the first British players to play in the Italian league – was the sinewy streak of lightning who could flit through defences that seemed impregnable; and Best was the darting, swaying winger who painted pictures on the pitch and who, as his colleague Paddy Crerand put it, left his opponents with their blood twisted.

They were the players who announced a new era. In the fifties, players had not been paid much more than a good working wage: some of them took summer jobs to supplement their income. But in the year that Best had his trial with United everything changed. The cap on wages was lifted after a court challenge by the players' union and Johnny Haynes of Fulham become the first £100-a-week footballer. When Jimmy Greaves signed for AC Milan in that same year he got a signing-on fee of £1,000, which was more than he had earned in England in the whole of the previous year.

The game was changing. Footballers were seen on television – in black and white in those days, and no games were broadcast live – and they were starting to become stars. Best fitted the mould. You only had to look at him to realize that he was a care-free character. He played with abandon, toyed with defences, became the cheekiest goal-scorer of them all. For five years after he was given a regular place in the team, he was the exciting boy who seemed to epitomize the reborn United. 'He used either foot,' said Busby, his manager. 'Sometimes he seemed to have six.'

And European football was stirring. For Manchester United the turning point was a game in Portugal in 1966 – the year England won the World Cup at home – when they became the first club to beat Benfica of Lisbon at home in the European competition, and by five goals to one. Best, at the top of his game, scored the first two goals and United were established, for all of Europe to see, as a brilliant side.

But, even then, there were intimations of what was to come. Interviewed by Ian Wooldridge of the *Daily Mail* towards the end of that golden year, Best spoke about the joys of being a star, and the difficulty of keeping his head. He was only 20, but he had three secretaries to answer his fan mail, drove a white Jaguar, had a pop star's wardrobe – and all on a wage that was probably about £160 a week. Later in life he would joke about these years – by the end it counted as very black humour – and said that in the sixties he once gave up women and drink. 'It was the worst twenty minutes of my life,' he'd say.

For him and his club, 1968 was The Year. They had won the First Division championship the year before, and had their eyes fixed on the European crown. In 1967 Celtic had become the first British team to win it, a triumph, in particular, for their manager, Jock Stein. Stein, like Busby and the great Bill Shankly at Liverpool, and later Sir Alex Ferguson, was hewn from solid West of Scotland rock and understood football as a game where unexpected flair and the flash of genius on the pitch came from teams that, first of all, were disciplined and dedicated. The game was everything.

Best was part of a team that had that spirit and in May 1968 – ten years after the Munich disaster – they became champions of Europe for the first time, beating Benfica 4–1 at Wembley. Best scored the second goal, weaving round the goalkeeper with typical insouciance. He was made European Footballer of the Year as well as Football Writers' Player of the Year in Britain. He was 22.

Few people watching from the terraces would have noticed over the next couple of seasons, but his discipline was going, his drinking was getting worse, and the strains of dating one Miss World after another seemed to be getting to him. The sixties decade of glory was nearly over.

And how quickly he fell. Busby, the father figure, retired in 1969 and Best began to look lost. In 1972, on holiday in Majorca, he announced that he was giving up the game. United scrambled him out of that one, but he was misbehaving on the pitch, the club was having to fine him for missing training, and in 1972 he committed the sin of failing to turn up to Charlton's testimonial match at Old Trafford. It was nearly over. The club put him up for sale – for £300,000 – and at first there were no takers. Everyone knew.

Tommy Docherty became United manager in 1972 and persuaded Best to try again, but it didn't work. He drifted to the United States, played for Stockport County, Fulham and Hibernian, among others, but by the eighties he was drinking himself to death. In 1981 he went into a rehabilitation clinic, in America, for the first time, though not for the last. He was declared bankrupt the following year.

The two decades afterwards were miserable and sad. In 2002 he had a liver transplant. But he continued drinking. Three years later he was dead, aged 59.

In Belfast he had a huge funeral. They named an airport after him. Everyone said he was a hero. Hadn't he once been a player of such skill that his party trick had been to place a coin on his heel behind his back, kick it over his head and catch it in his top pocket? But that was a long time ago.

George Best made the game more beautiful, but it killed him.

Germaine Greer

Germaine Greer did not invent sixties feminism in Britain; she just sounded as if she had.

With *The Female Eunuch* in 1970 she caused an explosion in thinking and writing about the place of women in a modern society that was heard in places that hadn't been touched by feminist argument before. This made her celebrated, something she greatly enjoyed, and also irritated many of those who might be thought to have been on her side. For them, she was an unguided missile, hitting some targets and missing others, and personalizing the women's movement in a way that some more sober feminists, concerned more with political theory, found unappetizing. The most unappetizing thing of all was that she was unavoidable.

Germaine Greer was born in Australia in 1939, and had a difficult relationship with her family. She wrote a memoir of her father in 1989, *Daddy, We Hardly Knew You*, which documented the sadness and distance in their relationship. For her whole life she has been writing about natural connections that aren't made: seeing the hidden barriers that she feels everywhere, and living like a bohemian as if to demonstrate that there isn't a single one of them that she can't break down.

She was a student in Melbourne in the fifties, then joined a libertarian set in Sydney, and by the time she arrived at Cambridge

University in the early sixties she was an irrepressible social force, as well as a Byron scholar. While she did her PhD there she was appearing in Footlights' student reviews, getting involved in the newly launched *Private Eye* – she contributed a gardening column under the byline 'Rose Blight' – and later writing for the magazine *Oz*, which had started in Sydney, survived an obscenity prosecution there, and in 1967 arrived in London, where it was eventually the centre of another obscenity case, defended by John Mortimer. Through the sixties Greer was a figure in the counterculture, writing for any magazine that mocked and attacked established ideas: in 1969, for example, editing the underground title *Suck*, published in Amsterdam, for which she posed naked. All the while, she was an academic at Warwick University, pursuing her passion for Shakespeare in particular.

The women's movement in Britain had a long and cherished history, from Mary Wollstonecraft on, through the suffragettes and their successors in the thirties. Greer's instinct, however, was to fight against any tradition: she is a dissenter through and through. In *The Female Eunuch* she was making a case that was very much her own. Her argument was not that 'equality' was desirable, for she thought that the men beside whom women might aspire to equal ambitions were themselves damaged and trapped. Instead she argued for the liberation of gender, for women to be themselves, her thesis being that they had been imprisoned and consequently desexed, asked to accept and be happy in a way of life that was out of date and frustrating.

When the book first appeared, bra-burning had been more of an American than a British phenomenon in the previous few years and feminist thinking was concentrated in intellectual, leftish circles. Greer became a bestseller, reaching young women and students in vast numbers with her assertions about why it was that fewer of them would become professionals than men and why manoeuvring within the established rules of a Western industrialized society wouldn't solve their problems. They needed to recognize that they had been lured into a subservient, desensitized way of life that had become a prison. As always with Greer, her writing was brilliantly polemical, and subjective. She used literature to help make the case for the shame that had been visited on her sex, defeminizing them, sapping their natural strength. Here was a woman who was not only willing to penetrate into the most private thoughts of women, single or married, but also to be a blazing public prophet in their cause.

Women, she said, had become like gelded animals: fat and docile. They needed to regain their vitality, not by dreaming of equality with men, who were enslaved by their own world, but by breaking away – and forgetting about traditional marriage, monogamy, the duty to rear children. The success of the book lay in its appeal to many women who didn't share Greer's radical objectives but found enough truth in the picture she painted to challenge some of the assumptions that held them back, in the workplace and perhaps at home too.

The times were already changing. At the start of the sixties in Britain only one in a hundred adults over 50 was living in a settled relationship outside marriage. Today the figure has risen from that 1 per cent to nearly 17 per cent. By the late sixties divorce reform had introduced an opportunity for women. Most petitions at that time were still being raised by men. A generation later, three-quarters would come from women. Above all, the sixties was the decade of the pill, the beginning of a slow revolution. Oral contraception was made available on the National Health Service in 1961, although at first it tended to be prescribed by doctors to older women who did not want any more pregnancies. Gradually that changed. In 1974 family planning clinics were permitted to prescribe the pill to single women, a decision that was controversial at the time. Abortion had been legalized, under strict conditions, in 1967, and the cumulative effect was to establish the right of women to take more control over sex and childbirth. It was against this background that Greer's call to arms was heard.

She had the good fortune to tap into a feeling for change that was already established – partly by the youth culture that had taken a grip – and to offer a tempting explanation for some of the frustration that young women, in particular, were feeling. Women, she said, had no idea how much men hated them. She used romantic fiction to help to make her point, telling the story of a portrayal of women that had seemed admiring but was in practice destructive.

After *The Female Eunuch* she became a figure on the American scene and in April 1971 in New York she had a famous televised confrontation with Norman Mailer, a writer for whom the macho world of boxing did the same as bullfighting had done for Ernest Hemingway, and who could be relied upon to face down any feminist with an iconoclastic, male left hook. She took him on, taunting him with his own put-down of D.H. Lawrence – 'no stud' – and matching his disdain at every turn.

But afterwards, in an article for *Esquire* magazine, she confessed that she had dined with Mailer after the show and found herself trying hard to win his affection. She wrote: 'I love you, I kept saying, with the unsaid corollary – "so why do you treat me this way?"' It was classic Greer, confessing her own vulnerability while charging into battle, playing with the ambiguities of her own emotions in the heat of it. Angry and skittish at the same time, because she couldn't resist it.

Greer herself describes *The Female Eunuch* as part of the second wave of feminism, and it influenced a whole generation of women. But her prescriptions for social change did not come about. By her standards, the social reforms that began in the sixties and touched women's lives were just fiddling at the edges.

In her time the consumer society got more of a grip, not less. The generation that had responded with alacrity to her irreverent assault on the male world, and women's 'castration', as she described it, may have succeeded in winning more independence for women, better rights in the workplace, and certainly more professional recognition, but if the point was to reject absolutely the consumerism of Western societies, and dismantle its social totems, then Greer has seen reaction rather than progress. She acknowledges it.

Greer has always been a disturbing figure, especially to some of those who are instinctively drawn to her. The only predictable thing about her is that she will do something unexpected. When she published *Sex and Destiny: The Politics of Human Fertility* in 1984, she retreated on some of her prescriptions about free love – which she herself had practised enthusiastically in the sixties – and to the horror of some feminists praised various child-rearing practices prevailing in the developing world. She was denounced by some of those feminists as a social conservative. That criticism reached a peak when, nearly thirty years after *The Female Eunuch*, she wrote *The Whole Woman*, declaring: 'It's time to get angry again.' Why hadn't the world changed as she said it should? If her anger had diminished in the intervening decades, no one had noticed. But in that book she appeared to condemn Western efforts to stop genital mutilation of girls in some societies, arguing that the practice had to be put in context, like breast implants or cosmetic surgery in the West. As she was well aware it would, this caused another blast of outrage.

And, most puzzling of all, why, having described *Big Brother* as 'as dignified as looking through the keyhole in your teenage child's bedroom door', did she agree to take part in the celebrity version in 2005? They shook their heads again: that's Germaine for you.

Her story is a long scream of rage, demanding reaction. She is also, however, funny and eloquent, a pungent and penetrating literary critic who will talk passionately for hours about Shakespeare or opera, with unquenchable zest.

But, if she suspects that all she is going to get in return is a polite critique, she will turn up the heat. As she says, and believes: 'The more people we annoy, the more we know we're doing it right.'

Robert Edwards

JUST BEFORE MIDNIGHT ON 25 JULY 1978, in a crowded operating theatre in Oldham General Hospital, a baby gave her first cry, produced a flood of relief in the room, and announced the birth of a new era. She had been delivered by Caesarean section, and the doctors were anxious to see that all was well. She was, after all, the first of her kind.

She was Louise Brown, who would always be known – memorably, though inaccurately – as the first test tube baby. Inaccurately, because it was not in a test tube that she was conceived. The procedure that allowed her mother's eggs and her father's sperm to come together took place in a glass petri dish. No matter. Louise Brown was the baby who would not have been born otherwise, and the man who made it happen was Robert Edwards.

As the first baby produced by in-vitro fertilization (IVF), Louise naturally became celebrated, but she was also the subject of a moral debate. Edwards, and his colleague Dr Patrick Steptoe, were in the thick of it. Were the doctors fiddling with nature, making laboratory babies? It was not only the Roman Catholic Church which expressed opposition; public misgivings about babies conceived outside the womb were widespread. Would they be healthy? Might there be long-term side effects that would come back to haunt us? More than three decades later most of those fears have subsided, and there is widespread acceptance of the moral justification for IVF births for parents who find it impossible to conceive children naturally. The same cannot be said for research on embryonic stem cells, which now produces a debate remarkably similar to the one that attended the birth of Louise Brown.

Edwards was awarded the Nobel Prize for Medicine in 2010; Steptoe, who would probably have shared the prize, was dead, and it is generally not awarded posthumously. When Edwards received another big prize, the Lasker Prize, in 2001, the biochemist Joseph Goldstein said in his citation: 'We know that IVF was a great leap, because Edwards and Steptoe were immediately attacked by an unlikely trinity – the press, the pope, and prominent Nobel Laureates.'

It certainly was a leap. In the last year for which figures are available, 2010, more than 45,000 women had IVF treatment in this country and nearly 13,000 babies were born as a result. Around the world, the number of people who would never have been born without it is around 5 million.

When Edwards began his research all this seemed a distant hope. His interest had been kindled first at the Institute of Animal Genetics at Edinburgh University, where he had studied for his doctorate in physiology, doing research on mouse embryos. By the time he arrived in 1963 at Cambridge University, where he spent most of his career, other scientists had pioneered in-vitro fertilization in mice, and he began to turn his attention to human embryos in the belief that the procedure was similar from mammal to mammal.

In the late sixties he became aware of an obstetrician and gynaecologist in Oldham who had worked on a way of obtaining human eggs. 'I read about this chap Steptoe in the *Lancet*, about his work with something called a laparoscope – a probe. He was writing about how he had managed to reach the fallopian tubes. I thought – if he can do that, he can reach the ovaries.' Steptoe had pioneered a way of extracting unfertilized eggs from the ovary by making minute incisions in the skin. Edwards realized that Steptoe was the ideal partner for him, because a practical, reliable way of producing eggs was needed for the procedure he was trying to develop.

They agreed to work together, and did so until Steptoe's death in 1988. But his method for extracting the eggs – with his laparoscope – was controversial, even among doctors. Steptoe later recalled being isolated at a gathering of clinicians who thought that he was operating beyond the pale. In 2001 Edwards wrote: 'Ethicists decried us, forecasting abnormal babies, misleading the infertile and misrepresenting our work as really acquiring human embryos for research.' That was one of the most damaging accusations of all: that they were bent on an unethical harvest of eggs for their own purposes, far beyond their stated purposes. It was tough. Funding for their experiments was cut – they were regularly attacked in Parliament as well as from the pulpit – and they stopped publishing regular reports on their research.

The most common accusation was that, far from promising help to infertile couples, they were planning to produce genetically engineered babies, to be produced by surrogate mothers. At that stage no such thing was in their minds. They were grappling, instead, with rather practical problems. For example, Edwards first believed that a woman's eggs took about twelve hours to mature outside the body. Strange though it is to remember it now, knowledge in this field was hazy. Eventually he came to realize that it wouldn't take twelve hours, but twenty-five.

By this time he and Steptoe were working together at Dr Kershaw's Cottage Hospital in Oldham. In the late sixties they had fertilized a human egg in a test tube for the first time, although it didn't develop beyond a single cell division. In 1972 they began to transfer fertilized eggs into the womb, on the assumption that the rate of implantation would be the same as had been found in farm animals when a similar procedure was used. It was not. There were problems. Hormones given to mothers to induce ovulation seemed to interfere with the growth of the embryo; injecting extra hormones to try to cure the problem turned out to make things worse: they induced abortion.

Both men were now determined to persevere with work that they were sure could overcome the practical difficulties that kept cropping up. Edwards was passionate about the benefits that could be available for infertile couples. In a talk in the United States, nearly twenty years after Louise Brown's birth and with huge advances in IVF treatment behind him, he said: 'I have not lost my drive, and I am passionately in favour of a man and a woman having the right to establish their family. That applies also to people who are post-menopausal. I firmly believe that merely because a woman has been unable to conceive for thirty years, that is no reason for us to refuse to help her now. She's fifty-five years old and wants to have a baby. I don't think it's up to me to say no.'

But in the early days some thought that it *was* Edwards's duty to say no. In the very year that he and Steptoe began to work together, 1968, Pope Paul VI produced his encyclical *Humanae Vitae* (Of Human Life), which laid down the Catholic Church's teaching on contraception. IVF was not mentioned, but it was clear where the Church stood on matters of procreation: any interference or interruption in the business of procreation through human sexual contact was wrong. Although many practising Catholics in the years that followed ignored the Pope's teaching on the contraceptive pill, for example, the encyclical became one of the pillars of the arguments against the work of Edwards and Steptoe.

But they carried on. By analysing a patient's hormone levels they could begin to work out the best time for fertilization in order to increase the chances of success. Throughout the early seventies they believed they were approaching the moment when their work might come to fruition. In their work with mice in 1972 they found a way of preventing the spontaneous abortion after the implanting of an embryo that had previously been a problem. Surely it could not be long before they succeeded with a human pregnancy.

Yet they tried more than forty embryo transfers without success. Then there was a partial success. But the pregnancy was ectopic, and failed.

Then, in 1976, they met John and Lesley Brown. The couple had failed to conceive over a period of nine years, and Mrs Brown had been referred to Steptoe in Oldham for advice. He discovered that she had bilateral fallopian tube obstruction. By luck she had found the right doctor. He suggested that she might be a good candidate for the experimental procedure he had developed, which he was sure was robust. She agreed.

In laparoscopic surgery a single egg was taken from one of Lesley Brown's ovaries and then Edwards did his part, supervising the addition of John Brown's sperm to the egg in the laboratory. A few days later the developing embryo was transferred to her uterus. The pregnancy progressed normally, and the baby was Louise Joy Brown.

The moral misgivings that were common currency were overwhelmed by excitement as the news of her birth spread around the world. For millions of childless couples, seemingly destined to go through life unable to conceive, there was hope. The second confirmed birth anywhere in the world was in Glasgow a year later: Alistair Macdonald was born on 14 January 1979. Then there was news from Australia: a girl born in Melbourne by the same process. The following year there were nine births. Work in the United States was progressing fast and soon doctors were able to freeze and subsequently thaw embryos. The procedure was becoming easier. There were still risks, but the lurid predictions of birth defects and uncontrolled multiple births did not come to pass.

By 2012 the UK's Human Fertilisation and Embryology Authority was estimating that for women under 35 years old the chances of a successful pregnancy after a cycle of IVF treatment were about one in three, and only slightly lower for women up to

37. The success declined with age, but even women in their forties could hope to conceive as a consequence of the work that Edwards and Steptoe had pioneered.

They'd had to show grit and determination to pursue their course against a good deal of public uncertainty and, from some quarters, outright hostility, but from the moment that the Browns' daughter was born in Oldham, there was no going back.

Speaking of Louise's arrival, many years later, her mother remembered the sound the two doctors had hoped to hear for so long, and which brought them a surge of relief and hope. She gave 'the biggest yell you have ever heard in your life'.

Jack Jones

JACK JONES WAS THE LAST of the trade union barons. He was a power in the land through a decade in which the balance between government and organized labour swung back and forth, and when sometimes they battled in the streets. When he retired, the unions were approaching a crisis from which they would emerge much weakened, and by the time he died, at the age of 96 in 2009, the Labour movement that he had known all his life had changed utterly.

Jones was the left's most powerful single figure in the late sixties and seventies, leading the Transport and General Workers' Union (TGWU) and finding himself in conflict with Labour as well as Conservative governments on industrial and social policy: a negotiator who became a leader of substance and was therefore respected, disliked and feared. He was the kingpin of the union movement for ten years from 1968, and therefore a bogeyman too. His members knew he would fight for the best deal; on the other side of politics he was seen as the embodiment of raw union power, often caricatured as the most powerful man in Britain, and most of the time a tabloid villain.

The generation that followed him, tortured by the dramatic fall of Arthur Scargill in the miners' strike that began in 1984, carried less clout, had a falling membership, and saw their position in the

Labour Party weakened. When Tony Blair left office in 2007 the original picture of the party as the parliamentary wing of the trade union movement was a quaint memory.

Jones was born, in Liverpool in 1913, into a different world. When he joined the Labour Party in 1927, the year after the general strike, it was still in its infancy, and starting work that same year as an apprentice engineer he was drawn naturally to the union activism and the ideological self-improvement that was such a strong undercurrent in working-class communities. He said he'd been inspired by Robert Tressell's novel *The Ragged Trousered Philanthropists*, plunged into Marxist theory, and then experienced the Depression, losing his first job in the year of the Wall Street Crash, 1929. It was natural that, after becoming secretary of Liverpool Labour College, joining his father as a docker, being elected to the city council, and being fired up by the consequences of unemployment and poverty, he'd find himself fighting in Spain.

The Spanish Civil War, which began in 1936, was a beacon for youngsters on the left, and acted as an ideological rallying point for those who felt the fight against European fascism, and Oswald Mosley's Blackshirt sympathizers at home, was a political imperative. Some had joined the Communist Party; others hadn't. Some were simply volunteers in a cause that had touched them. Life in the International Brigades of volunteers was messy and rough. Jones was injured at the Battle of the Ebro in 1938, but despite the factionalism and the military weakness of the Republican side, he never lost his belief that the Spanish campaign was one of the most important of his life.

That unflinching quality was obvious when he began to move into the hierarchy of the TGWU in the fifties, having become a full-time official on his return from Spain. Frank Cousins, the general secretary, who would serve uncomfortably in Harold Wilson's first government, from 1964, appointed him national officer of the union and, by the time Cousins retired in 1968, Jones was in pole position to be elected his successor.

Almost immediately he had to take up arms against the Labour government. Wilson had decided that he had to address public antipathy to 'wildcat' unofficial strikes led by shop stewards, which were pretty common. A commission led by Lord Donovan recommended changes to try to give full-time union officials more control over negotiations, but he also proposed new legal restrictions, including a compulsory twenty-eight-day cooling-off period before a strike could be called. Barbara Castle, the Minister for Labour, was given the job of selling it to the unions. She failed, not least because of a campaign against her inside the Cabinet, led by the Home Secretary, Jim Callaghan.

Her White Paper, quite tartly entitled 'In Place of Strife', divided the unions. Jones led the left in opposition, including the significant element of Communist Party members in leading positions in the union movement, along with Hugh Scanlon of the engineering union. The government succumbed. Castle was bitter about some of those on the Labour right, like Callaghan and Roy Jenkins, who hadn't stood by her in Cabinet; Wilson was badly wounded, and the débâcle helped to bring on his defeat in 1970.

Jones was in the thick of it. The efforts of Edward Heath's Conservative government to produce tougher union legislation than Wilson's were dogged with difficulty, not least because of the 1971 recession – the worst since the Second World War – which in little over a year more than doubled unemployment, to 1.6 million.

The celebrated sit-in against closure at Upper Clyde Shipbuilders led by the Communist Jimmy Reid was the prelude to several seasons of industrial chaos. A young Arthur Scargill broke onto the scene in February 1972 with a picket of the Saltley Coking Depot in Birmingham, using his miners to support other unions; there were factory occupations elsewhere. The government's Industrial Relations Act, meant to produce order, was encouraging the opposite.

The climax came when the industrial court set up under the act ordered five dockers to stop picketing a depot in East London.

They disobeyed, and went to jail. All the dockers in London walked out, sympathy strikes sprang up, and Jones successfully persuaded the TUC to call a general strike. On that same day, in July 1972, the law lords said the dockers had been jailed illegally, so they walked free.

The Heath government never recovered from the chaos, there were strikes everywhere, ministers had to introduce a compulsory three-day week, and in February 1974 Heath was persuaded to fight an election on the union question under the ill-advised slogan 'Who governs Britain?' The answer from the voters was: not you. The result was a hung parliament. Heath couldn't put a coalition together with Jeremy Thorpe's Liberals and Wilson squeaked in through the back door. In October of that year he held a second election and got a slim working majority.

For the unions, it seemed like a victory. Jones was the power broker – his union now had a record membership of about 2 million – and against the darkest of economic skies, with inflation reaching 26 per cent, he began to talk of a 'social contract' with government. For the Conservative opposition it looked like a surrender, with unions demanding pay deals that the public sector couldn't afford in return for an undeliverable promise of peace. It was caricatured as a time when union leaders would have beer and sandwiches at No. 10 and come away having chalked up another victory over ministers.

Jones always insisted that the achievement of those years was also in establishing mechanisms that no subsequent government, Labour or Conservative, has thought to dismantle, notably the Advisory, Conciliation and Arbitration Service (ACAS) – his idea – which has unquestionably established its place as an honest broker in preventing disputes that would otherwise have led to strikes. It was also he who pushed for strong employment protection legislation – subsequently more controversial – and the establishment of the Health and Safety Executive.

But the relationship with government was heading for the rocks. After 1976 it had lost its majority and under Jim Callaghan was a minority government, held together by an informal pact with the Liberals and bent on austerity: cuts and pay restraint for everyone. The Labour left was being led by Tony Benn inside the Cabinet, whose power to galvanize extra-parliamentary opposition terrified many ministers, and the unions were sour. By late 1978, the year of Jones's retirement, the mood was ugly. A series of public sector strikes was hugely unpopular, and left ministers looking as powerless as Heath's had seemed five years before. The 'Winter of Discontent' took a grip, and the era of Margaret Thatcher was about to begin.

Jones was 70 when he threw his energies into the National Pensioners' Convention, leading it for more than twenty years, still battling at every turn in arguing for a better state pension and more generous allowances. Ministers tangled with him at their peril.

The union world which he'd once dominated was changing very fast. The Thatcher–Scargill struggle over pit closures ended after many battles with defeat for the National Union of Mineworkers in 1985, now effectively destroyed, and its leader became an exile in Barnsley, convinced he had been right but talking to a shrinking band of followers.

The unions ceded their power. The days when Jones or Scanlon could command a Labour Party conference with their huge block votes would soon be over; Labour governments enthusiastically embraced Conservative legislation on strike ballots; the days of the big bosses had gone.

As the biggest of them, Jones could be austere, fearsome across a negotiating table, and often presented a steely, ascetic face to the outside world. But among those with whom he marched he was celebrated as a warm and resolute friend, a colossus in the Labour movement who never wavered, and wore his cloth cap proudly to the end.

He was absolutely a figure of the left, and in 2009 Christopher Andrew's *The Defence of the Realm: The Authorized History of MI5* revealed how the Security Service had long harboured deep suspicions about the closeness of his links to the Soviet Union throughout the Cold War. Oleg Gordievsky, once KGB *rezident* at the Soviet Embassy in London and a British double agent while in that role, went further and claimed that Jones had taken money in exchange for information over many years. Jones always denied that he'd been an undercover Communist (a charge that had been made against him in the early days by the leadership of his own union); but he never denied the depth of his socialist beliefs.

He lived almost his whole life in London in a modest block of flats, never accepted an honour, and – even his fiercest critics would acknowledge – sought none of the comforts or trappings of fame or power. As a union leader he was the last of his kind.

Roald Dahl

ROALD DAHL HAD A CHILD'S-EYE VIEW of the world, which meant that adults in his stories were usually silly, horrible or absurd. And those who were kind were excessively so, because they were the exception. It was a world with rules, and if you were young enough they made sense. He never broke them.

A generation was wrapped up in his books. They were the successors to the readers who had earlier grown up with Enid Blyton and maybe Richmal Crompton, worrying about the Famous Five in another scrape or William's latest bout of hand-to-hand combat with the lisping Violet Elizabeth Bott. Dahl's world floated somewhere offshore, leaving behind spreading farmhouses and ivy-covered public schools, and taking you to a kind of psychedelic realm where James would investigate the inside of the giant peach, or the master thief Fantastic Mr Fox went about his business, or the witches turned from grey-haired respectable women into bloodthirsty predators. It was full of colour, violence and transformation.

There was enough darkness, and enough glamour, in Dahl's life to make this natural territory for him. However, the reason for his success lay not only in the nature of his quirky imagination but also in the gift that was first spotted in him by C.S. Forester, author of the Horatio Hornblower sea adventures. Dahl was in Washington during the Second World War, working as an assistant air attaché at the British Embassy, and Forester had been commissioned to write up some rattling war experiences to help the effort. Dahl had knocked about a bit in North Africa as a fighter pilot – he'd been badly injured when his plane crashed in the desert – and they met for lunch. The author asked him for notes, which Dahl duly supplied, and Forester sent them straight to the *Saturday Evening Post*, where they were published for a huge readership. Forester wrote back: 'Did you know you were a writer? I haven't changed a word.' A cheque for $900 was in the post.

Dahl had a dizzying start. He wrote a book called *The Gremlins*, in which Walt Disney showed interest, and it was somehow noticed by Eleanor Roosevelt, the first lady. So Dahl found himself invited to the White House and to Hyde Park, the Roosevelts' country seat in New York State. He whirled through New York society, sweeping up socialites like Clare Boothe Luce as he went, and became a favourite of William Stephenson – later immortalized as the Man called Intrepid – who ran a shadowy British intelligence outfit in the United States and pumped Dahl for interesting gossip from the tables and bedrooms of the powerful. Dahl apparently produced a regular supply. And he became a short story writer.

American magazines were hungry for classy writers, because they cared about the short story, and Dahl entered a gilded circle. He became a friend of Ernest Hemingway and (it's said) a lover of his wife, Martha Gellhorn. He was writing prolifically, and in the early fifties Alfred Hitchcock asked him to produce scripts for his television series of spine-chilling tales. A typical short story was 'Lamb to the Slaughter', in which a woman beat her husband to death with a frozen leg of lamb, then cooked it and served it up to the policeman who arrived to question her. Tasteless? 'I thought it was hilarious,' said Dahl. 'What's horrible is basically funny in fiction.' He would discover that children agreed with him.

Dahl was an imposing man, six feet five and three-quarter inches tall. He was born in Wales of Norwegian parents, and from an early age his life was punctuated by tragedy. A burst appendix killed his older sister when he was only 3, and his father died prematurely soon afterwards. He could have been forgiven for thinking that it set a pattern. He was nearly killed in an air crash in North Africa in the war; his four-month-old son Theo was gravely injured and brain-damaged when he was hit by a car in New York; his first wife, the actress Patricia Neal, had a stroke in the early sixties aged only 39; his eldest daughter, Olivia, died from the complications of measles; and he had to put up with a long series of spine operations as a result of his wartime injuries. It isn't surprising that he is often thought to have developed his macabre, black humour from his own experiences. Unhappiness was never far away. He'd recall, for example, his English boarding school, where the headmaster would beat the boys until blood ran down their legs.

For him, the grotesque was sometimes a way of dealing with a haunting memory, or the unbearable. Take the experience out of the world – give it wings – and the child's mind will make sense of it. He had a gift, he once said. 'The mind of a child is a dark wood. It is full of secret, half-civilized thoughts that are forgotten like dreams a short time afterwards. And it is no easy matter for the adult to recall totally and with absolute clarity some forty or fifty years later what it was like to be a little boy or a little girl.'

'I can do it.'

When, at the start of the sixties, he began to make up bedtime stories for his daughters, he had experience of a life that was already touched by tragedy and also by excitement, and the skill of a writer-craftsman whose words came naturally and who knew how to manage them. As Hemingway himself had told him, passing on what he thought was a trick of the trade: 'When it's going good, stop. Never write yourself out.'

The result was *James and the Giant Peach*, published in America in 1961, and it set the pattern. James was an orphan with terrible aunts as guardians. His real friends looked like insects, and lived inside a giant peach. They let him escape, taking him to enjoy the thrills of New York.

Charlie and the Chocolate Factory followed three years later, a fairy tale of success visited on the most unlikely hero, and a come-uppance for those who would do him down, with the classic Dahl quality of effervescent fable. It sold 2 million copies in its first Chinese edition twenty-five years after it was written, a story that spoke to everyone, eventually. From there he seemed never to hit a dud note, with high points including *The BFG*, *Danny the Champion of the World*, *The Twits*, *The Witches* and *Matilda*, which in 2011 became a West End and international musical hit in an adaptation by the comedian and musician Tim Minchin.

He became the world's best-selling children's writer, working away in a white shed at the bottom of his garden in Great Missenden, Buckinghamshire. Visitors did not find it a particu-larly appealing nest for a writer who by then could have had anything he wanted. Through the primrose yellow door there was a room with the walls stained with nicotine, old heaters that apparently didn't work too well, and a collection of odd objects scattered around – at one stage, bits of three artificial hips that he'd gone through.

He spoke to interviewers with a weary air, suffused in smoke from his Cartier cigarettes, appearing to enjoy confirming the image that had taken hold: that he was difficult, sometimes unpleasant, and cynically inclined. Yet he said that when he was in his hut he always had a good time. For him that meant sharing 'the slight sense that people are quite nasty' and that adults are the enemy of the child because of the obligation that's placed on them to try to civilize the thing that is born 'as an animal with no manners, no moral sense at all'.

But of his own moral sense, he said that it only had one purpose: to teach children to read. The most important thing was to make sure that they weren't daunted by books. 'Wherever you are going to be you are going to have to have books.'

Dahl, who died in 1990 aged 74, gave his readers a means of escape from a world that he himself didn't seem to like very much. He may have been blissfully happy in his shed, where he could inhabit a different place, with Matilda or James, or the kids who turn the tables on the witches and send them scurrying for the hills, but his misanthropic side can't be denied. Away from the shed he was a less contented man, stuck with a world that he still liked to see through a child's lens: a place often threatening and usually absurd.

He didn't find that odd. He used to say that he had more love for children than many who wrote for them, claiming that Beatrix Potter disliked them so much – having none of her own – that she had even been known to throw things at them in the street, in a display worthy of Mr McGregor coming into the garden with his scary rake to chase away the rabbits. His dislike was for the real world, not the one he imagined, where he was at home with the darkness, the cruelty, the surprise.

No one in his time touched so many children's imaginations. After the Blyton era, he opened a window to a different place, as if he were opening the door to his shed. As J.K. Rowling would do in the nineties with a wholly unexpected return to magic and fantasy that hypnotized a new generation of readers, Dahl wrote in a style that was inimitable, as vivid as the unforgettable accompanying illustrations by Quentin Blake that imprinted pictures of those weird adventures on every reader's mind.

He told them what he thought the world was really like, and they understood what he meant.

David Bowie

Ziggy Stardust came into the world in 1972. David Bowie opened a concert at the Royal Festival Hall in London with the words, 'I'm Ziggy', and he was. His alter ego, who wore platform shoes, weird jumpsuits or multi-coloured leotards, and sprouted carrot-red hair, became what he called, with his love of the glamorous and the absurd, 'the most talked about man in the world'. But the alien, rock-star spaceman from somewhere else was also a monster whom his creator wanted to disown, after only about a year. He left a question that's still unanswered: who exactly is David Bowie?

He is certainly not David Jones, which is what his parents called him in south London, where he was born in 1947. He abandoned the name in the sixties when he started recording with Parlophone – he led Davy Jones and the Lower Third – because he wanted to avoid confusion with Davy Jones of the Monkees, the band created for television. He was also more than the singer whose first solo album included tracks like 'Please Mr Gravedigger' and 'The Laughing Gnome' because his cockney persona, reminiscent of Anthony Newley and the novelty song, was only a warm-up. It was when he became unearthly that he started to get a musical personality.

He had a lucky break in 1969 when the BBC used his 'Space Oddity' as part of the programme soundtrack for the Apollo 11 landing. Major Tom floated through space in a tin can, about to step out into nothingness. It was a time when space was an obsession. Visits to the moon studio between regular programmes became a national habit and the whole country learned the first rules of space travel at the feet of Patrick Moore, resident astronomer and archetypal dishevelled man of science, whose eyebrows performed a nightly St Vitus' dance as the astronauts headed for Tranquility Base on the moon, where they landed on 20 July.

Bowie, who took his name from the American Western hero Jim Bowie for reasons no one has satisfactorily explained, turned that fame into an original journey of his own. His album *The Rise and Fall of Ziggy Stardust and the Spiders from Mars* was released in 1972. When he said afterwards that the character arrived at 'the rightest, ripest time', he hit the nail on the head. He was the performer who'd broken away from the rock and pop mainstream established by the end of the sixties: an outsider, with a decadent glamour that was weird because he fitted none of the stereotypes. 'That dear creature,' says Bowie. 'I loved him.'

He told *Melody Maker* afterwards that he worried, because he thought the worldwide hype had occurred before the artist in him had really proved himself. That's why he saw Ziggy as a monster, who grew and grew before his eyes, with Bowie himself as Dr Frankenstein in the laboratory. 'Ziggy follows David Bowie very closely, but they are indeed two different people. What have I created?' he said. He wasn't sure.

He plucked ideas from the air, he said, and only later looked to see what he had plucked. There was Ziggy, then Aladdin Sane – the album cover with the livid red slashes across his pale face – then Jean Genie. The moment you thought you'd caught him, he was transformed again.

No wonder he took to the mime artist Lindsay Kemp, who said, 'I taught David to free his body.' Kemp was in at the birth of Ziggy Stardust, teaching Bowie his moves and orchestrating the sinuous and sometimes menacing camp routines that created the persona on stage.

Bowie may indeed have worried about the hype, which seemed to come from nowhere, but through his songs he was creating a personality that was real. Tracks like 'Oh! You Pretty Things', 'Queen Bitch' and 'Rebel Rebel' established him as the shining emblem of glam rock – Marc Bolan and Freddie Mercury became devotees – and a sparkling precursor of punk as well, when others would turn his psychedelic glitter into black.

He was now the leading gender-bender of his time. Rock stars in the early seventies hadn't yet been fully released from the shackles of sexual convention: they might be renowned for wild behaviour on the road, and even occasionally admit to a drug habit, but sex was usually more private. There was none of today's easy discussion of homosexuality. Bowie was having none of it. He said that he was bisexual – indeed at one press conference, asked if he was gay, he said, 'I always have been' – and with his first wife Angela he swapped clothes for photographs, adopting Ziggy's androgynous character. Bowie's persona at that time could be summed up by something he said about Angie: 'When we met, we were both laying the same man.' He said afterwards that he regretted what he'd said about his sexuality, because it became such an obsession for everyone who interviewed him or wrote about him, but he certainly didn't regret the fact itself. How could you understand the chameleon performer without it?

He moved from cult status to the rock mainstream in the United States in 1975, when his album *Young Americans* accompanied his move to New York and he joined the rock aristocracy. He co-wrote 'Fame' with John Lennon, who sang backing tracks with him, and was the epitome of glamour. His early days in rhythm and blues in south London in the sixties were far behind, and instead of the pre-punk Ziggy he became the white soul boy, dressed in fifties hipster clothes, though one still in search of decadence. He wanted nothing to be permanent, everything to churn around him. For a while he called himself 'the thin white duke', but before long it was time to move on again. In one interview he said that he adopted a character for whatever he happened to be doing at the time. 'I've said that so many times, I'm getting used to trotting it out. I might look like Zsa Zsa Gabor next month, or Marlon Brando, you can never tell – 'cos I don't know what I'll feel like then.'

He did feel like a blast of Berlin, so he moved there in 1977, and it was bad for him. His marriage was coming apart, and he developed a serious cocaine addiction. The trio of albums from the late seventies, despite his collaboration with the innovative musician and producer Brian Eno, seemed to be taking him up a siding, and by his standards they weren't successful. It was only when he moved back to the United States at the end of the decade that his life stabilized.

He found that he was still capable of surprise. Who would have thought that the man who lived inside Ziggy Stardust would ever sing a corny duet with Bing Crosby, who admitted that he'd never heard of Bowie? But he did, on TV in 1977, and again in 1982 for a Christmas single.

There was nothing he wouldn't try. He started to dress like the young Sinatra, which horrified some of the rock writers who'd been so excited by his glamorous inventions of a decade earlier, and he had fabulous successes: 'Let's Dance', 'Modern World', 'China Girl'. And then came a famous collaboration with Mick Jagger. Their version of Martha and the Vandellas' song 'Dancing in the Street', shown at the Live Aid concert in 1984, was a huge hit around the world the following year. Between them they seemed to recapture the edgy atmosphere of the sixties, when Jagger was the thrusting, impossibly agile life force of the Rolling Stones and Bowie was beginning his journey of experimentation. They were still performers with access to a magic source of energy, whose antics on stage had entranced a generation. Bowie's first wife Angie once said she had come across them naked and asleep in bed together, exhausted. She assumed after sex. A natural pair.

Watching them in the eighties was to remember how far they'd come, Jagger still fronting the rock band with the longest record of success in rock history – which would still be touring twenty-five years later – and Bowie, carrying with him every twist and turn of his seventies fame: the sexual ambiguity, the drugs, the colour and movement of an individual artist who resisted imitation. By the eighties he had succeeded in establishing the fact that rock 'n' roll was a pose: 'My statement is very pointed – except that it's very ambiguous. Rock 'n' roll is walking all over everybody.'

He had the capacity to hypnotize an audience. Madonna said that he changed her life when she was 15 and sneaked away from home without her father's permission to attend her first rock concert, watching Bowie in Detroit. 'I was just your normal, dysfunctional, rebellious teenager from the Midwest, and he truly changed my life …' When she put on her high platform shoes and a long black silk cape and hitchhiked with a friend to the forbidden concert, nothing could be the same again.

Bowie's originality lit up the seventies and throughout the eighties he was still recording intensely. He is reckoned to have sold more than 140 million albums. Although in the nineties it was fairly clear that his most productive days were probably behind him, his place in the pantheon was assured. When he was inducted into the Rock 'n' Roll Hall of Fame he was described as an artist who'd been glamorous, perverse, fun, sexy and confusing. 'He was both a kind of shrink and a priest, a sex object and a prophet of doom,' his citation said.

He was an innovator, a style icon and a performer of extraordinary originality. He is also a serious man, an art collector who has bought Tintoretto and Rembrandt as well as contemporary painters like the Glasgow artist Peter Howson, whose examination of mental torment and portraits of war have captivated him. Though he has liked to appear unsettled, sometimes even skittish, throughout his career, Bowie has always taken his music seriously.

It may all have been a pose, but he has meant it. 'I never had much luck telling people I was an actor,' he once said, 'so I let everyone else figure it out.'

Talaiasi Labalaba

THE NAME OF TALAIASI LABALABA is almost unknown in
this country, except where some soldiers gather. He is a secret
hero. He even has a statue in his honour, which the public never
sees. He was a British soldier, killed in action, and his death, too,
was almost a secret. Telling his story is like pointing to the tomb
of the Unknown Soldier and opening a book.

For Labalaba has a significance quite like that representative,
nameless figure buried at Westminster Abbey and celebrated as an
emblem of a military life and death. His own brief life under arms
illuminates a dark and dangerous part of our military history
since the Second World War, and also the way the army's role has
changed in our time. After his death, in 1972, the kind of operation for which he was trained became more common and rather
better known. His regiment was the SAS.

He was a sergeant, known by all his fellow soldiers as Laba,
and he was killed in the Battle of Mirbat, an engagement in the
Gulf state of Oman during a long war between the Sultan (who
trained as a soldier at Sandhurst) and communist-supported guerrillas, in which Britain, officially, was not involved. But it was one
of the proxy struggles of the Cold War, with at stake the prize of
access to the Gulf through the Strait of Hormuz. British officers
had advised the Sultan in the coup in which he deposed his father

in 1970 and, with the Saudis and the Shah of Iran in support, as well as India and Pakistan, the British government was committed to preventing the birth of a People's Republic of Oman, certain to transfer its loyalty from Western powers to the Soviet Union.

In the SAS, the Battle of Mirbat is celebrated as the exemplar of the regiment's skill and courage. It was short, lasting from dawn until noon, and the casualty figures were low compared with the contemporary killings every week around the world in seemingly ceaseless urban warfare. For the SAS, however, Mirbat became a legend. Nine men, with a few local warriors to help them, faced hundreds of guerrillas in a battle for control of an important coastal town. They were ill-equipped for the fight, and the chances of their holding out until air support could be organized were remote.

It was 19 July 1972 and the team were due to go home the next day. But that morning there was a guerrilla attack from the mountains surrounding the town. They had to fight for survival. It was Laba who made the difference. He had been born in Fiji, a fighter who was known by his colleagues as a gentle giant, a man of iron loyalty and formidable courage. He manned a twenty-five-pound gun which would usually require between four and six men to operate. While he was assisted for brief periods, he was largely operating it on his own. He held out while under attack, repelling wave after wave of the enemy. Without him his colleagues could not have survived.

In other circumstances he would surely have been decorated, perhaps with the highest award of all. But it was a secret war. Laba was mentioned in dispatches, and other awards were announced two years later, but not for Laba. Yet his regiment is particularly proud of his gallantry and valour, and every SAS soldier is told his story. The regiment believe that his deeds speak for themselves.

The Oman operation, conducted over several years with no publicity, would be familiar to a later generation reared on news reports of guerrilla warfare, seemingly permanent insurgency in one continent or another, suicide bombings. That was a different time. To anyone uninitiated in military ways, the SAS was unknown. This changed in the spring of 1980. At half past eleven on the morning of Wednesday, 30 April, six armed Iranians over-powered PC Trevor Lock of the diplomatic protection squad as he stood guard outside their embassy, got inside, and took twenty-six hostages. They were protesting against the regime of Ayatollah Khomeini which had come to power the year before, after the fall of the Shah, and said they would execute the hostages one by one, and blow up the embassy, if ninety-one political prisoners in Iran were not released. They demanded a plane to fly them, and their hostages, home.

The crisis lasted for six days, with the nation watching and listening. By the weekend five hostages had been released because they were ill or hurt, and two deadlines set by the attackers passed without shots being heard. Contact had been made by police with the leader of the gang, apparently the only one who spoke English, but on Monday the atmosphere changed. They wanted confirmation that all their demands would be met, but didn't get it. An Iranian hostage was shot and his body was pushed through a door into the street just after seven o'clock that evening.

The Home Secretary, Willie Whitelaw, then authorized the attack on the building that had been planned in the preceding days, and millions of television viewers – it was a Bank Holiday Monday – saw the SAS in action for the first time. Men in black were seen dropping from the roof, and were inside the embassy within a minute. Explosions were heard. Within seven minutes a white flag was being waved from a window. Nineteen hostages were rescued, with two of the survivors injured. Five hostage-takers were killed; only one survived, and he would later receive a life sentence for his actions.

The Prime Minister, Margaret Thatcher, made a triumphant statement to the House of Commons the next day.

The operation brought into the open a regiment that had always prized its anonymity. Ken Connor, who served with the SAS for nearly twenty-five years and wrote a history of the regiment, said that well before 1980 the commanding officer used to tell troops who'd survived the famously gruelling selection course: 'Rank? Forget it, you're not getting any. Career? If you stay here you won't have one. Pay? If you want money, you'll get none.'

After the Iranian Embassy siege, the regiment became a source of fascination. Naturally, its activities fitted into a world in which anti-terrorist operations seemed to be the military preoccupation. In that sense the Falklands conflict in 1982 was an exception: the dispatch of a vast task force to the South Atlantic to fight a conventional war with Argentina over the islands looked like a throwback to an age that most people, including the Royal Navy, thought had gone. Most military crises seemed to be different. After the hijacking of a German airliner by a Palestinian in 1977, when the SAS had helped to rescue hostages at Mogadishu, people spoke of an 'age of terrorism', and the siege at the London embassy introduced a television audience to a new kind of conflict.

For the SAS, it was hardly new. Since being formed by Colonel David Stirling in the Second World War the regiment had been involved undercover in the Malayan emergency from 1948 onwards, in Muscat and Oman, Borneo, Aden, from where the last British troops left Yemen in 1967, and elsewhere. And from 1969, when troops were deployed on the streets of Northern Ireland, SAS soldiers were involved in civil conflict throughout years of bloody and divisive struggles that took more than a generation to come to a political settlement.

Most of the history of the SAS was played out against the background of the Cold War, when every civil war, each terrorist kidnapping, was projected against the background of a struggle for supremacy between East and West. The paradox was that for the majority of British military personnel in that time, the most testing active service was in home streets, in Belfast or Derry or Crossmaglen. The Falklands conflict notwithstanding, in which 255 British servicemen died, the Cold War years were not a time of conventional fighting.

It was only after the collapse of the Soviet Union that British troops began to go to war in large numbers. In 1990–1 they were in Kuwait and Iraq in the first Gulf War, the following year in Bosnia, back in the Gulf in 1998, then to Kosovo in 1999, Sierra Leone in 2000, and, immediately after the attacks on the World Trade Center in New York on 11 September 2001, dispatched to Afghanistan, scene of bloody and inconclusive imperial war at the end of the nineteenth century. In 2003 war came to Iraq, the most politically divisive military intervention in living memory. Tony Blair, who had been Prime Minister for six years when it began, took responsibility for more military campaigns than any Prime Minister since the Second World War. No one knows how many civilians died in Iraq, but the number was huge. By the middle of 2012 more than 500 members of the British forces had died there and in Afghanistan.

The action in which Laba died in 1972, a British operation about which the public knew almost nothing, was a template for what would follow a generation after him: covert operations, guerrilla warfare that swung back and forth, asymmetric conflicts in which the armies of big powers were engaged and tormented by tiny groups or individuals, bent on a variety of campaigns which soldiers' mothers and fathers back home could hardly be expected to understand.

A quarter of a century on, the world of Laba's SAS, and the expectation of the army and the other services, seem simple by comparison. The reason for his special place in the history of his regiment, and for his statue that stands at their base, is that its founding principle was that danger would come in unexpected ways and that bravery and the command to risk everything would often come with no promise of reward. And the reason why Talaiasi Labalaba helps to tell the story of his time is that it has turned out to be even more obviously true forty years on than it was when he died.

Jocelyn Bell Burnell

WHEN JOCELYN BELL BURNELL made one of the most exciting discoveries in modern astronomy they called it in the laboratory 'Little Green Men', just in case. She had picked up signals from deepest space that hadn't been seen or heard before. They were a mystery. No one knew where they came from; what produced them. Were they freak reflections from a planet, or even our own moon? Was some man-made satellite probe, lost in space, emitting a last message as it sped away?

It was November 1967, and at least one astrophysicist in her lab at Cambridge University wondered if they were the most suggestive evidence yet of an extra-terrestrial intelligence. Half in fun, she called them LGM, her Little Green Men. But within a few weeks she had established that they weren't messages from other beings. Hard on the heels of the first traces, she discovered others – coming from somewhere else in space. It was unlikely that different extra-terrestrial intelligences had chosen exactly the same moment to send similar messages. Goodbye, LGM.

Then she noticed a pattern in the way the source of the signals changed position, staying fixed with respect to the position of the stars. Jocelyn Bell, aged only 24, had discovered something quite new: star-like objects pulsating radio waves, beams of energy, the first that had been found. Pulsars. They were the first, new, unexpected and genuinely strange discovery to come through the new window on the universe opened by radio astronomy.

It was the astrophysicist Thomas Gold who proposed that these pulses were actually emanating from rapidly rotating neutron stars. They are produced in huge stellar explosions, weigh thousands of millions of tonnes, and from them beams of radiation sweep through space as the dead star spins at a bewildering rate. The signal from the first of them was a set of pulses that occurred precisely every 1.337 seconds, as regular as the most regular clock that had ever been built on earth. It mattered because it later helped to prove part of Einstein's theory of gravity in his General Theory of Relativity, which predicts that as masses move they create tiny ripples in the structure of space and time. Just as the Higgs Boson identification in 2012 confirmed a theory that was waiting for confirmation and signalled a new era in research, the discovery that the pulsar was a starburst proved to be revolutionary. Astrophysicists around the world saluted the PhD student who was telling them something they didn't know, and opening a new window in space.

Jocelyn Bell was born in Belfast in 1943 and educated at a Quaker boarding school in York. She took her first science degree at Glasgow University, then went to do research in Cambridge. In the course of it she helped to build a huge radio telescope, which she described as looking like a field of hops, with 1,000 nine-foot-high wooden posts covering an area of four and a half acres, strung with copper wire and cables. It was the equivalent of a radio telescope with a 500-foot dish.

One day she spotted something that occurred during the night, a radio source that had been picked up in a part of the sky that was in the opposite direction from the sun: a tiny interruption on the printout from the telescope, only half an inch of 'scruff', as she called it, in the three and a half miles of paper produced over months. She was intrigued and began to investigate. Day by day she analysed ninety-six feet of printout, looking for tiny bursts of interference that might have been missed.

She worked backwards, and concluded that the source was neither terrestrial nor solar. Then she pinpointed the timing of the signal, worked out its position in the sky, identified a pulsar, then another. After she'd found four, she went back and studied miles of paper – they weren't using computers – looking for an inch or two of 'scruff', like a tenacious beachcomber looking for treasure.

When her results were published in the journal *Nature* in 1968 they caused an astronomical sensation. Around the world, researchers began to search for new pulsars because of what they revealed about mass and gravitational force in space. A thousand are now known to exist in our galaxy; there may be more than a million in our solar system.

For Bell, who married in 1968 and became Bell Burnell, the attraction of astronomy had always been the lure of the unknown: she has always loved the surprising results that keep rolling in. You can never know it all. When will we have understood the mystery of so-called 'dark matter' that makes up 95 per cent of the universe that we know? To illustrate the extent of the unknown, she uses the image of a vast building, like St Paul's Cathedral. If you put three grains of sand on the floor, St Paul's would be more full of sand than the universe is of stars.

Her enthusiasm was fed by her parents, who took her to the Armagh Observatory, not far from their home in Northern Ireland, and there she developed a fascination that has never left her. She has been honoured around the world, became Dame Jocelyn in 2007, and remains Visiting Professor of Astrophysics at Oxford University. One prize, however, eluded her. In 1974 her PhD supervisor, Professor Anthony Hewish, received the Nobel Prize for Physics, along with Dr Martin Ryle, for their work on pulsars, but she was not included. Many of her peers think she is one of the most notable omissions from the Nobel list. Astronomers like Sir Fred Hoyle condemned her omission, but she has always made light of it. 'At the time of the prize, I had a child about eighteen months old and was trying to keep working and it was proving very difficult. In those days, mothers didn't work – so a bit of me said, "Yes – men get prizes and women look after babies."' She says she harbours no grudge.

Throughout her life Bell Burnell has promoted the cause of women in science, and tried to make it easier for them to progress. In her physics class at Glasgow University she was the only woman, outnumbered fifty to one. In the early sixties it was standard practice for male students to bang their desks and whistle when a woman walked in. Change was slow to come. When she was appointed Professor of Physics at the Open University in 1991, the number of women holding chairs in the subject doubled, to two. By the end of the decade it was 36 out of 650. 'Clearly,' she said, 'there is still much work to be done.'

She was the first woman president of the Institute of Physics, but attitudes were entrenched. Larry Summers, the former American Treasury Secretary, caused a stir when he was president of Harvard by suggesting that there might be a biological reason for the domination of men: 'a different availability of aptitude at the high end when it comes to science'. Bell Burnell said he was confusing nurture with nature, and pointed out that in south-east Asia it was perfectly normal for women to study science and engineering. If there was a difference, they hadn't noticed it there.

Bell Burnell describes herself as 'a role model, a spokeswoman, a representative and a promoter of women in science in the UK'. Her tone, however, is not one of sour complaint. She is noted for her calm. Perhaps it is connected with her Quaker background, an important part of her life. She was once asked what people might be most surprised to know about her, and the answer was: 'I am religious. I'm an elder in my church, which is the Quakers, the Religious Society of Friends. A lot of people think that scientists aren't religious. It isn't true.'

She finds a parallel between the Quaker approach to life and the scientific method. 'I find that Quakerism and research science fit together very, very well. In Quakerism you're expected to develop your own understanding of God from your experience in the world. There isn't a creed, there isn't a dogma.' In science, 'You have a model, of a star, it's an understanding, and you develop that model in the light of experiments and observation, and so in both you're expected to evolve your thinking. Nothing is static, nothing is final, everything is held provisionally.'

Quaker practice treasures silence and patience, no one speaking at a Friends' meeting house until they have something to say. For Bell Burnell, a laboratory creates the same atmosphere and the same possibilities. 'I don't have to carry all the baggage of a Christian God ... it doesn't require God to be in charge of the world. I believe and work on the perfect tightrope.'

She was also balancing the life of a wife and a professional. 'A lot of my working life has been driven by family circumstances. I worked part-time for eighteen years and was married to a peripatetic husband who moved around an awful lot, so I sought whatever job I could get in astronomy or physics wherever he was ... although we are now much more conscious about equal opportunities I think there are still a number of inbuilt structural disadvantages for women. My research record is a good deal patchier than any man's of a comparable age.'

But her work did have a blazing start, and it put her in the pantheon of modern British scientists – with the likes of Stephen Hawking, who has offered new explanations of time and space, Lord Rees, who explored quasars and dark matter, Peter Higgs, whose long quest for the 'God particle' proved successful in 2012, and a host of other tenacious and innovative thinkers, internationally renowned, whose work is less well known outside the lab.

The neutron star may not bear Jocelyn Bell Burnell's name, only the prosaic label PSR B1919+21, but it was the first of its kind to be known. As recently as June 2012, astronomers identified a pulsar that may be the fastest of them all, spinning through space at perhaps 6 million miles an hour, the remnant of a vast supernova explosion in a distant world. Without her we might never have known it existed, and pulsars would remain beyond our understanding. Instead we're watching them, tracking them through space, and learning from them.

Roy Jenkins

R OY JENKINS INFLUENCED THE SHAPE and tone of the politics of his age more than anyone else who did not become Prime Minister. His career was a zigzag, taking him near the top and from time to time leaving him adrift, but it took him to the heart of great arguments – on social reform, Europe, the role of liberals and the left – and stamped his inimitable character on events, sometimes as man of government, as biographer, and always as sage bon vivant.

He presided as Home Secretary over a lightning series of reforms in the sixties that changed the social character of the country, played a pivotal role in the arguments over Britain and Europe that convulsed the two big parties and split them for a generation, and then, in the eighties, led an unexpected and often messy upheaval in party politics that reworked the pattern that had dominated the House of Commons for most of his lifetime.

Jenkins described himself in his autobiography as having had 'a life at the centre'. He also divided opinion – in the Labour governments in which he served, in the Social Democratic Party that he co-founded – and he was an innocent source of fun, whether for his love of claret, his voice and orotund style, or his apparent loftiness. Everyone in politics, however, knew him as a big man.

He was part of a remarkable generation. When he went from school in South Wales to Oxford, in 1937, Edward Heath and Denis Healey were fellow undergraduates at Balliol College (their three lives would be intertwined) and he found himself in an intellectual powerhouse, fired by the angry politics of the thirties. He did time at the code-breaking school at Bletchley Park during the war and in the forties followed the path into Labour politics taken by his father, MP for Pontypool until his death in 1946. Through his party's wilderness years in the fifties he formed his most important early political alliance with its leader, Hugh Gaitskell, and aligned himself permanently to the social-democratic Labour tradition, away from the left.

Gaitskell's unexpected death in 1963 led to Harold Wilson becoming leader, and the start of an uneasy, ambiguous relationship with Jenkins. But Wilson knew quality when he saw it, and when he won the 1964 general election he gave Jenkins a ministry: aviation. Within a year Jenkins became Home Secretary. Partly with his own legislation, and by encouraging private members' bills, by giving them the priceless gift of parliamentary time, he supervised two years of startling reform.

The divorce law changed, homosexuality was brought in from the cold, abortion was taken from the back streets by David Steel (his future political colleague), even the ancient power of the Lord Chamberlain to censor the theatre passed away. Jenkins used his office to make the case to promote reform as the spirit of the time. To the voices complaining of a tide of permissiveness, he had a characteristically blunt put-down: 'The permissive society has been allowed to become a dirty phrase,' he said in 1969. 'A better phrase is the civilized society.'

It may have been Jenkins's most productive period in office. He became Chancellor of the Exchequer after the débâcle of the devaluation of the pound in 1967, when he swapped jobs with Jim Callaghan, and had the job of steadying the ship. This he did rather successfully, more so perhaps than Wilson wanted, refusing to contrive an electorally enticing budget in 1970 and thereby giving his old student friend Ted Heath the chance to lead the Conservatives to an unexpected victory.

In the late sixties Wilson had conceived the notion that Jenkins was plotting to replace him, an idea that had little substance, but revealed how successfully his Chancellor had rallied a gang of supporters for whom he represented a particular strand in politics. It was unashamedly intellectual in tone: his biography of the Liberal Prime Minister H.H. Asquith in 1964 had established his credentials – liberal and internationalist by instinct and, to those of another stripe, infuriatingly smooth. Jenkins believed that part of Wilson thought that one day he would be his successor at No. 10; but only part.

Their crisis came in opposition. As Prime Minister, Heath had one dominating ambition. Since the thirties, when he'd travelled to Germany as a student and seen Hitler in action at a Nuremberg rally, he had cherished European unity. Jenkins had the same cast of mind; Wilson had not. He'd swung back and forth on the question in the sixties, managing his party's disagreements, and he was determined to exploit Heath's troubles with his own backbenchers.

Jenkins, elected deputy leader by Labour MPs in 1970, was having none of that. To the fury of his leader, and of the left, which was largely opposed to joining the Common Market, he led a Labour rebellion of sixty-nine MPs, big enough to set Heath up for a European victory. For the deputy leader to hand such a prize to the Conservatives seemed to many of his colleagues high treachery. After that rebellion – despite entreaties from sympathizers who had followed him into the 'Aye' lobby, like Roy Hattersley and David Owen – he resigned the deputy leadership to free himself for the European fight. Hattersley said afterwards that it was then that he lost his last chance of becoming Prime Minister.

Instead, he ended up in Brussels. Wilson's 1975 referendum, with Cabinet ministers allowed to campaign for 'Yes' or 'No' as they wished, confirmed British membership of the EEC. But as a 'recycled Home Secretary' – in his own phrase – from 1974 to 1976, Jenkins was uneasy. Denis Healey was Chancellor, and Wilson showed no inclination to give Jenkins the Foreign Office, which he wanted. The offer came to be the first British President of the European Commission, and when Jim Callaghan succeeded Wilson in March 1976 and the Foreign Office eluded Jenkins again, he was off.

They were years in which the first European monetary system was conceived, and Jenkins relished the high politics. As his Brussels diaries reveal, he also enjoyed the gastronomy and the diplomatic whirl: the flavour is rich and even louche. But as always with Jenkins – whose image belied a disciplined working life – there was restlessness. When he gave the Dimbleby lecture on BBC television in November 1979 he distilled some of his thoughts about a realignment in British politics, his estrangement from the Labour Party being almost completed by then.

Events moved fast. Tony Benn's ability to electrify the left meant that after Margaret Thatcher's election in 1979, Labour moved decisively away from the social-democratic path that Jenkins represented. By 1981 three serious Labour figures – David Owen, Shirley Williams and Bill Rodgers – were ready to break out and, with Jenkins, they established the Social Democratic Party, the 'Gang of Four'.

Michael Foot was now leading a wounded Labour Party, caught in the force field of early Thatcherism, and a third party seemed more of a runner than anyone would have thought a few years before. Jenkins, to the surprise of the whole political class, tramped the streets, first trying to win a by-election in Warrington, then succeeding in Glasgow Hillhead in March 1982.

But the SDP was still an idea and not a reality. Many of the Labour MPs who defected to it in the first year or two were eccentrics, or second-raters. And relations between Jenkins and Owen were bad: they rubbed each other the wrong way. Jenkins's ease with the Liberals – still led by David Steel – irritated Owen, and the 1983 election campaign, with Jenkins and Steel leading a

Liberal–SDP Alliance, was awkward and painful behind the scenes. The first-past-the-post system also held them back. They got more than 25 per cent of the vote (less than 3 per cent behind Labour) but only 23 seats out of 651.

Yet, in a phrase of the day, they broke the mould. The coming-together with the Liberals was difficult, with Owen holding out defiantly, but the parties merged in 1988. Jenkins, who had lost his seat the year before and gone to the Lords, as Lord Jenkins of Hillhead, had brought his third party into being. He was content, almost as content as he had been to be elected Chancellor of Oxford University a year earlier – defeating Edward Heath.

After it was done, although he served as the Liberal Democrat leader in the Lords, he gave even more time to writing, producing a prize-winning life of Gladstone in 1995 and finishing a life of Churchill in his eightieth year. By then he was watching the Blair government with a weary eye: the enthusiasm he had worked up for the young Blair – some called him 'Blair's history tutor' – was on the wane.

He was writing to the end, lunching enthusiastically, indulging many of his unlikely passions – weather forecasts, train timetables, croquet – and acting as an enthusiastic host to friends young and old. He died in January 2003 at his home in East Hendred, Oxfordshire, leaving an indelible mark on his time.

And the twinkle never left his eye. The writer Robert Harris, a close friend in later years, asked him not long before he died how much he regretted not reaching the topmost rung. Jenkins replied: 'I rather think I would have liked being Prime Minister in retrospect, rather more than I would have enjoyed it at the time.'

Vivienne Westwood

VIVIENNE WESTWOOD ONCE SAID that she wasn't comfortable defending her own clothes, which is an unusual posture for a fashion designer. From her, it seemed normal and entirely predictable. Throughout her long career she has specialized in a kind of gaudy outrage, whether as an in-house style guru for punk rock, the debunker of her own industry, or as the Buckingham Palace guest who couldn't wait to tell the world that she had deliberately not worn any underwear for her visit to receive her OBE.

She oscillates between innovation and eccentricity, and in the course of a loud and usually garish career she has managed to keep up that energy, which means that although she has often flirted with absurdity she has never quite disappeared from public view. One of the reasons is that after she had spent a couple of decades helping the young to dress down, and to practise a rebellious counter-culture, she appeared to turn against the whole enterprise and announced in the nineties that giving the young self-expression had created a generation of morons, 'hooked on an endless appetite for rubbish'.

It hadn't seemed like that in the sixties, when she met the man who would lead her into that world, Malcolm McLaren, most famous as manager of the Sex Pistols. By the early seventies they

were opening a shop in King's Road in London devoted to retro-
spective celebration of the teddy boys and then the mods and
rockers who'd strutted along that same street in the fifties and
sixties, on scooters or big bikes, depending on their orientation,
and spent bank holiday weekends bringing mayhem to English
seaside resorts with their pitched battles on the beaches and
promenades. Westwood and McLaren sold memorabilia and old
clothes and changed the name of the shop from Let It Rock to
Too Fast To Live Too Young To Die, which caught something of
their approach to life.

By 1974 they'd opened Sex, a shop selling fashions associated
with sex fetishes, and the following year came Seditionaries, a
place that might be said to have been the birthplace of punk,
where after a year or two no self-respecting customer would be
seen without torn jeans and safety pins about their person.

Sedition was indeed the idea. The clothes and the style were
nihilistic, rejecting every norm, and the assumption was that you
approached a world of chaos with no expectation of anything
other than rejection. Sex was about fetishism, particularly sado-
masochism, and the only appropriate way to face life was with
spiky hair, ragged, dull clothes, and piercings everywhere. The
approach had a subversive power that made Westwood and
McLaren unlikely monarchs of all they surveyed. She was the
fashion designer who was anti-fashion, the stylist for those who
loathed style.

Westwood was born in 1941 in Tintwistle in the Peak District
and, by her own account, moved to London with her parents
when she was 17 without any knowledge of music or art. She
went to art school, she said, to avoid all the geeks who went to
university. 'I wanted to have fun with men.'

She had a brief marriage to Derek Westwood, whose name she
kept, but the radical McLaren swept her away after a couple of
years. She was espousing left-wing causes and interested in
subversion. McLaren, she said, seemed to know everything she
needed to know at the time: she'd started making jewellery and

wanted to learn about art and the theatre, go to galleries, think about creativity and political protest. At the time, in the mid-sixties, she was able to tune into an anti-establishment movement that suited her mood, and let her artistic instincts flourish. There was something different to be done, and she began to think of clothes design. To her own surprise, it was popular.

With McLaren's swaggering presence alongside her, she was a success. Everyone began to watch her. Years later the designer Jasper Conran gave an appropriately warm but rather back-handed compliment: 'Vivienne's effect on other designers has been rather like a laxative. Vivienne does, and others follow.'

In fact, her first formal fashion show wasn't until 1979. This was the so-called 'pirate look' that became associated with the New Romantics. But long before that she'd stamped her over-sized personality on day-to-day street wear, in the years when punk began to become the forbidden culture that replaced the sixties youth culture, which by the mid-seventies seemed impossibly tame to the follow-on generation.

Throughout the eighties Westwood never produced a collection that wasn't described by someone as perverse, irrelevant or unwearable. It hardly bothered her. By that stage she was not only very well-off, but could rightly say that, in a wacky, irrepressible way, she had shaped the styles and ideas of that part of the seventies generation who needed to learn how not to belong: she was the fairy godmother of punk, outrageous and unpredictable, but always there when you needed her. She really wanted no more.

The period was marked by some ludicrous overstatement – in keeping with the Westwood–McLaren style – as if she had changed the world, which she hadn't. The singer Adam Ant described her sex shop as 'one of the all-time greatest shops in history', just because he'd never come across anything like it before.

Westwood was happy to sell T-shirts with images combining the swastika and the face of the Queen, or referring to underage sex, and to be prosecuted for selling shirts with pictures of two cowboys revealing rather too much of themselves. She explained the shop by saying it was necessary to 'seduce people into revolt', but in truth the revolt that she wanted was never entirely clear, except that it should be some kind of grunt of rage against everything that seemed settled.

That rage was expressed in piercings, safety pins, ripped clothes, distended shoes and wildly pointed heels, towering platform heels and straps, belts and buckles everywhere. She invented a fashion world looking as if it was at an early stage of construction, with nothing quite ready and everything about to fall apart. She and McLaren said they wanted to 'plunder the world of its ideas' and as a couple they managed to encourage the cynicism that McLaren's Sex Pistols brought to a climax in the late seventies.

Through it all Westwood herself specialized in an over-the-top camp glamour, getting more fevered as she got older, so that someone described her as 'Miss Marple on acid'. She was sometimes as impossibly coiffured as the grandmother of the romantic pot-boiler, Barbara Cartland, and often a carefully contrived mess that deliberately knew no bounds.

The constant theme was confrontation. Politics was always a conspiracy of some kind. Other designers were always unoriginal. Had you forgotten that you had a duty to reject everything you'd been told? When she designed everyday clothes based on sexual fetishes – all rubber and leather and buckles – she said: 'The bondage clothes were ostensibly restricting but when you put them on they gave you a feeling of freedom.' Not everyone knew what she meant, but there were enough who did, or at least who wanted to try it.

By the time the eighties came along, there was a whole cohort of the young dressed in conformity with Westwood's idea of freedom. And, soon, of course, she was off. It was part of her style that she couldn't sit still. In the eighties she distanced herself from everything she'd represented in the previous decade. Looking back later to the Sex Pistols, and their lead singer, Johnny Rotten, she said: 'I actually think John wanted me to mother him. But I could never be bothered.' Who knows? Maybe both parts are true.

Nothing could exist without eventually being debunked. She criticized designers who followed her lead, dismissed any avant-garde art – 'Andy Warhol, Tracey Emin – I couldn't give tuppence for it', said all feminists were puritans, and by the start of the new century was proclaiming her loss of faith in young people. 'I don't waste time trying to communicate with them,' she said.

She remains the anti-heroine, refusing to defend even that which made her rich and famous, whether clothes or ideas, politics or taste.

The only obligation, it seems, is to continue to surprise. Whether she is a wild radical spirit accepting a damehood from the Queen, or supporting the Prince of Wales in his campaigns for sustainable environmentalism, she has always balanced the deliberately provocative with the surprisingly predictable. She is a highly successful businesswoman, with a substantial fashion empire, who is convinced that the system which continues to support her will destroy everyone in the end. 'We're going to be killed. The human race faces extinction,' she said in 2011, and much of her energy is now put into environmental campaigns.

However effective some of them might be, it will not be for this that Vivienne Westwood will be remembered. Her creativity was channelled deliberately into cultural destruction, out of which she believed something would emerge that might be fun: she never pretended to know what it might be, maybe even not what it might look like, just that it couldn't be worse than what was all around us. She turned impatience into an obsession, and turned the cultural currency of the seventies into rejection and a love of emptiness.

In her designs she even got quite close to the enemy: haute couture. And she always had an eye for a good stunt, as when she posed for the cover of *Tatler* in 1989, made up as Margaret Thatcher and wearing clothes that the Prime Minister had ordered but not yet worn. The Iron Lady was furious, Westwood amused. A picture of her life. Why take it too seriously?

After all, she once said of fashion that it would eventually lead to us all being naked.

Jayaben Desai

THE NAME OF JAYABEN DESAI is attached to one company
whose story is inseparable from the upheavals of the seventies, and the political ebb and flow of the time. Many of those
who don't know her name will remember the firm for which she
worked in north London and which, for a couple of years, was
synonymous with the argument between left and right about
employment rights and union tactics, and with the birth of
Thatcherism: Grunwick.

It was Desai who led a strike there in 1976 that became the
fulcrum for the debate about union power. Although there were
many bigger disputes – Ted Heath's Conservative government
had been destroyed in effect in 1973–4 by a miners' strike, and
Jim Callaghan's Labour government was emasculated by the
'winter of discontent' in 1978–9 – Grunwick sits at the centre of
the story. The unions said the strike there was a fundamental
struggle for rights that had been won generations earlier; for the
company it was an emblem of the freedom of employers to resist
the collective power of a workforce.

Few people outside north London had heard of Grunwick in
August 1976, even if it processed their holiday photographs,
which was its business. After Jayaben Desai decided to walk out
on an argument about pay, with as many of her fellow employees

as she could muster, that changed. For two years the plant was the scene of a political struggle, sometimes a street fight, that became a crusade, an awkward political problem, and – depending where you stood – a political godsend.

There is another reason for Grunwick's resonance. Jayaben Desai represented a new strand in the British workforce. She was born in Gujarat in India in 1933, and in 1955 married Suryakant Desai from Tanganyika. He was manager of a tyre factory, and they settled there the following year, long before the country united with Zanzibar after decolonization and became Tanzania. Husband and wife were children of the Empire, then citizens of the Commonwealth. They came to Britain in the late sixties, thanks to an immigration policy here that was unintentionally liberalized by the repressive regime of Idi Amin in Uganda. He expelled British passport-holders of Asian origin, and they came to Britain, with many others from east Africa.

The experience of the Desai family wasn't unusual. In Tanzania they had enjoyed some status – Suryakant was a manager and, relatively speaking, they were comfortably off – then suddenly they found themselves at the bottom of the heap. It wasn't a happy transition, and soured further by post-colonial bitterness. Why couldn't they make their way like British people at home? They had the same passport after all.

Jayaben Desai found work at Grunwick. Not surprisingly, in north-west London, there were many like her in the firm: immigrant women glad of any work. Desai, however, was determined that the workforce should have the right to join a union, so that they could bargain for better conditions. George Ward – Anglo-Indian proprietor of Grunwick – was determined to resist that. He ran a profitable company that offered employment and his line was simple: come and work if you want to. Otherwise, don't.

The walk-out came in August 1976. Desai's son was arguing that he had been unfairly dismissed; she said she refused to work overtime. The event was hardly national news – though the press called them 'the strikers in saris' – but it quickly emerged that

Desai, four foot ten and an endless source of eloquent energy, was going into battle with style. The words with which she confronted her manager became famous in trade union circles: 'What you are running is not a factory. It is a zoo.' She said that in a zoo there were monkeys, but there were also lions, among which she counted herself, who could bite his head off. The battle lines were clearly drawn.

A strike began three days after the walk-out and the postal workers in nearby Cricklewood decided to support it, a pretty serious matter for Grunwick, whose business was mail order. Enter John Gorst, Conservative MP, and the National Association for Freedom, who asked the High Court to intervene, with the support of the leader of the opposition, Margaret Thatcher, who'd been leading the Conservatives for less than eighteen months at that point.

It was largely due to Desai's persistence that the strike kept going. 'Would Gandhi give up?' she'd say at meetings. By late autumn Grunwick had become the front line of a political argument in which Mrs Thatcher had decided she wanted to engage. On the other side, the trade unions had taken up Grunwick as a symbol. In August 1976 the TUC organized a march of 20,000 people to the gates of the processing factory. Everyone was investing capital in the fight.

Then it changed. By the very fact that it became a cause célèbre for the left, the Labour government was caught in embarrassment. So was the TUC. Desai's eloquence about the pay and conditions at Grunwick turned the dispute into a rallying point. The Callaghan government was already struggling with the consequences of an austerity policy that had split the Cabinet in 1976 and was deeply unpopular among Labour supporters. Grunwick provided a focal point for those who thought that the government needed to be reminded of its history in the union movement. The Trotskyite Socialist Workers Party was in the vanguard, and Paul Foot was preaching class war in the streets of north London.

The government hurriedly organized a commission of inquiry under the judge Lord Scarman, which recommended reinstatement and union recognition for the sacked workers, but things had gone too far. Throughout the summer of 1977 there were mass pickets outside Grunwick, with the police holding back trade union protesters. The Conservative employment spokesman, Jim Prior, later to be dismissed as a 'wet' by Mrs Thatcher, had been privately sympathetic to the principle of union recognition at Grunwick, but events had moved too fast. It was a deep divide.

Shirley Williams, Labour Cabinet minister on the right of her party, visited the picket line, because her own union, APEX, was involved, but she complained later about a rent-a-mob of pickets.

Mrs Thatcher pointed to union power in the streets. The police were being drafted in in greater numbers to restrain the demonstrators and pickets; George Ward was saying that the company was being denied the right to trade. 'We won't surrender,' he said. 'I think we've shown ourselves to be the great survivors.' The press was overwhelmingly sympathetic to that side of the argument, and from the instigators of the walk-out there began to be heard complaints about the ambiguity inherent in the TUC, where the General Secretary, Len Murray, was privately very worried about the left.

Yet Desai carried on. A picture from the height of the dispute, carried by every newspaper, showed her confronting police lines, her sari perfectly straight, a handbag over her arm, and a calm look on her face. Her most memorable remark from that time was about the value of official backing from the trade union establishment. It felt, she said, like honey on your elbow. You knew it was there, you could touch it and even see it, but you couldn't taste it.

Looking back to Grunwick from our own time, it seems entangled in battles that defined the politics of the previous decade. The public mood at the time of the Heath government's struggle with the miners was divided, but in the two general elections of 1974 it came down against the Prime Minister – just. The economic travails of the last Wilson administration from 1974 to 1976, however, were grim, and by the time Grunwick came along it was clear that a substantial part of the public was persuaded that the policies of the big unions had been a hindrance rather than a help. The consequence was that when police and pickets were seen to struggle outside Grunwick (there were more than 500 arrests) there would be only one political winner in the end.

That end came in 1978. There was a drift back to work, a claim of betrayal by Desai directed at the TUC, a short, sad hunger strike of defiance, and then defeat.

Desai failed, but she was the first of her kind. Through the sixties a great many immigrant workers had arrived in the United Kingdom from many parts of the Commonwealth. Quite apart from the inevitable disadvantages of language and culture, not to mention colour, many of them had few skills and were destined for poor-paying jobs or unemployment, finding it pretty hard to make their way. Others, like Desai herself, found that expectations which they had thought reasonable because of their status in a previous existence were painfully unrealistic.

She was one of the most notable representatives of post-war immigrants to make a political mark, not least because she was a woman, and caricatured as the leader of that 'sari protest' when the whole thing began. That her name is not widely known now – she died in 2010, at the age of 77 – is no indication that the Grunwick arguments weren't important. She continued to support political-industrial causes when she thought them justified, but her significance in our time comes from those torrid summers of the mid-seventies.

It was a brave thing to do what she did. The government and the TUC found it impossible to go as far as she wanted, and they believed that the dispute had been hijacked by the hard left as a cause which, in the end, damaged the likes of those whom Desai took her stand to protect. That argument will never be settled.

What can't be doubted is the importance of the Grunwick episode in the election campaign that followed in 1979, in which the Thatcher era was born.

Desai herself believed all her life that, whether Grunwick was won or lost, the walk-out and then the strike revealed to everyone, far beyond her own community, the reality of a life of which they knew little. In her last interview, not long before she died, she said she was proud of what she did for that reason. 'They wanted to break us down,' she said. 'But we did not break.'

Stuart Hall

MORE THAN HALF A CENTURY after he arrived from Jamaica to study at Oxford at the very beginning of the fifties, Stuart Hall looked back and said that for the first time in his adult life he was beginning to feel like a dinosaur. Asked if he felt defeated, he said that the points of reference for his political world had disappeared. He clung to hope, he said, but events seemed to conspire against it. There is no one who can sing the song with more feeling: the lament of the sixties leftist.

Hall was an intellectual force on the left for decades, a theorist who promoted ideas of multiculturalism and championed cultural studies in universities, and a writer who tried to get a generation to examine the complicated question of what 'Britishness' means. He has never been engaged seriously in party politics – the Labour Party of the late twentieth century was anathema to him – and instead remained a thinker and teacher, in a country where the idea of the public intellectual (of right and left) has so often been derided. And over forty years or so he saw the course of events turn decisively against socialists like him: globalization and individualism became the guiding stars. The world had gone the other way.

Hall's story begins in the West Indies. He remembers sitting at Paddington Station in London watching members of the

'*Windrush* generation' – immigrants always associated with that famous cargo ship – trying to find work and accommodation in London, a city in which their assimilation would often be difficult and painful. He naturally felt like an outsider: when he arrived from Jamaica he'd never met anyone from Trinidad or Barbados, never mind Oxford.

Yet within ten years Hall would be a force. He was influenced above all by two figures who changed many people's thinking about British society in the post-war period, which was inevitably a time of reassessment: Raymond Williams and Richard Hoggart. They wrote about culture, not as something handed down on a plate but as something that was always changing, day by day, with new influences working on the old. Hoggart's book *The Uses of Literacy*, published in 1957, described the emergence of a mass culture and offered an explanation of how it might change the way people thought, spoke, communicated with each other. For young idealists like Hall it opened a door. His generation, attracted by Marxist ideas, faced a particular problem: the Soviet Union.

The Soviet invasion of Hungary in 1956 was a seismic event for many who would otherwise have been attracted by the Communist Party, as so many had been in the thirties. The Soviet Union itself had begun to admit the extent of Stalin's policy of murder and terror, and for many of Hall's generation the totalitarian model was exploded. He and others began to cluster round the journal the *New Left Review* in search of a new way of expressing their ideas. Hall's contribution was to try to make a connection between the political intellectual – interested in institutions – and the creative artist who was interested in the moral and emotional life of individuals. As a result he became, in the sixties, a pioneer of what became known as cultural studies.

In later life, Hall was sceptical about some of the directions this discipline had taken. 'I do want to go on thinking about cultural studies,' he said in 2006, 'but not as a field. I never defended it as a field. I think that as a field, it contains a lot of rubbish.' He had

THE NEW ELIZABETHANS

thought of it more as an opening up to new influences, specifically to ideas of identity which were close to his heart, for obvious reasons. He was talking in the sixties about ideas of 'Britishness' which are eerily familiar in today's discussion of the impact of devolution on different parts of the United Kingdom, and the independence debate in Scotland. He was trying to define how different cultures coexisted in British society – particularly if they were based on ethnic identity – and what the consequences were when they collided.

He said that people needed to understand that Britain was not homogeneous, and the country had never been without conflict. 'The English fought tooth and nail over everything we know of as English political values – rule of law, free speech, the franchise.' And for him the biggest gap in our understanding of our own history was in the story of empire. 'Euroscepticism and Little Englander nationalism could hardly survive if people understood whose sugar flowed through English blood and rotted English teeth.'

Hall's ideas have developed in part from the thinking of the Italian Marxist Antonio Gramsci, who was more interested in a cultural critique of society than a purely economic one, and Hall has tried to analyse the ways in which power operates through cultural values. His own beginnings, after all, had not been in Marxist theory but in the literary criticism of F.R. Leavis – about as far from a left-wing intellectual as you could get – which saw literature as, in part, representing a whole experience of life.

For thinkers like Hall, the sixties were bliss. A particular kind of political tradition – deferential, socially and politically conservative – was passing away. A youth culture was beginning to encourage free thinking (or at least social rebellion) and in the United States the trauma of the Vietnam War from 1966 onwards had a galvanizing effect. To a degree that students in the eighties and nineties would find hard to comprehend, the radical left had a field day. By 1968, when Paris was the scene of street battles and the fall of a modern *ancien régime*, going on a demonstration

232

for students was as much a part of life as punting on the river might have been for the Brideshead generation. For many of them, it was what you did.

One of the reasons was that writers and polemicists like Hall were able to argue that the simple account of what Britain was, and how it had come to be, was inadequate. For many students, that seemed self-evidently true. So there was a flowering of left-ism, channelled into the usual feuding sects, which duly battled with each other. In contrast with continental Europe, however, there was almost no representation of that movement in parliamentary politics, which remained almost impervious.

Hall's work's as a social theorist and cultural commentator took him into youth sub-cultures and his became an original voice on the left. He never shared the views of those who believed that an economic transformation on some Marxist model was a holy grail which, one day, they were bound to find. Instead, he was more interested in the questions that students might ask about their own history as a way of changing our idea of community, and his intellectual influence was the greater for the fact that he could not be pigeon-holed. He has always been his own man.

The Labour Party's struggle with itself, lasting for about fifteen years from the early seventies, was an institutional battle that was resolved, in the end, by the party accepting the electoral impact of the Thatcher years, and adapting to it. For intellectuals on the left like Hall, the arrival of Tony Blair was the proof that they had failed. Their only comfort was that they had predicted it all along. For them, parliamentary politics had never offered anything.

Of New Labour, Hall said: 'Community is in their mouth every day. Reform has been absorbed by them and re-used in quite a different way ... that linguistic move that New Labour has made which presents anyone who is trying to make a critical approach with a tremendous problem. What terms can you use to speak about your objections?' For him, by the time the Blair years were over, the concept that he attached to the word 'social' had been destroyed, to be replaced by something marked 'private'. It was as simple as that.

It was a long way from the sixties idealism which Hall had tried to underpin with an intellectual analysis. Politics had taken the economic arguments in quite a different direction, and even if intellectuals on the left could look at the collapse of international markets in 2008 and say 'I told you so', they were aware that the response was quite different from the one they would have liked to expect when they were storming the citadels of capitalism in the sixties. The left alternative that they had dreamed of was notable by its absence.

Hall's battle also encompassed the word that is the focus of another divisive argument: 'multiculturalism'. He was a member of the Commission on the Future of Multi-ethnic Britain, set up by the Runnymede Trust, which reported in 2000 and argued for a reassessment of our idea of Britishness, because of the ethnic diversity now established across the country. When Hall said that the teaching of history needed to reflect that fact, he found himself under attack, and in the years since the report was published 'multiculturalism' has been attached to an idea of national coexistence that has become unpopular in the political mainstream. The pendulum has swung, and too much diversity is now thought to be unhelpful. Hall is phlegmatic about this: he's used to it. Years as a teacher – at the University of Birmingham, the Open University (where he was Professor of Sociology for nearly twenty years) – and a lifetime's writing as a political theorist have left him unsurprised by political shifts in the wind.

He is, however, a figure who – a couple of generations ago – placed ideas in the minds of students and the wider public that have taken root, even if the consequences are not what he would have predicted or wanted.

Does he still hope? He said a few years ago: 'I think things are stuck. I am not so disillusioned to think that history is finished … but I do think that the balance of social forces is very powerfully against hope.'

David Attenborough

NO ONE HAS DONE MORE TO EXPLAIN the natural world to modern Britain than David Attenborough. Since he first popped up in jungle clearings on television in the fifties, he's gone in search of the bird of paradise, watched insects mating on every continent, and fraternized with apes. He has run with the wildebeest and the lemmings on their last journey, and taken us to the hottest and the coldest places on earth. Attenborough is everyone's favourite teacher, the one who inspires with his humanity. Without him, imagine how much we wouldn't know.

It came as no surprise that when Radio 4 listeners were asked to nominate figures who might feature in *The New Elizabethans*, Attenborough's name was immediately at the top of the list, and stayed there. It's impossible to look back across the decades and not see his footprints, or hear his voice whispering from some tree hut from where he might get a glimpse of a newly born chimp or a snail that everyone else thought extinct. These are precious memories for everyone who's followed him on these journeys, because they touch our instinct for discovery, for surprise, and sometimes for danger. Therefore he is cherished.

Attenborough's own excitement is, of course, genuine. 'One of the great things, much more exciting than going to the moon,' he once said, 'would not to have been Darwin, but Captain Cook.

On his first and second voyage, he went round the Pacific and went to Tahiti, where he saw a new brand of humanity, and a completely new set of animals and plants. That must have been mind-blowing.'

His enthusiasm started early. He was born in 1926 and grew up in Leicester, where his father was principal of University College. By the time he was 10 he had a collection of fossils and things that intrigued him: ammonites, brachiopods, bits of Roman pottery, and a whopping snakeskin about two and a half feet long. As a boy in short trousers he found endless romance in the idea of a rock inside which there might be a perfect shell which had never been seen by another human being, and on which the sun hadn't shone for 350 million years.

He took a degree in natural sciences at Cambridge and after national service in the Royal Navy he got a job – at the second try – at the BBC. It was 1952. He didn't own a television, but the service was in its early days and that hardly mattered. His boss thought his teeth were too big to let him be seen on the screen, so he became a producer, working on an animal programme with the naturalist Julian Huxley and as a consequence making a happy connection with the reptile keeper at London zoo, Jack Lester. Why didn't they go on an expedition together? said Attenborough. They did, and during the first series Lester fell ill. His producer stepped in and made his first television appearance, in *Zoo Quest*.

Those of us who remember those years, the black and white television flickering in the corner of the room, and television being rationed by nervous parents, will recall the sight of him in the second series in South America in 1959, introduced by music that conjured up a wild, faraway world where anything might happen. He'd poke around in bushes and anthills, even stick his hand down an armadillo's burrow to see what might be in there. You felt like hiding behind the sofa.

He was a khaki-clad version of the explorers of old, Indiana Jones without a gun, stepping on twisted vines that might turn out to be poisonous snakes, lying in wait for beasts that would surely turn nasty. But all the time he was revealing a world where ancient ways held sway, where loggers in Paraguay still went about their business without raping the rainforests, and there seemed to be a fearful respect for nature. It was the most entertaining education you could imagine.

The pattern was set. More than fifty years later, Attenborough, in his eighties, was wrapped up in the Arctic to film for *The Frozen Planet*, explaining the pattern of life in the polar regions and taking his viewers on another journey that, they felt, would have been impossible without him. And by then, after decades of growing environmental awareness – and with the noisy debate about global warming in the background – the exploration had a different character. You didn't expect animals to be put in boxes and shipped back to London Zoo for examination like those armadillos; it was an invitation to contemplate the reality of a different place, connected to our own and important to it, but somewhere that should be left alone.

Down the years, Attenborough's journeys and films have charted the changing attitudes to the environment, and have played a part in them. *Life on Earth*, broadcast in 1979, and the follow-up, *Living Planet*, in 1984, were almost certainly the most widely consumed accounts of animals in our natural world that we have ever known. Attenborough was knighted in 1985. As ever, he made no inflated academic claims for this work. He simply presented a picture, as accurately as he could, and told us what he knew. At the start of *Life on Earth*, he said: 'There are some four million different kinds of animals and plants in the world. Four million different solutions to the problems of staying alive. This is the story of how a few of them came to be as they are.'

By the early eighties, an Attenborough series was a landmark event. But that had not been inevitable, and the chance that made it possible had come twenty years earlier. He'd left the BBC staff to study social anthropology at the London School of Economics, filming when he could. Then he'd received an enlightened offer: would he like to come back and take control of the new TV channel that was about to be launched, BBC2? He said yes. He was 39.

Television was expanding fast, and it was fortunate for the BBC that Attenborough returned. He had a passionate belief in the BBC's founding purposes and spirit – it remains as strong in him today as it ever did – and he set about running a channel that would inform, educate and entertain with as much determination (and a good deal more good humour) as Lord Reith himself would have wanted. There was *Call My Bluff* and *Chronicle*, *Man Alive* and *The Old Grey Whistle Test*, *Monty Python's Flying Circus* and *The Money Programme*. Snooker arrived properly when colour came along in 1967. And Attenborough conceived the idea of a string of programmes that might deliver something television had never managed before.

The first was *Civilisation*, in which Kenneth Clark explored Western art, and then came Jacob Bronowski's *The Ascent of Man*. They were innovative, confident series, pedagogical in style without apology, dazzling in their exploitation of the medium of colour, and all gilded with the eloquence of Clark and Bronowski. After Attenborough's time, Alistair Cooke's *America* followed the same pattern, and all these programmes remain some of the greatest achievements of television in that era. Moreover, they revealed Attenborough's own understanding of the possibilities of the medium.

But now he wanted to do more by himself. He'd been made Director of Programmes at the BBC in 1969 and it was natural that when the post of Director-General came up in 1972 he was a front runner. It made him think hard. He spoke to his brother Richard, actor and film-maker, and confessed that he had no appetite for the job, despite the chance it would give him to run the Corporation. No, he wanted to make programmes, particularly the natural history epic that had been taking shape in his mind. So, bravely, he pulled out and became a freelance programme-maker once more.

He went on various filming expeditions until *Life on Earth* was finally commissioned – with American backing – in 1976, and the great project began. The filming was extraordinary, with all the skills and patience of the BBC's Natural History Unit in Bristol stretched to the limit, and for broadcasters around the world the series and its successors – *The Living Planet*, *The Life of Birds*, *The Life of Mammals* – set a standard that has never been surpassed. It was in 2008 that the project reached its natural end, with *Life in Cold Blood*, and Attenborough acknowledged that he had never expected it to last. 'The evolutionary story is finished. The endeavour is complete,' he said. 'If you'd asked me twenty years ago whether we'd be attempting such a mammoth task, I'd have said – don't be ridiculous.' He hoped that, perhaps fifty years on, people might still think the programmes said something about the world we lived in.

The programmes provided a treasure-trove of memories, but often his viewers remember most the personal moment, a tousled Attenborough in the wild, crouched and whispering, eyes aflame, and smiling, as when he exchanged glances with a gorilla in Africa, and said he wasn't scared.

Such moments remain, permanent as a specimen in the glass case of a Victorian museum, and with the same magic ingredient of intimacy. Everyone who saw it might have been having a private audience with the man, taken behind the curtain to see something that they might never set eyes on again. And always, stamped on every shot and threaded through every script, his passion for discovery. 'There is no deeper pleasure than the contemplation of the natural world,' he says.

And under the boyish enthusiasm that he still carries with him, we know the sense of urgency that he's brought to his work, which has sharpened through the years: a feeling that there is now more danger, more destruction, a greater need for humanity in our dealings with our planet and its creatures. At the end of *State of the Planet* he said that the future of life depended on our ability to take action: 'I've been lucky in my lifetime to see some

of the greatest spectacles that the natural world has to offer.
Surely we have the responsibility to leave for future generations
a plant that is healthy, inhabitable by all species.'

That's why David Attenborough is still travelling, still filming,
and telling us the story of our planet.

Margaret Thatcher

O N THE EVENING OF 20 NOVEMBER 1990, in a room behind the Speaker's chair in the House of Commons, one of the most notable political careers of modern times came quickly to a close. Members of the Cabinet were led in one by one so that the Prime Minister could speak to each of them alone. When they had done, at about half past eight, she walked a few yards to her car and was driven up Whitehall in the dark to Downing Street, where, without delay, she made the arrangements for the resignation that she knew must now come. The age of Thatcher was over.

Only twenty-four hours earlier, at a meeting of world leaders in Paris, she had declared that she would fight on in the Conservative leadership election, having been denied outright victory in the first ballot by a mere four votes. But the tide she had taken at the flood for so long was ebbing faster than she knew. Although most of her Cabinet told her that they would vote for her in the second ballot as a matter of duty, she learned from them what she had been one of the last in the government to accept: that her authority had gone. She faced them in the Cabinet Room the next morning to say she was resigning – breaking down as she read a statement – and drove to Buckingham Palace to tell the Queen that she would leave office as soon as her party had chosen a successor.

The manner of her fall was appropriate because, like her eleven years in office, it was fashioned as high drama. The Thatcher years were a breathless time: fast, provocative, sometimes ruthless, often dangerous. Underneath the carapace of the Iron Lady there was a greater capacity for pragmatism and compromise than her loudest supporters would acknowledge, but she was convinced from the start that governing was mostly a matter of will, the exercise of a personality that would not be denied. Until that balance between judgement and will was skewed after her third election victory in 1987, and lurched so far towards danger that her government and party fractured, she could justly claim to have been a Prime Minister who had changed her country.

Thatcherism became a byword for individual enterprise and an accompanying suspicion of an overweening state. She campaigned against collectivism in all things (especially when represented by trade unions) and revived a post-imperial nationalism which enthused the right of the Conservative Party, giving it an energy that it hadn't known in government in modern times. All this, of course, meant division and conflict too. But Margaret Thatcher's trump card was her relish for those consequences. She thrived on them, sometimes appearing to believe that the more fervent the opposition, the more it proved she was right.

Her personality and her politics were inseparable, government seeming to be an extension of her own passions or, as critics would have it, prejudices. Britain's first woman Prime Minister did not want to be a political manager, but a crusader. Doubt became a synonym for weakness, and she made the point by gradually picking off the Tory 'wets' in her Cabinet, equating their unease at her economic policies with a lack of backbone.

That was why the wholly unexpected and unpredictable Falklands War in 1982 was so important for her. In the months before it began, her government was hugely unpopular. She was easily portrayed as a Prime Minister who had divided the country, because she had. Victory in the Falklands gave her a chance to claim that she was leading a national renewal: Britain had found herself in the South Atlantic, she said.

It was enough to give her a commanding majority in the 1983 election and when she prevailed in the long miners' strike which began the following year she seemed impregnable. No one was neutral about Margaret Thatcher, which was how she liked it, but the majority was still on her side. When she survived the bomb attack by the IRA on the Grand Hotel in Brighton, during the Conservative Party conference of 1984, and appeared on the platform a few hours later, defiant and calm, the picture was complete. A leader who would not give way.

Once it had all seemed so unlikely. Chosen by Conservative MPs after Edward Heath's defeat in the two elections of 1974, she had a stumbling start. Easily caricatured for her voice and manner, and with only a modest and brief Cabinet career as Education Secretary behind her, she was a slow learner as leader of the Opposition, finding Jim Callaghan a wily operator in the Commons, deliberately affecting an avuncular style to dampen her fire. But events moved in her favour, with the Labour government racked by trade union militancy, suffused in economic gloom and sapped by a constitutional failure over devolution to Scotland and Wales. Callaghan himself confessed to one of his advisers just before the election in 1979 that he believed that once in every three decades or so there was a shift in what the public wanted, and approved of. 'I suspect there is now such a sea change,' he said. 'And it is for Mrs Thatcher.'

He was right. With most of Fleet Street cheering her on, and the Saatchi brothers producing the most effective political advertising campaign Britain had ever seen, she capitalized on a public mood for change. Her government began to talk in new political language, changed the rules of the game: from the abolition of exchange controls in the first year, the era of privatization, the sale of council homes to their tenants, tax reforms, especially for high earners, to the 'big bang' that loosened the culture of the City of London. And Thatcher herself carved out a persona that was partly Action Woman – going where a man wouldn't dare – and partly a defiant throwback to the 'Victorian values' of self-reliance that she pinned as a badge on her father, Alderman Roberts, the grocer in Grantham.

Her determination was legendary. Political life in her time was active, rich and pulsed with surprise. You can't tell her story, of course, without painting some of the personality and the hypnotic effect the woman leader had on the male politicians that she encountered. François Mitterand said of her that she had 'the eyes of Caligula and the mouth of Marilyn Monroe'. David Owen, officially a political opponent, wrote in his memoirs of the excitement he felt walking through a Commons corridor late at night and sensing the odour of a particular perfume and whisky, which meant that she had passed that way.

But the price of a premiership fashioned on such a personality was that its temperament waxed and waned with her mood, and crackled with unpredictability. After Michael Heseltine walked away in 1986 – accusing Thatcher of undermining cabinet government – the strains got worse. Nigel Lawson – Chancellor through the glory years of Thatcherism – decided that a wilfulness had set in. Later he wrote in his memoir: 'She had become reckless over Europe, reckless over the poll tax, reckless over what she said in public, and reckless over her colleagues.'

The poll tax – the government had failed to make the term 'community charge' stick – was a political disaster, as Lawson had warned his colleagues it would be, reforming the rates but shifting the burden of paying for local authorities from the better off to the poorest. But, far from stabilizing her government in the crisis, the Prime Minister lurched into bitter and ultimately fatal battles with her two Chancellors, Lawson and his predecessor, Sir Geoffrey Howe.

Lawson resigned in 1989 when Thatcher refused to sack her personal economic adviser, Sir Alan Walters, who was opposing Lawson's exchange rate policy. And the following year Howe, feeling demoted and personally humiliated in Cabinet, could take it no more. In his resignation speech to the Commons, the killer punch was his critique of the Prime Minister's conduct to her colleagues. He had wrestled with his conflict of loyalty for too long, he said; he invited others to consider what they should do. The next day Heseltine announced that he would contest the leadership, and the endgame began.

On the evening when Thatcher saw the Cabinet one by one and heard the truth, Alan Clark, conservative in outlook, a loyalist, and the master diarist of his age, saw her leave the Commons and get into her car, and the interior light go out as the door closed and the car slid away. He knew what was happening, and wrote that night: 'I came in with her, I go out with her.' He said: 'A terrible sadness envelops me – of unfinished duties and preoccupations, of dangers and injustices remaining, of the greed, timidity and short-sightedness of so many in public life.'

The authentic spirit of Thatcherism: impassioned, certain, always ready for betrayal, because that was the fate of the mighty.

Margaret Thatcher dominated and divided, because that was her instinct. She changed a way of thinking, shone a different light on her country, spawned a generation of politicians – including prime ministers – who move in her shadow, and could claim to have been a leader who rose above the throng. Her achievement is that believers and non-believers alike accept that.

David Hockney

IT WAS PERFECTLY NATURAL FOR David Hockney to mount an exhibition of Yorkshire landscapes a few years ago for the beautiful people of Los Angeles far away. They'd first known him nearly half a century before when he painted swimming pools, the young men cavorting in them, and the shadows of the Californian sun. But, for the painter, surprisingly little had changed in that time, although he had swapped Beverly Hills for Bridlington and become fascinated again by gnarled English trees and dales instead of beach houses and the empty spaces of America's far west. The pictures of spring coming to Woldgate Woods seemed quite at home in a Hollywood gallery, because he was the same man, and they couldn't have been painted by anyone else.

Although he has experimented ceaselessly with technique – he took to making pictures on his iPad with the enthusiasm of a child – and has always enjoyed being an awkward swimmer against the tide, he is also a traditionalist. His interests have remained portraiture, landscape and still life, and in the whole of his work you can see his inheritance as well as his personality. His faces – dozens of his own among them – place him in the line of portrait painters stretching back to the old masters, and he has been devoted to the contours of landscape (usually without people) since he started to paint. He revels in traditional forms like the very English 'conversation piece', even if in his pictures the people often look as if they aren't talking to each other, and may not want to.

His feeling for colour is his own. There are particular blues and yellows and greens that are a kind of badge for Hockney, and a purple that seeps through many of his landscapes. He fell in love with the Californian light in the sixties, and the dazzling brightness that made its spaces seem infinite. When he was heading into his seventies he plunged into the countryside of Yorkshire and produced a series of vast canvases capturing the changing of the seasons. The palette seemed familiar: his colours were the same as they'd been on the sun terraces overlooking the Pacific, or when he first tried to pin down the ceaseless movement of colour in the Grand Canyon.

When the Yorkshire pictures went on show at the Royal Academy in London in spring 2012 more than half a million people went to see them. It was one of the most attended shows in the Academy's history, an indication of Hockney's place in the public's affection. He was the established outsider, a painter whose luminous, airy style was not only recognizable at once, but seemed to be a commentary on everything that had happened since the sixties. The young artists of BritArt might be building their installations, or dipping their sheep in formaldehyde, but he was still drawing, and searching with his brush for just the right colour.

Hockney was born in Bradford in 1937, and studied drawing and painting at college there before going to the Royal College of Art in London in 1959. A year or so later he saw the Picasso exhibition at the Tate Gallery, and it was an experience that shaped him. Just as the Fauvists like Henri Matisse attracted him because of their commitment to the primacy of colour and feeling, so he was inspired by the Cubists' fascination for changing form and perspective in order to analyse them and tease out their inner life.

Hockney's individual style leaps out of his earliest paintings. In a series of teenage self-portraits, in watercolour and pencil, one stands out, from 1954. He's staring straight ahead, sitting on a bed set against bright-yellow wallpaper, his hair still dark and cut in a boy's pudding-basin style, but the wide, round glasses and the downturned mouth prefigure the man we know; and the line and colour in the picture ring with confidence. It couldn't be anyone else. Within ten years of painting that picture he was the talk of London and New York.

Nineteen sixty-three was his year. He'd already visited New York, done a series of etchings in a modern reworking of Hogarth's 'The Rake's Progress', and left the Royal College with a gold medal. Now he had his first solo exhibition in London – a sell-out. The *Sunday Times* commissioned drawings of Egypt for its new colour magazine, he won a graphic prize at the Paris Biennale, and went back to New York, where he encountered Andy Warhol and his circle. 'By the summer of 1961 I'd spent a few months in New York,' Hockney said. 'As soon as I got there I realized that this was the place for me. It was a 24-hour city in a way London wasn't. It didn't matter where you were from. I absolutely loved it, and when I went to LA I liked that even more.' London, he said, was for a few people. LA was for the many, 'which I preferred'.

The gay writer Edmund White pointed out that when Hockney encountered LA and the sybarites who flitted through it, he found no difficulty in being himself. 'He took up gay subject matter before almost anyone else – and the amazing thing is that he got away with it,' White wrote. The scene was so intoxicating – swimming pools under vivid blue skies, a spacious freedom that seemed a dream – Hockney's eye and his imagination were let loose, and nothing could stop them. He said: 'It's very British to go about, to see something unusual and paint it. I'm always excited by the unusual, never by ordinary things.'

Just as Matisse had painted the bright colours and bathers of Nice, under striped awnings and waving palms, Hockney produced images of the hedonism of southern California that were washed in special colours and etched in simple forms. Rich hues, sharp angles, wide spaces and beautiful bodies. Whether it was the line of a friend's back as he lay by the pool or emerged from the water, or the spreading vista through a glass wall, his excitement was aroused by freedom and space. His California pictures – like his double portrait of Christopher Isherwood and Don Bachardy – are also about the feeling of Los Angeles for itself.

He says that he caught, by chance, the last great years of Hollywood, and, in a tableau like the picture *The American Collectors* (*Fred and Marcia Weisman*) of 1968, you sense an artist with the cinematographer's eye. Everything is perfectly composed, the colours meticulously delineated, and everyone is frozen for the moment of the picture. As with all the double portraits, of which he painted so many, the background says as much about the relationship as the people do. They often look at the artist, not each other. Sometimes, as in many of his portraits, the figures look as if they are about to try to escape.

Hockney painted his parents often, and there is one famous double portrait. His mother sits to the side, facing the artist, expressionless, her hands placed neatly on her lap. His father leans forward in a chair on the other side of a bright-green cupboard, reading intently, his head down. There are flowers between them, and a mirror reflecting some pictures from another wall. They seem, each of them, in their own world, showing no connection to the artist, although to his mother, especially, he was very close. He captures their milieu, the social conformity of Bradford, perhaps the seriousness of the house: his mother was a devout Methodist, his father a man of strong socialist beliefs. Their appearance in the picture is solid, rooted, and without a flicker of the unexpected. They exude steady, independent permanence.

He sometimes paints very fast, and sometimes very slowly. Lucian Freud he sketched quickly, because the great man didn't have much time. But when Hockney sat for Freud, for a portrait, it took 120 hours, during which he watched the master's method. He later compared it with the video portrait of a sleeping David

Beckham done by the contemporary artist Sam Taylor-Wood when they were exhibited at the National Portrait Gallery at the same time. The video was based on an hour's observation. 'You don't see it in layers,' he said. That's why he wants the real thing, and why the Freud painting was more interesting for him: it was accumulated knowledge built up over time.

With Hockney that accumulation emerges in patterns that recur: the depths of the Grand Canyon re-emerge in his Covent Garden sets for Richard Strauss's opera *Die Frau Ohne Schatten*, where the landscape turns and twists like a dream painted in the brightest hues, and then it's back to Yorkshire in, for example, his painting of Garrowby Hill, which looks like an extension of that Strauss backdrop, and where the woman without a shadow might still be walking.

And in recent years that home territory is where all his visual power has been concentrated with an enthusiasm as great as ever. He says his visual sharpness has increased through the years while his hearing has dulled, and in his seventy-sixth year he seems, as an artist, to be speeding up while others are slowing down, still producing at an extraordinary rate. He wants to catch the landscape of home once and for all.

There is the countryside and above all there are the faces: the sketches, some done in a trice, so many of himself and close friends, who reappear again and again, and rich portraits that reveal his insight and his devotion to painterly technique. His fascination with technology is really misleading. In a way he's been in a battle with the camera for decades, proving that it can catch a moment but never time.

His paintings seem timeless because his canvases now are from the same hand that sketched and coloured the sixties. Yet what they have is a feeling for those layers that Hockney watched Freud patiently constructing on his own face through those long hours, like the wonderfully coloured geographical strata of the Grand Canyon, where he has sat for so long with a canvas in front of him.

He loves his camera, his iPad, the fun of artworks built from their images. But in the end it won't do. Only a painter can see the layers underneath. 'The photograph isn't good enough. It's not real enough.'

Billy Connolly

Y<small>OU CAN TELL THAT</small> B<small>ILLY</small> C<small>ONNOLLY</small> is a funny man, because he doesn't look at all odd wearing a coat of many colours, a straggly beard, giant yellow banana boots, and carrying a banjo. When he isn't laughing he looks as if he is about to. When he tells a story he never seems to know where it will take him before he steers it home, but goes along for the ride. And you know that he's amused most of all by the fact that he is now a Scottish laird, with an estate that is only a few glens away from Balmoral.

Connolly is the living link between music hall and the stand-up comedians of the 1990s, a patter merchant who could have topped a variety bill at the Glasgow Empire in its grim glory days, and is just as much at home standing on a lonely stage – or in a football stadium – for two hours on his own, telling tales from Glasgow and touching young audiences, or reminding grannies of the time they heard him tell a story about sex or the Pope (or both together) or the perils of breaking wind in a space suit, when they found that they were creasing up, in spite of themselves.

None of our modern comics so rooted in one place has become a bigger international star. In the early seventies he was propelled in a whoosh from cult story-teller, who'd sprung from the folk and blues scene, to an entertainer who was opening American concerts for Elton John (although the first time round was a disaster). Part of his appeal lay in his visible surprise at what had happened to him. When he took his show to Australia or Canada, or even London, and found them tuning into his Glasgow patois, and wanting more shaggy-dog stories about sex and religion, he squeaked with delight as if he couldn't believe it. That was genuine, and Connolly's trick has always been his authenticity.

He was born on the third floor of a Glasgow tenement in 1942 – as he tells it, landing unexpectedly on the linoleum. He worked in the shipyards after he left school, apprenticed as a boilermaker, and became a jobbing musician, picking on his banjo and enjoying folk and bluegrass. Those of us who saw him with Gerry Rafferty in the late sixties in the Humblebums knew an irrepressible raconteur and party animal, who never stopped, even after he had left the stage (when it often got even better). In the seventies luck shone on him in the form of Nat Joseph of Atlantic Records, who took a risk and released two albums.

The risk was not only commercial. The second album had a long rambling sketch called The Crucifixion in which Connolly relocated the Last Supper to a favourite Glasgow pub, the Saracens' Head – or, more recognizably, the Sarry Heid in the Barras Market – and broke every taboo in the book. But the time was right. A year later, in 1975, he turned up on Michael Parkinson's Saturday night television chat show and found a vast new audience with one long joke. A man had murdered his wife and decided to make use of the corpse by burying it face down in the outside wash-house, with her backside sticking up. He wanted somewhere to park his bike. His manager had warned him it might be too much, but Connolly thought the chat was going well and said to himself, stuff it, or words to that effect. He was a star.

He had a gold disc with his take-off of Tammy Wynette's country and western hit 'DIVORCE' – then two more gold albums – and set off abroad, especially to where there might be audiences of exiled Scots to act as mass translators and – with the exception of the Elton John tour in 1976, when he mystified the American crowds – he was launched on a career that never dipped. He could tour Scotland whenever he liked, fill the biggest hall in London, be the star of *The Secret Policeman's Ball*, and have a more or less permanent pass to *Parkinson*, on which he appeared a record fifteen times.

Connolly was the friend who'd just heard another mad story on the bus, or seen a Glasgow policeman behaving badly; or remembered the stories they used to tell in the yards on the Clyde. It all poured out, one long spinning yarn, that established him as an unruly, singing, giggling national hero. He wasn't a breakaway from the tradition of comedy that preceded him, but a kind of homage to it. He'd seen the lugubrious masters of deadpan comedy at the Glasgow theatres of his youth, and they were the clowns that inspired him, just as the next generation of stand-up comedians learned so much about technique, stamina and style from him. Eddie Izzard, Michael McIntyre, Jimmy Carr – the lot. He was the first of them.

Glasgow's secret, of course, is its obsession with itself. It loves the self-image of a place of sentimentality with a flinty crust, where conmen and shambling drunks are the poets of the streets, offering a running commentary on their lives in a rich, intoxicating language of their own. Connolly's ear had been tuned to it all his life, and he plunged into it with a bubbling affection, whether he was mocking middle-class pretension or working-class sensitivity, gasping with delight at his own memory of all the stories he'd heard and remembered.

This was different from the established patter of the television funny men like Jimmy Tarbuck or even Morecambe and Wise, who still wore suits and told great gags in the old way. He was crude and rude, using words that the grannies who loved his albums thought they'd never hear in their living rooms, let alone on television in the presence of their offspring, and happily paddling into forbidden waters: bodily functions of every kind, masturbation, ministers and Popes, sexual disasters he had known. The secret is that he is always the soft-hearted critic, merciless but never cruel. He loves the people he finds funny, and knows that pomposity always conceals something better.

It turned out that he had concealed quite a lot himself. After his first marriage fell away, he lived with Pamela Stephenson, whom he'd met when he was a guest turn on *Not the Nine O'Clock News* on BBC television, and they had troubles. He was drinking heavily – later he said that he was probably looking forward to dying – and she forced him to stop. He did, and didn't backslide. Then, on the day his father died, in 1988, he broke down and told Pamela what he had never told anyone else: that his father had abused him sexually over a period of years when he was very young.

Her written account *Billy*, of his life, and theirs, is a story of survival as well as fame, and it reveals the fragility that Connolly felt throughout most of his life when he was drinking hard, making people laugh, but almost deliberately driving himself down a steep and rocky slope. It also charts the recovery from those days: he is dry, although no less funny for it, and remarkably unstained by the memory of his father's weakness. 'I have no lack of love for my father,' he says. 'I love his memory now as much as I loved him when he was alive. It was disloyal of him to do that to me. But there were other facets of his character that were great.'

In that book, Connolly emerges as a stronger man, perhaps someone who's grateful for the rough days of the past. The changes in his life did, however, lose him some of the closeness he had with his background. Some Scots, with a weary predictability, thought the guy who'd moved to Hollywood with Pamela – where he lived next door to David Hockney and partied with the stars – had decided that Glasgow wasn't good enough for him. And when he started to have friends in the Royal Family, well, that suspicion in some minds was confirmed. It was the stuff of a Connolly joke: there were some attitudes that would never change, a few hang-ups that would never disappear.

He spoke himself about a negative attitude to him in parts of the Scottish press that was like a disease, from which he had to escape. 'It was time for me to leave, in millions of ways,' he said. There were other things to do, maybe most memorably in the film *Mrs Brown*, in which Judi Dench played Queen Victoria and Connolly was her gamekeeper, companion and soulmate at Balmoral, John Brown. He was funny, poignant and proud in that film, understanding that it was a relationship that maybe couldn't be portrayed in any other way.

Whether he is being funny, and absurd in his big welly boots or banana boots, or with his banjo long ago, or whether he's being serious for a moment and lamenting the tabloids or the celebrity culture or the British tendency to negativity, Connolly is above all a funny man who has understood the sadness of so many people. In a way, what he tried to do – with a shaggy-dog story or a warm but dirty joke – was to lift it, let it fly away, even if only for a few minutes. It was always worth it.

He knew quite a bit of sadness himself, and suffered a good deal of personal anxiety. It's one of the reasons why he was certainly amused just before his sixtieth birthday to be able to buy a beautiful house and estate in Aberdeenshire where, once a year at the Lonach Gathering, he has the ancient task of setting the kilted posse of the Lonach Men on their ceremonial march down the glen to the annual highland games, there to toss their cabers and make merry. For him it's orange juice these days, but more fun than ever.

Who would have thought it?

And that is the invisible punchline to most of his stories down the years, and he is living one of his own fancies.

The giggle still bubbles up without warning, and he'll still pull that beard and start on a story from the streets he knew, still find people as perplexing and endearing as ever. Still laughing after all these years.

Ralph Robins

RALPH ROBINS WAS THE ENGINEER who experienced the near-collapse of British manufacturing industry, battled with government over nationalization, and fought the City over investment. By the time he stepped down as chairman of Rolls-Royce in 2003 he could say that it was a world-class company, but also that it had been a damned close-run thing.

His career mirrors the roller-coaster history of British industry since the Second World War, and perhaps also catches the flavour of the financial crisis that was building up at the time of his retirement, ready to blow like a volcano five years later and leave governments, business and ordinary citizens ploughing through lava that covered the landscape. He is one of the most intriguing and influential figures in our recent industrial history. After his retirement, one of the papers said of him that he was that rare animal, a British engineer who had successfully run a big company and kept it independent, when others had been gobbled up or lost the fight to the Japanese or the Americans. For that he deserved his place in the corporate history books more than most.

The first important thing about Ralph Robins, industrialist, is that he trained as an engineer. When he joined Rolls-Royce as a trainee in 1955 after graduating from Imperial College London, management in business and industry was quite different from what it was when he reached the top. The idea of training for management at the business schools that have proliferated in recent decades would have seemed quaint. There were remarkable men – and they were all men – who built companies and ran them, but in too many of them managers had neither the skills that they were meant to manage in the workforce nor any particular talent of a different kind. By the end of the sixties it was a political commonplace that one of the reasons for industrial decline was the weakness of management, and a culture changed. In the fifties that seemed a long way off.

The company that Robins joined in 1955 was a success. Since Henry Royce had built his first car in 1904, and met the salesman Charles Rolls that same year, they had done pretty well. They built their first aero engine – the Eagle – in the First World War, opening up new territory, and by the time the Second World War came along and the company had developed expertise and market power in the field, it was ready with the Merlin engine for the Spitfire and the Hurricane. By the end of the war the company was prepared for the age of commercial aviation. So Robins was part of a success story. With Armstrong Siddeley its main competitor, Rolls-Royce was providing engines for the airline companies that were catering for a market that was expanding at a speed no one had expected. It was almost exactly in the middle of the fifties that for the first time more people flew across the Atlantic in one year than travelled by ship, and by the start of the sixties Rolls-Royce engines were powering planes large and small around the world. The Comet and then the Boeing 707 were the international planes that did the heavy work, and Rolls-Royce drove them. With a name that carried an echo of elegance and style from their cars, the company was confident, successful and looking forward to an expanding future.

But by the end of the sixties it had all gone wrong. After the merger with Armstrong Siddeley – now called Bristol Siddeley – in 1966, Rolls-Royce was preparing to service the generation of wide-bodied jets that would offer the next opportunity. The answer was a family of engines called the RB-211, first designed for the Lockheed TriStar. But the costs went up and the company found itself in trouble. Soon after it was elected in 1970 Edward Heath's government discovered that it had a nightmare on its hands. Might it have to nationalize Rolls-Royce?

The idea cut across the very appeal that Heath had made to the electorate, that Labour's affection for a substantial public stake in industry was outdated. But political theory didn't solve the problem. Rolls-Royce's development costs had got out of control. The question was whether the country could afford to lose a world-class aircraft engine manufacturer even if its management had made a mess of the RB-211. The answer from the Conservative government was: no. It had to be saved. So, in 1971, the company was nationalized after going into receivership, divided into separate aero and car companies. It would remain in public hands until Margaret Thatcher's government put it back in the private sector in 1987.

Nationalization was the nadir for a company that had once seemed impregnable, and came at a time when Britain's confidence about its industrial future was at an exceedingly low ebb. The Wilson government had been defeated in 1970 on a promise from Ted Heath of economic regeneration, but that did not come about. His government, in turn, was mired in arguments with the trade unions and inside his Cabinet a group of ministers, led by Sir Keith Joseph and including Margaret Thatcher, were beginning to construct a free-market argument against what they saw as a policy that was, in the end, indistinguishable from Labour's. For them the rescue of Rolls-Royce – though the government thought it had no choice – was a consequence of long-term industrial decline that had to be reversed.

Inside the company, it was a long road back. Robins, who became commercial director in the mid-seventies, was deeply affected by the government rescue. He was a committed company man. His initial interest had been in the product – the engines – and he came to management with a feeling for the history of innovation that Rolls-Royce represented. A generation later, figures like him would have arrived from a business school, fast-tracked to the top, with a grasp of all the current theories of management. His style was quite different, and it would play an important part in the life of the country.

One of his colleagues says of Robins that he's a born engineer. He loves tinkering with classic race cars, and the long-term scale of engineering projects is reflected in the way he invested in the company. He was one of the first to champion Rolls-Royce, even through the dark days of bankruptcy and nationalization. He is the great unsung hero of British industry.

Throughout the seventies, in a difficult economic climate, the priority was to continue to develop new engines. Robins took one particularly clever gamble. The Hong Kong airline Cathay Pacific wanted an engine for its new fleet of 747 aircraft, and he offered them a concession on one order in the hope of getting more. It was a much more generous deal than airlines were used to getting, and a risk for the company. But it worked. Cathay expanded fast, and flew with Rolls-Royce engines.

On the back of that success came an important deal with British Airways in the eighties, privatized by Margaret Thatcher's Conservative government. Rolls-Royce had a deal with the American giant General Electric to make a joint bid for an engine contract, but, to the fury of GE, Rolls-Royce also offered a stand-alone deal for the RB-211 and won. The consequence was more work for Britain – almost all the parts came from domestic plants – and a big increase in the company's market share.

The commercial work done by Robins was vital in getting Rolls-Royce to a position from which it might hope to be floated by government – ministers would need the guarantee of a good return for the taxpayer – and be able to run itself, without the involvement of the Department of Trade and Industry. It came in 1987, and the following year Robins, then managing director, signed a $1 billion contract with American Airlines that took the company into the US market in a big way for the first time.

But a turbulent decade lay ahead. Deals at the end of the eighties, when Robins had become chief executive, were mixed. There was American expansion, but a takeover of Northern Engineering Industries for £300 million went wrong. But, just as he'd done the Cathay Pacific deal in 1979 when the company needed some good news, so the development of the Trent engine turned out to be a success.

When Robins became chairman in 1992, it was inevitable that there would be ups and downs, because the reputation he had made in the company was as a shrewd deal-maker – 'gambler' would be too strong – but a man of convictions who often felt it difficult to keep them quiet. It was sometimes an advantage, and sometimes dangerous. Sir John Rose, who served under him as chief executive, put it rather pithily: 'Ralph had balls of steel.'

Through the nineties, however, Rolls-Royce became what it hadn't been since the sixties, a world-ranking manufacturing company of a kind that Britain seemed to have been in danger of losing. In the recession of that decade it did cut thousands of jobs, however, and saw its profits fall. Without the non-aero-engine business – power generation and mining equipment, for example – it would have been in serious trouble. It was Robins who turned that round. And he had another strong card to play. The company had considerable interests in the nuclear industry, which meant government money and a good deal of protection from potentially hostile business predators.

Richard Lambert, former Director General of the CBI, says Robins is a hero of British industry. He was willing to be blunt with institutional and individual shareholders. Robins would say: 'What do you want – a world-leading company in a dozen years' time, or a bigger payout today?' The trouble was that the answer often came back: 'Give us the money.'

Robins had exactly the same argument with the City of London. Throughout the nineties he was warning of the problem that become a commonplace criticism after the financial crash of 2008: short-termism. When he retired in 2003 he said that his greatest regret was that the company had never been, in his view, properly valued by the City. He wanted investment, and he wanted shareholders to be patient. Neither was easy. The City wanted a fast buck.

In 2000 Rolls-Royce had to issue a profit warning, and had the embarrassment of slipping out of the FTSE 100 share index. 'The disappointing thing is that people today want a very quick return,' said Robins, but this is a long-term business. We are the last engineering company in this country that is global and can take on the world but sadly that is not reflected in our share price.' His regret, and his warning, have a poignant quality nearly ten years on. The short-termism was another aspect of the mentality that filled the financial bubble, now routinely regretted but at the time the unchallenged orthodoxy.

The City gave Robins a send-off that some might think cheeky. The share price rose 12p on the news of his retirement. When he went, after forty-three years, he was the company's longest-serving employee. And he could reflect that, more than anyone else, he had saved Rolls-Royce.

Amartya Sen

Amartya Sen says he was born on a university campus and seems to have lived all his life on one. He never had an interest, however, in seclusion in an ivory tower. His academic prowess was driven by a desire to apply intellectual rigour to problems that might affect the life of the world. He is notable for having achieved the highest academic distinction in the service of tackling some of the most intractable problems of our time, poverty, famine and population.

When, in 1988, he became Master of Trinity College, Cambridge – where he'd been an undergraduate – he had already taught in India, at Oxford and in the United States, and had a reputation among economists that placed him in a category of his own. That was the year in which he was awarded the Nobel Prize for his contribution to welfare economics, the citation noting that his work had been directed at some of the most impoverished members of society. One newspaper even called him the Mother Theresa of Economics. Crowds were said to follow him 'wanting to touch his fountain pen'.

It was not surprising that Sen should be aware of the needs of the downtrodden. He was born in India in 1933 in Santiniketan in West Bengal and grew up in Dhaka, now the capital of Bangladesh. He was therefore aware of poverty all his life, and when he was 9 he saw the effects of the Bengal famine which took the lives of between 2 and 3 million people. It had a profound effect on him, and by the time he went to Cambridge for the second time, as a fellow of Trinity in the late fifties, he was convinced that what he called 'the eccentric charms of economics' had to serve a purpose in understanding how problems of that kind might be solved.

His first experience of Cambridge had been when he was 19, arriving to take a degree in pure economics. He realized that the economists in the university were grouped in two camps. The Keynesians and the neo-classical economists profoundly disagreed on macroeconomic theory and how governments could best produce prosperity. To the young Sen, much of that debate, though it was absorbing as an intellectual exercise, was irrelevant. He said, however, that he was lucky to be at Trinity because it was something of an oasis in the ideological battle, where economists of different outlooks could rub along very happily.

Sen returned to India in the early fifties, was immediately appointed a professor, and was asked to set up a new department of economics at the newly created Jadavpur University in Calcutta. 'I was not yet 23,' he says. 'This caused a predictable – and entirely understandable – storm of protest.' Graffiti popped up on the university walls saying that the new professor had been snatched from the cradle. When he returned to Cambridge two years later on a fellowship, which allowed him to study whatever he liked for four years, he decided on philosophy. He wanted to harness it to help him solve some fundamental economic problems, and he became an academic convinced that original thinking was not simply enjoyable, but urgent.

There was another reason. Sen brought to Britain, like many artists and thinkers from India, a cultural perspective that influenced many of his university colleagues. His grandfather had taught Sanskrit at the university in Santiniketan that had been founded by his friend the Indian poet and thinker Rabindranath Tagore. Sen's mother performed in many of Tagore's dance dramas and Tagore actually helped to choose Amartya's first name, which means 'immortal'.

Tagore and his followers argued strongly against the idea of the separate identities which was encouraged in India by the presence of different religions and cultures (and which, not long after Tagore's death, would produce a great deal of violence after the country's independence and partition). That cultural background was one that greatly influenced Sen. He had also seen sectarian violence and knew its consequences. He would tell the story of a man who came through the gate of the Sens' house in Dhaka screaming pitifully and bleeding. He was a Muslim who had been knifed on the street by thugs in the Hindu area. As he was being taken to the hospital by Sen's father, he went on saying that his wife had told him not to go into a hostile area during the communal riots. But he had had to go out in search of work to get some money because his family had nothing to eat. 'The penalty of that economic unfreedom,' says Sen, 'turned out to be death,' for the man later died in hospital. He adds: 'The experience was devastating for me, and suddenly made me aware of the dangers of narrowly defined identities, and also of the divisiveness that can lie buried in communitarian politics.' His subsequent intellectual development was shaped by that cultural background as much as by his natural aptitude for ideas.

Sen was glad to get back to India at the start of the sixties, and in Delhi he managed to find colleagues who shared his interest in a field of study for which he'd found little appetite in Cambridge: social choice theory. Put simply, it was the question of how individual choices and different preferences in society could be measured. The puzzle was how to gather information and create mechanisms for policy-makers that would offer advantages to people who were crippled by poverty or isolation as well as to those who started from a better position.

Beyond the theory of social choice – how could you provide choice for everyone in a free society, when their preferences and circumstances were so radically different? – was the memory of famine in India, and the belief that democratic societies must be better equipped to prevent it.

By the time he published *Collective Choice and Social Welfare* in 1970, Sen was established as an intellectual trailblazer. His thinking involved meticulous observation: he remembers weighing every boy and girl between the ages of 2 and 5, one by one, in two large communities in West Bengal.

In a lecture for Radio 4 in 1976 called 'The Art of Economics' he argued that, because of the misery and agony it caused, starvation must surely be the greatest economic problem facing the world. Many economists would have given a different answer. He then argued that it was inadequate to see the problem as a population that was growing faster than the production of food. If that were true, why was it that in some of most underdeveloped countries the increase in food production was greater than the increase in the number of people?

And what were the social rules or the institutions that governed the system of exchange? Start to examine them and you might make progress. Since then Sen's ideas have informed the policies of governments and organizations around the world when food is in short supply. This has encouraged them to keep prices stable and, beyond alleviating immediate suffering, to provide the poor with opportunities to earn money.

Sen also believed that measuring the GNP of a country – its wealth – was too simplistic for assessing the standard of living, and although he was concerned that one figure could not capture the complexities, he worked with the Pakistani economist Mahbub ul Haq to create the United Nations' Human Development Index. This became the most authoritative international source for welfare comparisons between countries. It is an attempt to shift the attention of policy-makers onto human, rather than economic, well-being. Sen has also recognized that gender must be addressed and has long argued for investment in the education of girls in order to help them lift their families out of poverty.

When he published *The Idea of Justice* in 2009 he argued that the world of the twenty-first century had to understand that there were injustices whose removal was as important as the abolition of slavery was in the early nineteenth century.

It is inescapable that the clarity of the argument that Sen brought to academic life in Britain was developed far away, in the India of the empire in which he was born and where he absorbed a culture quite different from the one that he encountered at Cambridge. The school which he attended in Santiniketan had been founded by Tagore with the purpose of fostering curiosity rather than promoting competition. He remembers one of his teachers saying of another pupil: 'She is quite a serious thinker, even though her grades are very good.' Years later, teaching in the West, where obsessions about examinations and grades had become all-consuming, that memory remained precious to him.

Sen is still an Indian citizen, because that is where he comes from, and maybe it is the good fortune of some of our more self-confident academic institutions that they have been exposed to the spirit of Santiniketan.

Salman Rushdie

NO WRITER IN MODERN TIMES has had to hide from his readers for longer than Salman Rushdie. For nearly ten years he lived in seclusion under armed guard while fundamentalist Muslims who had sentenced him to death promised to hunt him down. It placed him at the heart of an argument about religious tolerance and artistic freedom, made him a celebrated victim, and turned the theme of so much of his writing into a matter of life and death: the question of identity.

When it happened, Rushdie was already a novelist celebrated around the world. At the moment *Midnight's Children* won the Booker Prize in 1981 he was propelled to the front rank of writers. Malcolm Bradbury called it 'a new start for the late-twentieth century novel', and for Rushdie, who was 34, it was a thundering triumph. Overnight he became one of the masters of magic realism – fusing fantasy and myth with reality – and this style seems in the book to be not at all contrived, and a natural way of telling the story.

That story was the birth of India as an independent country in 1947 and its tentative, sometimes painful emergence from the shadow of empire, through the experiences of Saleem Sinai, one of the 1,001 children born in the hour of independence and gifted, as a result, with magical powers. They give Rushdie the chance to move back and forth across the pencil-thin line that in India divides the business of day-to-day life from a rich world of religious symbolism, myth and the supernatural. And to spin a saga that has the gleaming quality of *Tales from the Arabian Nights*, playing with memory and imagination and flashing with dazzling colours.

The fact that Saleem's history is imperfect illustrates Rushdie's own distance from his past: living in London and remembering the India of his childhood through a clouded lens. He was writing about himself as well as his own country, and he carried the theme forward in his next book, *Shame*, in which the family at the centre of the story live in an ancestral home in which the windows only look inwards, into the dark and violent experience of Pakistan, which came into existence with India's independence. Inevitably Rushdie is often seen as the first in a line of writers from India whose books have explored the post-colonial era in south Asia – Arundhati Roy, Amitav Ghosh and Anita Desai among them – and who have been read enthusiastically in Britain because they probe the cultural undercurrents that flow back and forth from East to West.

As a young man Rushdie loved the writing of E.M. Forster, whom he was lucky enough to meet, and particularly *A Passage to India*, but he said he wanted to get away from its cool, controlled language, which he admired but said didn't reflect the India he knew. 'India isn't cool, it's hot, and I began to wonder what the language might sound like that was not cool but hot – that was noisy and vulgar and crowded and sensual.'

He therefore established himself before he was 40 as a writer who could probe the British fascination with India and reveal some of its secrets, the layers that give its life a texture so different from the Western experience. When he was writing *Midnight's Children* he couldn't be sure that his own enthusiasm would be shared. 'It was all right, and I'd done something which I liked, but I had no idea if anybody on the planet would agree with me, let alone buy it.'

The book made him famous, and well-off. But it was the events of 1989 that gave Rushdie a different public character, turning him into a writer swept up in the politics of religion. Although it was a draining and dangerous experience, he often reflected on the piquancy that it had all happened to an atheist.

He wanted to write about Islam from the perspective of a man brought up in a Muslim middle-class family who had lost his faith. He has spoken of his writing being an effort to find the precise shape of the God-shaped hole in his life. In *The Satanic Verses*, published in 1988, he decided to apply his love of fantasy to his religious heritage. From the first time he picked up a pen as a boy and tried to write a story, he'd been attracted by fairy tales: he called his first short story 'Over the Rainbow', because he loved *The Wizard of Oz*. And he applied those same instincts to this subject, with incendiary consequences.

He remembered an apocryphal episode in the life of the Prophet Mohammed in which the devil appears to him disguised as the Archangel Gabriel and hands him some satanic verses which later have to be expunged from the Koran when the deception is revealed. So Rushdie's theme would be the difficulty in telling the difference between angels and devils, good and evil.

The book begins with a piece of vintage Rushdie invention. Two Muslims are in a hijacked plane over the English Channel, which blows up. But they're miraculously spared and as they float downwards they're transformed, one into Gabriel and one into a devil. The rest of the story has an eerie familiarity, a contemporary fable written before its time, encompassing terrorism, the fate of illegal immigrants, a world gripped by competing fundamentalist beliefs, and a sense of loss by individuals caught up in the chaos. Unfortunately for Rushdie his explorations were dangerously timed.

There was anger in the Muslim world, book burnings and protests, and then the religious authorities, in power in Iran for ten years, took a hand. As Rushdie put it much later: 'It wasn't the first time they didn't like what I'd written, just the first time they'd tried to kill me.' On Valentine's Day in 1989 a declaration was issued in Teheran, unmistakable in its intent. For those of us involved in the news it was a dramatic day. I was presenter of *The World at One* on Radio 4 on that day, and it was the programme that told him of the threat to his life. He went into hiding that same afternoon.

The security advice was so clear that he could not avoid doing so: the threats were serious and he could expect potential assassins to pop up and try to find him. A death sentence from the Ayatollah Khomeini was not a rhetorical flourish but, to some followers, a command. Rushdie could joke about it later – 'I wasn't writing for the Mullahs. I didn't think they were my target audience' – but that was many years away. He had to find a way of keeping himself safe. With the help of friends he disappeared from view.

The bounty on his head from one religious group was £1.5 million, and they were after him. The man who translated the book into Japanese was killed. His Italian translator and Norwegian publisher were both injured. The author himself moved through more than two dozen safe houses over the next year, spending more time in the folded hills of mid-Wales than anywhere else, but as the years went by he popped up from time to time at London parties, with security guards never far away.

Through his years in hiding, with the apparatus of a daily routine removed from him, it was natural that he'd continue to worry away at the theme which had already marked his writing: rootlessness and the shock of losing touch with a culture. He likes to say that there are more people now living in countries in which they weren't born than at any time in the whole of human history, and is fascinated by the trauma of losing a sense of place, having to use an alien language and living in a different culture. What did you get from the world in which you live, and what was retained from the place from which you came?

Although Rushdie had support from writers outraged by his fate, and public sympathy was generally with him, it was not universal. Germaine Greer, feminist and left-wing humanist, refused to sign a petition against the fatwa in the early nineties, and Rushdie was outraged. He accused her of describing him as 'a megalomaniac, an Englishman with dark skin', well aware that in some quarters he had got a reputation for preciousness which he thought quite undeserved. But it kept recurring. He was accused of vanity when he had an operation to correct a condition that was causing his eyelids to droop down, giving him a heavy and sinister look. And his enjoyment of a good one-liner never helped. He once said: 'I don't think this would have happened to Beryl Bainbridge.'

He'd been advised by his friend the writer Julian Barnes not to let the experience of enforced internal exile turn him into an obsessive, and he largely succeeded – although it caused him to think particularly about freedom and security, and about the press which he said was vicious in its treatment of writers in Britain in a way that he found hard to understand. In the febrile world after the attacks of September 2001, after the fatwa had been lifted, he spoke about the danger of a rush to excessive security, and a suspension of liberties, even in the face of serious threats of the kind that he'd had to live with for so long. And continued to live with.

Even in 2012 at the Jaipur literary festival in India he was told to keep away for fear of murderous attack. A number of writers read from *The Satanic Verses* in an act of defiance, the book still being banned in India.

However, he retained the ability to be funny, especially in his books for children: *Haroun and the Sea of Stories* in 1990 and *Luka and the Fire of Life* in 2010. He had been after all the young copy-writer in an advertising agency in London who'd coined the slogan for cream cakes 'naughty but nice'. He took to Facebook and Twitter with a relish that very few high-minded writers could manage, played scrabble with Kylie Minogue and her sister, never missed a good party if he could help it.

Yet Rushdie remains a novelist with a serious intent. He has called his latest memoir *Joseph Anton*, taking the pen name from his two favourite writers, Conrad and Chekhov – the name was also his alias while under police protection – and says he remains convinced that writing is an argument with the world. That argument, in his case, put his life in danger.

As well as becoming a novelist who painted an unforgettable picture of the Indian experience, seen in retrospect from the seat of empire, he experienced for himself the preciousness of artistic liberty. 'What is freedom of expression?' he once said. 'Without the freedom to offend, it ceases to exist.'

Anita Roddick

IN THE LATE SIXTIES, anyone trying to sell banana shampoo, or coconut hair gloss, or grapeseed serum, let alone hemp hand butter or peppermint foot rescue, could have expected to be treated like a snake-oil salesman selling dodgy potions from the back of a cart, and chased out of town. Most people wouldn't have wanted a pot of strawberry exfoliator in the house. Environmentalism had its limits. Yet within a few years Anita Roddick was opening her first Body Shop, convinced that the time had come, and building a worldwide business where once there had been nothing.

The first shop was in Brighton. She couldn't get a loan from the bank – she thought it might have been because she was wearing a Bob Dylan T-shirt when she went to see the manager – but succeeded in getting £4,000 to start up. She'd become convinced that there was a market for new body products after she'd watched Polynesian women, when she was travelling in the sixties, who rubbed cocoa butter onto their breasts and bellies and seemed to have beautiful velvety skin. Why not? she thought to herself.

She got the name of the shop from the sign outside a panel-beater's, though she had some trouble from local undertakers who didn't want a place advertised as the Body Shop next door to them. It gave Roddick her first burst of publicity, and she was soon selling fifteen different products, some of them in recycled urine sample bottles, which were cheap. It didn't matter: the customers began to roll in. She concocted the products in her kitchen, and displayed pictures in the shop of the exotic places from which she'd picked up the idea and sourced the raw materials.

Her husband, Gordon Roddick, had a business brain and when he got back after fulfilling a long-standing dream of riding a horse from Buenos Aires to New York he set about devising a financial structure for the business, and establishing a system of franchises by which the chain could begin. It was fast. Within two years they had opened a franchised shop in Brussels, and high streets all over Britain were beginning to have a Body Shop. The design seemed fresh and colourful, and Roddick liked the idea of telling the story of her products: where the plants come from and how potions and remedies were used by native peoples. Nothing like it had been done on this scale before.

From the start Roddick said that her products would be environmentally friendly. In Britain, that was new. Green thinking was some way off, and the kind of environmental concerns that a lot of shoppers have today were the preserve of enthusiasts who, in the seventies, had to accept that many people regarded them as cranks. It was a time when even health food stores were outposts of eccentricity. Roddick wasn't at all bothered. Much later she described herself as having been 'a ballsy, truth-telling, free-thinking, heart-bleeding, myth-debunking, non-conforming and hell-raising activist'. She needed that spirit, because a sober business appraisal of her idea would probably have been gloomy.

Instead, she managed to turn her personality to good use, being the innovating woman who refused to be put down. That guaranteed her a good deal of publicity, and the expansion took place with remarkably little national advertising. Requests for franchises poured in. The deal was that a shopkeeper could use the Body Shop name and logo as long as all the products were bought from Roddick. She found that a substantial number of potential franchisees were women. They liked the idea, and believed they could build local markets for the products. It wasn't long before they were proved right, and the chain grew and grew.

One of the attractions, though Roddick saw it as a principle rather than a marketing ploy, was that she spoke of her business as being ethically sound and committed, for example, to products that did not involve cruel testing on animals. The soundness of that approach would be questioned from time to time through the years, but there was no doubting Roddick's spirit. She was in part a crusader against the big cosmetic companies, thereby putting herself on the side of women who felt patronized and used by them, and a regular champion of causes that were gaining public support. She was an early supporter of Greenpeace, her shops promoted Third World development (as it was still known), and she wasn't nervous about filling those shops with leaflets promoting the causes she had taken up.

The formula worked. By 1984, when Body Shop was floated on the stock market, it was valued at £8 million. Roddick had established herself as a figure from the counterculture who nonetheless connected with women, particularly young professionals, who appreciated her get-up-and-go style and her commitment to the environment, even if most of her shoppers might not have shared all her political views. It was a time of expansion. There was an irony in Thatcherism being good for Roddick, for she was the polar opposite of the Prime Minister in many ways, but it was. And yet they did have one feature in common: unstoppability.

By now Roddick was wealthy, and that made her even more enthusiastic about her causes. 'Wealth obliges you to be generous,' she once said. 'For me that generosity means supporting the men and women – the grassroots activists – who are campaigning to bring about positive social change. This means anything from investing in a hemp farm in Ontario to helping fund *Mother Jones*, a radical magazine in San Francisco, to getting the *Big Issue* started here in the UK.'

Roddick was one of the most successful businesswomen Britain had ever seen. Boardrooms were notoriously free of female influence, and the sight of a shrewd and successful company boss who was not only a woman but had liberal-left views as well was a rarity indeed. She said in the mid-nineties that, partly because she always made herself available for interview, she reckoned that Body Shop racked up £2 million in free publicity every year through editorial coverage.

Naturally, that made her an irritating as well as a successful figure. A high moral tone is always a two-edged sword, and she had plenty of detractors, who resented the impression that she was alone in promoting an ethical approach to retail. It also produced particular difficulties in the United States, where the first Body Shop appeared in 1988. It was one thing to display anti-whaling posters in a shop in Hampstead, quite another to put up pacifist posters in American shopping malls during the First Gulf War of 1991, as she did. Her US marketing director got board approval to take them down, because of the assumed public reaction.

That difficulty was soon followed by a damaging legal fight with Channel Four, which broadcast a documentary that cast doubt on Body Shop's boasts about its opposition to animal testing. The programme claimed that the policy was not as strict as it appeared, and the effect on the business was immediate. The accusation was that one of its founding principles was flawed, and the shares plunged. The Roddicks sued and won, but it was a wearing fight, accompanied by hostile publicity in the United States, which they had never faced before. After the company was sold to the French firm L'Oréal in 2006 for £652 million, some of Roddick's strongest supporters were dismayed to see it in the hands of one of the big cosmetic firms of the sort that she had railed against when she started out. But for some time the special quality that had been attached to the chain in the early days had been diluted. Body Shop was not the only one in the high street selling environmentally friendly products, and some shoppers evidently felt that the stores had lost the early zest that came with the feeling that they were part of a crusade.

The story, however, was one of success. Roddick was an undeniable force in the retail industry. Her theory of business was simple: 'In the end, the best advert is a good product, a good shop, staff that are thrilled by what you do, and customers not hyped out or overmarketed or overwhelmed by advertising.' It was a measure of her success that this model was widely copied, and the market for environmentally friendly cosmetics, with limited animal testing, expanded hugely.

She continued to campaign all her life, even after the business was sold. 'Business doesn't interest me any more,' she said. 'I was a one-song person. What saved me was that I never went to business school and I don't know who Milton Friedman is. I was a teacher and a researcher – and I knew how to tell a story.'

It was an honest assessment. Roddick had started out as a teacher in the sixties, and it was indeed a story that she wanted to tell. The success of Body Shop was never separate in her mind from the campaigns that ran alongside it. When she died, in 2007 at the age of only 64, many retailers who had learned lessons about the power and popularity of ethical trading acknowledged their debt. Stuart Rose, chief executive of Marks & Spencer at the time, who was developing a green future for the business, said of her: 'She was one the first ethical traders, and was twenty years ahead of her time in ethical trading.'

Roddick changed the habits of her customers, and also the behaviour of her competitors. She did so by imagination, belief and a good deal of bloody-mindedness. She was once asked by a newspaper what she thought the most over-rated virtue and she replied honestly: 'Self-effacement.'

Norman Foster

NORMAN FOSTER HAS LEFT a more visible mark in more cities around the world than any of his countrymen in the post-war era. Flying to Beijing you land at one of his airports, German parliamentarians sit under the glass dome of his Reichstag in Berlin, his taste has shaped the skylines of London, Tokyo and Hong Kong, and if you drive to the south of France you will sail into the sky over one of his bridges, which is higher than the Eiffel Tower and is generally reckoned to be one of the most beautiful in the world.

Lord Foster of Thames Bank is the British architect of his age, along with Richard Rogers, with whom he once worked in a partnership. He is a winner of the Stirling Prize – the architects' Blue Riband – and a string of awards around the world, during a career in which he developed his own modernist style, an airy high-tech fusion of innovative engineering and bold lines that made his practice one of the world's most successful. Whether with the 'Gherkin' in the City of London or the HSBC headquarters in Hong Kong, Foster has been at the forefront of much commercial urban redesign for more than thirty years.

He became an architect, however, by a circuitous route. As a boy in Manchester he was mad about planes and trains – there was a railway line at the back of the house where he grew up in a working-class part of the city – and a lifelong fascination with engineering and design was beginning to develop. But his first job, after he left school at 16, was as a trainee in the clerks' department in Manchester Town Hall and it was because the son of one of his supervisors was training as an architect that he started down the road to his profession. After national service in the Royal Air Force – more planes – he ended up in an architect's office only because he'd been turned down for a job with an office machine company.

After that it happened very fast. Quickly he was off to Manchester School of Architecture and then, in the early sixties, on a scholarship to Yale, where he met Richard Rogers. Back in London they established their own practice in 1963, the proving ground for two men who would become, separately, the most prolific and celebrated architects in Britain.

Foster was greatly influenced by encounters in the United States with Buckminster Fuller, an architect and designer celebrated for his unorthodox thinking and his utopian cast of mind. His great project was the geodesic dome, which could sustain its own weight without any visible means of support, and anyone who glances at Foster's work – his love of space, the way he maximizes light, the elegance of his lines – will see Fuller's passions replicated. Fuller was also a generation ahead of his time in thinking about the uses of solar power and dreaming of electricity produced by the wind. He would talk of his work as contributing to 'the sustenance of all humanity', and ideas that seemed a little wacky to his contemporaries would be mainstream by the time Foster was trying to develop environmentally sustainable buildings.

Foster Associates, his own practice, was founded in 1967. From the beginning he began to think of architecture as overwhelmingly practical. 'The subject is too often treated as a fine art,' he once said, 'delicately wrapped in mumbo-jumbo. In reality, it's an all-embracing discipline taking in science, art, maths, engineering, climate, nature, politics, economics.' He speaks of what he has learned about buildings from his passion for flying, saying that the best lesson in aerodynamics he ever had was in a glider when he climbed through a thermal at the same time as an eagle, and saw how it combined its strength with an apparently effortless lightness.

There is a metaphor there for much of Foster's work. By the time he'd become internationally renowned in the eighties he was already addressing the problems that would increasingly dominate the thinking of planners and designers by the end of the century: the sustainability of buildings and communities, the need to combine technical innovation with low-energy, environmentally friendly design. By the time he came to produce the building that was his first big international success, the headquarters for HSBC in Hong Kong, opened in 1986, he was thinking ahead.

That building made his name, just as his former partner Richard Rogers (working with Renzo Piano among others) was celebrated for the Pompidou Centre in Paris, opened in 1977. The HSBC building – the tallest skyscraper outside the United States when it opened – was a combination of meticulous detail and startling style, with its supporting structure on the outside. Natural sunlight is the main source of internal lighting, with huge mirrors built into the atrium as reflectors, and Foster created a feeling of spaciousness in the midst of one of the most crowded urban landscapes in the world. Within a couple of years he was designing a Millennium Tower for Tokyo, the tallest tower in Barcelona, and getting to work on the Reichstag for the new parliament in Berlin that followed German reunification.

Foster's hallmark has been an elegance that contrasts with the much-derided brutalism associated with much sixties urban architecture in Britain, which left a legacy of streaked concrete walls and bleak, windswept walkways. By the time he came to build Stansted Airport in 1991, Foster's use of steel, his soaring curves and his determination to maximize space and light gave him an unmistakable identity. Critics have said that the airport terminal – he has designed many of them – is the template that never leaves his mind, and sometimes becomes too much of a guide. For him, it has always been a question of practicality: making the building work by providing space and light. The headquarters of his own practice in London makes the point. A converted warehouse between Battersea and Albert bridges on the Thames, it has no dark corners, no unnecessary walls, and offers vistas from every window.

Contemporary architects in Britain have had their battles, of course – mainly with the Prince of Wales. When the Prince first began to reveal his feelings about some modern buildings, especially in London, it was inevitably a challenge to anyone working in a modern idiom. He declared his dislike of Sir Denys Lasdun's National Theatre, and in a famous speech in 1984 attacked the design for an extension to the National Gallery in Trafalgar Square as putting him in mind of a 'monstrous carbuncle' on the face of a much-loved and elegant old friend. It was changed. There followed a period in which he was portrayed as an enemy of any building that wasn't neo-Georgian, and any architect pursuing a modernist style was considered his enemy.

In fact, some common ground was reached, and Foster's buildings were partly responsible. Ten years on from that speech Prince Charles spoke of how he had simply been trying to prevent what he once called a 'welter of ugliness' across the country, and said that he wanted to recover 'an architecture of the heart', in which an essence of feeling and a sense of place and atmosphere were in the forefront of architects' minds. He feared 'an age without spirit', and was at pains to say that he appreciated buildings that possessed style. In the same year as those comments, 1994, one of Foster's designs made the point as eloquently as anything else he ever produced.

A bridge was opened in the middle of southern France, on the way from Clermont-Ferrand to Béziers, which was conceived as a way of allowing cars to avoid the famous traffic jams that built up in the town of Millau on the A75 when the rush to the Midi began in the summer. The bridge would take them over that road. Foster's design was breathtaking: a viaduct more than one and a half miles long, its towers reaching a height of more than 1,000 feet, with seven elegant piers and a roadway that seems impossibly narrow and delicate. The bridge is intensely practical, and exhilarating as a piece of design on the landscape, catching the contours of the valley and giving them a spectacular lift. Foster said that anyone driving over it should feel as if they were flying a car over the River Tarn. 'A work of man must fuse with nature,' he said. 'The pillars had to look almost organic, like they had grown from the earth.'

It would be hard to think of words from an architect that could more easily be put in the mouth of the Prince of Wales, and Foster's language about the purpose of architecture and the responsibilities of designers and builders to the environment – its appearance and its protection – have been passions all his life. Such sentiments didn't stop the old battle from flaring up again from time to time. A Richard Rogers design for the site of the former Chelsea Barracks in London produced an appeal from Clarence House to the site's owners, the Qatari royal family, in which the Prince said his 'heart sank' when he saw the design. It was blocked, despite a protest letter in support of Rogers signed by Foster among others.

But between them Foster and Rogers – both given peerages, both winners of the Stirling Prize, each celebrated on several continents – had been largely responsible for the hugely enhanced position of architecture in the public mind in Britain by the turn of the century. This they brought about by demonstrating the importance of environmental awareness, by their commitment to innovative style, and most of all by emphasizing the necessity for a constructive and sensitive debate about urban design and the future of communities.

Norman Foster's buildings have changed the appearance of many of the world's cities, and he has taken their people with him.

Charles Saatchi

CHARLES SAATCHI MAKES AN UNLIKELY LINK between two of the otherwise unconnected public phenomena of his time: Thatcherism, and the wild young turks who made a new kind of conceptual art for Britain at the end of the twentieth century, who asked the public to appreciate, among other exotic objects, the allure of an unmade bed and a shark floating in a glass tank full of formaldehyde.

He is the advertising man who became one of the world's most restless art collectors, buying and selling modern pieces, making young careers, and filling his own London gallery with a provocative rolling show that became the playground for a new movement: the Young British Artists, also known as BritArt.

Saatchi's freedom to become a collector on such a vast scale came from his success in advertising, which reached its zenith in 1979. He and his brother Maurice ran the agency which was asked by Margaret Thatcher's Conservatives to devise the posters and slogans for her election campaign. It was ruthless and brilliant, hanging a slogan around the neck of Prime Minister Jim Callaghan in late 1978 that became an emblem of the time and one that he couldn't cast off. One of the posters showed a long queue of unemployed people, with the words: 'Labour Isn't Working.'

Never mind that some of the unemployed in the photograph were volunteer Young Conservatives, the effect was powerful. The government had spent the winter of 1978–9 embroiled in bitter disputes with public sector unions over pay, and seemed helpless to prevent strikes that affected vital services. By the time it fell, in a Commons vote at the end of March 1979, the Saatchi & Saatchi campaign had already drawn much blood, and in the month that followed before polling day it became the tune to which Mrs Thatcher marched to victory.

Working with Gordon Reece – the cigar-chomping Svengali whose achievements included getting Mrs Thatcher to make her voice more appealing by taking it down a few semitones, hiring a National Theatre voice coach to help – the Saatchis were installed as pillars of the new Conservative establishment. Their business boomed, because their political connections gave them access to the top, and their touch was sure. Reece may have said – to Rupert Murdoch's delight – that 'it was the *Sun* wot won it', but the Saatchis had built the image which the Prime Minister never lost, through bad times and good. They helped to make her what she became.

Charles Saatchi was born in Baghdad, the second of four sons of a well-to-do Iraqi Jewish family in a community in the capital that was once substantial. The name means 'watchmaker' in Iraqi Arabic and Persian. In the 1940s, however, their comfortable life was changing: Saatchi's father, Nathan, realized that things were going to become increasingly difficult under the Sunni Arab government – in the end tens of thousands of Jews would flee – and he took his family to London in 1947. Charles was 4 when he arrived in Britain.

They had money. Nathan bought two textile mills, settled in the North London Jewish community, and the boys grew up in comfort. Charles gives very few interviews, rarely talks about himself, seems reclusive, but he does recall a happy childhood and a teenage infatuation with many of the habits of the day: collecting cigarette cards, the occasional nudist magazine and Superman comics. He listened to American rock 'n' roll and says that the event that changed his life was a visit to New York during which he saw an exhibition at the Museum of Modern Art and first set eyes on a painting by Jackson Pollock. He was hooked on the spot, by its abstract boldness and its force.

After studying in London he entered the thrusting world of advertising as a copywriter, getting recognition at one of the leading agencies of the time, Collett Dickenson Pearce. His contemporaries there included David Puttnam and the film director Alan Parker, who recall his competitiveness in everything: he was the first to buy an E-type Jaguar and when someone followed suit he went out and got himself a Ferrari.

Parker said of him that 'he was always ahead of us with regard to ambitions in life', and by the time he was 24 he had set up his own consultancy with the art director John Cramer, and his career began to grow. Three years later, with Maurice – three years his junior – he set up Saatchi & Saatchi and they began to make waves. Among the early financial backers was the fashion designer Mary Quant. On the side, Charles was already buying art.

The brothers started to collect clients. There's a story – maybe apocryphal but with a ring of truth to it – that when one potentially lucrative client visited them to discuss an advertising contract, Saatchi went into the street and hired a dozen strangers whom he persuaded to sit around the office, giving the impression it was rather busier than it was. True or not, they got the contract. They'd also hired a smart media director called Tim Bell and were showing some skill in spotting talent. Martin Sorrell, later a City, then worldwide, star, arrived in 1975 to help their programme of acquisitions, and when the company was only six years old it was floated on the stock exchange, and money rolled in.

But even with ground-breaking and controversial campaigns – remember the picture of the pregnant man for the Health Education Council ad warning against unwanted pregnancy – Saatchi was frustrated with the limitations of print. He told the

BBC's *Panorama* in 1971: 'You just can't go on pumping facts into people for ever and I think once the facts have sunk in you want to build on those facts and perhaps use an emotional approach and it needs television, no doubt about it.'

'How much money do you get a year now?' the interviewer asked him.

'We're working on a budget of £100,000,' he replied.

'And what would you need to do what you'd like to?'

'A million.'

'Do you think you're going to get a million?'

'No.'

But they did, and by the time they landed the multi-million pound British Airways account in the mid-eighties Saatchi & Saatchi could rightly claim to be the biggest advertising agency in the world. But the speed of its rise was matched by the dramatic collapse of the empire. The brothers had been ruthless and they were paid back: they were forced out of the boardroom of their own company.

Meanwhile, Saatchi had become a notable art collector. In 1985 he opened his first gallery, a huge space in a former paint factory in St John's Wood, North London, and published a four-volume catalogue of his collection that had been growing for nearly twenty years and was already extremely valuable. He'd been buying minimalist paintings but at that stage he was also acquiring pieces by Leon Kossoff, Lucian Freud and Frank Auerbach, reflecting a slightly more traditional taste that he would not exhibit in years to come. But it was all a little risky.

Many of the paintings were owned by the company, and the combination of falling profits and a costly divorce settlement with his first wife, Doris, meant that Saatchi had to be a shrewd as well as a bold buyer and seller. By 1990 his books were show-ing a $20 million profit from art sales. One Irish artist, Sean Scully, whose work Saatchi sold for a huge profit, fumed about his success. 'He's really a commodities broker,' he said. 'He claims to love art but his is the love a wolf has for the lamb.'

Although he would never deny his ruthlessness in business, Saatchi sees no distinction between his passion for art and a good deal. He once said that since Renaissance masters were supported by the patronage of the rich and the Church, and became wealthy as a result, it might be true that even at that time in Florence people were more fascinated by how much art fetched than the pictures themselves.

He has described himself as 'a gorger of the nearly new' and he has now been feasting for more than forty years. In 1990 he bought his first 'gruesome' piece from Damien Hirst and that relationship became famous the following year when he gave the artist £50,000 to get hold of a tiger shark, preserve it, bring it back to London, and then display it under the title *The Physical Impossibility of Death in the Mind of Someone Living.*

This formed the central part of the first series of exhibitions that turned into the beginning of a movement. The shows were called *Young British Artists I–VI*, from which sprang the acronym that became the talk of the nineties, YBA.

Saatchi was now investing in a great many young artists – usually in quite small amounts – and soon he had collected hundreds of pieces. The result was an exhibition in 1997 called *Sensation*, which produced precisely what it said on the poster. More than 300,000 people went to the Royal Academy in London to see it, and it became notorious. An image of the Moors murderer Myra Hindley by Marcus Harvey caused demonstrations in the streets outside, and a Virgin Mary exhibit brought more ordure flying in Saatchi's direction. *Sensation* toured to Berlin and New York, but the director of the National Gallery of Australia decide to cancel its invitation, not on the grounds that the exhibits might offend people but because he thought the show was 'too close to the market'.

This complaint was familiar by now: that Saatchi might well be an enthusiast for art but that he was as much a wheeler-dealer as a patron. He hardly bothered to reply, remaining resistant to interviews and even public statements. He preferred to let people make up their own minds, and usually didn't even attend the opening of his own shows on the grounds that he didn't attend opening parties at other galleries and thought it appropriate to treat himself in the same way. He prefers to stay at home, with his third wife, the writer and cook Nigella Lawson, and their children. And as for his effect on the market, he describes himself as a causing a 'strange distortion' when he decides there is a painting or a sculpture that he wants. 'I think it comes from a desire to show an artist at their best,' he says. 'Some people are reluctant to let them go unless you pay them a very, very high premium. So I do. That's how I get them.'

The results can be seen at the Saatchi Gallery of contemporary art, housed in a former Army barracks in Chelsea, which in the three years up to 2011 was home to seven of the ten most visited exhibitions in London. In 2010 Saatchi donated it to the public as the Museum of Contemporary Art for London, and the collection continues to startle, to satisfy and to bore visitors, as all his galleries and shows have done since the eighties.

Charles Saatchi, advertising man, has always enjoyed engineering a shock, having discovered long ago that it works.

Goldie

THINK OF THE DIFFERENCE between the music at the opening ceremony at the London Olympics of 2012 and the scene
when the flame last burned in the city, in 1948. At the earlier
games the performers were military bands. Splendid, but traditional. In 2012, at both the opening and closing ceremonies, the
theme was, in part, the change in our musical culture in those
intervening decades. There was the sound of the sixties from Paul
McCartney and the Who, of course, but on the opening night
there was one notable performance that caught a more contemporary spirit. One of the stars was a young rapper called Dizzee
Rascal, and his sound, a mix of grime and hip hop, is a direct
descendant of drum 'n' bass, one of the dominant strains of
modern pop music and quite different from its antecedents. If you
try to find its origins in this country, you come face to face with
Goldie.

Clifford Joseph Goldie was born in Wolverhampton in 1965
and his childhood was rough. Brought up in foster care, he knew
the streets. His recreation was spraying graffiti, and he represents
the kind of childhood that governments spend their time worrying about and trying to correct. But Goldie survived. He became
a musician, producer, DJ, the pioneer of a new sound, and a
phenomenon. In 2009 his first orchestral piece, *Sine Tempora*,

had its première at the BBC Proms in the Royal Albert Hall. The previous year he'd been a star in the BBC's conducting talent competition, *Maestro*, although he'd had no formal musical training.

He does, however, have a rich musical personality. It is one that is remote from an older generation, because his style springs from the streets and it's overlaid with the rough, violent language of the rapper and the patois of gang culture, but his music is surprisingly familiar. The drum 'n' bass genre has become ubiquitous in its influence, the heavy pulse and thumping rhythms almost as familiar to people who've never heard of Goldie as to those who think of him as a hero.

The style marked one of the changes that let music turn a corner, just as noticeably as when the pop music of the first wave from the sixties changed to the heavy, complicated, rich inventions of Pink Floyd and Led Zeppelin in the second wave. Drum 'n' bass was more than a tweak to an existing style: it turned into a style of its own. And it is inseparable from the dance culture of the early nineties that got a grip in the way that the first disco craze, more than a decade earlier, had hypnotized another generation.

One reason for its distinctiveness, and its threatening tone to outsiders, was the culture that grew up around it. This was the world of raves and weekend musical binges, warehouse parties in 'Madchester', obsessive clubbing, drugs, all to the thumping bass sounds of the likes of Goldie. He explains it like this: 'There are some similarities between classical music and drum 'n' bass – if you don't know it, you don't get it.' And he uses the cultural references of the street to explain its grip: 'I wanted to show the seriousness of the gang-related, the multicultural. Just like the ruckus on the street and mobile phones on the street, there's a loada wannabees out there and people have to understand that whole thing: if you live by that, you die by that.'

He's talking of a time in the nineties when youth culture changed in two particular ways. The mobile phone arrived, and suddenly there was interconnection of a kind that had never been available before. Over the past decade or so there has been a revolution in the way music is provided. The days are pretty much gone when you buy a CD in a record shop. Now there are iTunes, and countless websites that offer instant and virtually free downloads. No generation before ever had access to such a wide range of sounds: a paradise of music, in every style imaginable, and enough of it to satisfy anyone. For the first time it's a twenty-four-hour-a-day commodity, pouring out of headphones everywhere, and it's possible to live almost your whole life with the sound of music in your ears. Irritating it may be to people standing next to you in the street who don't want to hear it, but as Goldie would say: Hey! Times have changed.

He sprang from a raucous street culture. He had a Scottish mother and a Jamaican father, and it was a violent and broken childhood. He went into a children's home when he was three, and grew up as an outsider, the kind of kid often described as feral when people are expressing worries about anti-social behaviour and the growth of gangs. It's not surprising then that he absorbed musical influences from the American gangsta-rap culture that so appealed to him.

In the early eighties he'd been a member of the breakdance crew Westside in Wolverhampton and made his name as a graffiti artist, which took him in the end to – where else? – New York. He spent a while there during that decade – making money in the unusual trade of selling gold caps for teeth to the hip-hoppers of the city – and when he came back he immersed himself in the then underground world of breakbeat and jungle music, as it was called. He was an innovator, at the forefront of the evolution of British drum 'n' bass, and from the start of the nineties he made a name for himself working with some of the best artists in the genre, setting up in 1994 his own pioneering drum 'n' bass record label, Metalheadz.

His musical breakthrough came in 1995 with his album *Timeless*, remarkable for mixing breakbeats and heavy bass lines with orchestral overtones and soul vocals and even featuring a twenty-one-minute symphonic track. It became quite a surprise best-seller and Goldie, the outsider who spoke in street language and was comfortable with the idea of a violent culture around him, was suddenly a star. His remix of a song by the band Bush topped the UK and American charts in 1996 and – in an illustration of where his kind of music was heading – his second album, *Saturnz Return*, again included an orchestral piece featuring drum 'n' bass, which this time lasted more than an hour. The album was also graced with an appearance from David Bowie.

By this time Goldie had developed into quite a distinctive character. He's been described as a myth made from experience and desire, an image that he clearly enjoys because he likes to talk – or, rather, shout – in metaphors and riddles, and to change his persona, from street kid to swaggering high-roller, in the blink of an eye. 'I'm a chameleon. I can change shape any time I want. I'm a complicated character, shape-shifting all the time,' he once said. It's an image that he has nurtured, managing to keep people in his world wondering what he'll do next. Appear in a TV reality show? Write for an orchestra, even though he can't read music properly? Produce some new art? Find a new star to play with? He's done it all, again and again.

Goldie is significant not because he's a giant of a musician, but because he is a true innovator. He was one of the characters in the early nineties who took music by the scruff of the neck and gave it a violent shake. With the proliferation of genres, all pursued by crowds of devotees, the music scene was dividing up into a plethora of competing fashions. Drum 'n' bass was important because it became the soundtrack for the dance culture of the nineties and was inseparable from a particular style of clubbing and rapping until dawn.

It would be wrong, though, to think of Goldie's kind of music as something that touched the dark side, with no resonance outside its own boundaries. The reverse is true. It became a style that insinuated itself into the mainstream in a way that many sub-genres never could. An older generation who'd be quite unfamiliar with the bewildering language of contemporary music, who like their crowded supermarket shelves stacked carefully into product classes, might be surprised to realize how Goldie's thudding rhythms are heard everywhere.

He has spoken of many musicians – fascinated by electronic possibilities – who cut themselves off: 'We turned into these bedroom people working on our own. But then we realized – hang on, you need to share your idea, which is what classical musicians still do when they play together in orchestras. But I realized – God, there's no money in it. When I think how much money I make DJ ing in a week – I can make ten to fifteen grand in a weekend – and these people maybe get paid that in a year. They are doing it for love, they really are.'

As well as musical creativity, Goldie represents a side of our culture that is difficult to confront without seeing in the mind's eye a stereotypical picture of a gang, maybe a rapper out of his head on drugs, a hopeless kid who never takes out his earphones and comes out of clubs long after the sun is up, violence everywhere. But Goldie is more complicated than that. After a struggle, he is clear of drugs. He took a course at the Hoffman Institute, which promotes personal development by way of going back to childhood and adolescence and asking the question: why do we become like our parents? For him, it worked.

In his mid-forties, he's creative and rough-edged; a thrusting, perplexing figure who can justly claim to have been a pioneering influence and someone whose own music will last. He's calmer now, and he dates that to a water-skiing accident, of all things, from which he still bears long scars. 'That was a useful accident,' he says, 'because I started making music again, and painting, because I couldn't run around. And also because it's the left side, the feminine side, that I really need to address. So that really calmed me down and I thought, OK now, I know what to do.'

And you never knew that Goldie, the drum 'n' bass king, had a feminine side.

John Hume and David Trimble

T WO OF THE MEN WHO MADE POSSIBLE a peaceful political settlement in Northern Ireland have ended up as prophets
with little honour in their own land. David Trimble saw his Ulster
Unionist Party destroyed by rivals who'd fought him all the way.
John Hume, whose whole life in politics as a democratic nationalist was a fight against Sinn Fein and the IRA, had to hand them
the fruits of power. Yet the power-sharing government is in large
part their achievement, just as they can claim to have given the
people of Northern Ireland something that was denied to a whole
generation: a glimpse of normality.

They are not alone. If Gerry Adams and Martin McGuinness
had not decided that it was time for the IRA to find a way of
talking openly with a British government, if the Reverend Ian
Paisley had not in the end been willing to abandon a lifelong
pledge and break bread with Republicans, then the hope of
change would have been lost. Successive British governments
took brave steps forward – including the one led by Margaret
Thatcher, whom the IRA nearly succeeded in murdering – and all
of them learned how difficult it was to demonstrate and give
voice to a truth that British generals had told their Prime Minister
soon after the modern 'Troubles' began in the 1960s: that only
politics, not a military campaign, could produce a settlement.

Hume and Trimble were given the Nobel Prize for Peace jointly in 1998, because by then the groundwork had been done and the road mapped out. Everyone knew that dissenters on both sides of the fight would resent the deal and some would try to fight it in the streets, but they also knew that for the overwhelming majority of the combatants there was no way back, because people in Northern Ireland had decided this for them. When Paisley and McGuinness agreed after the elections of 2007 to lead an administration together – a notion previously unthinkable to them, and to everyone else in Northern Ireland – all but the most cynical or battle-hardened were tempted to think that what they had been told was true: it was over.

The poet Seamus Heaney, whose work is in part a subtle lament for the Troubles, calls Hume and Trimble the hedgehog and the fox. In Aesop's fable the fox knows many things, and thinks that they will get him out of the trouble he's in. The hedgehog knows one big thing, and that's all. For Heaney – raised in the nationalist tradition – Hume understood the big truth, that justice had to prevail, while Trimble had, as Heaney puts it, the 'intellectual clarity and political courage' to work for an accommodation with nationalism.

When the Good Friday Agreement was signed in April 1998, for a devolved government in which nationalists and unionists would share power, Trimble said that even twenty-four hours earlier he had doubted if they would get there. Each inch of progress in the previous twenty-five years had been tentative, ambiguous, and often doomed to be reversed by a bomb or a veto, or a speech saying 'No', and this one teetered on the edge to the last.

But it didn't fall. Daunting difficulties remained, for example about whether paramilitaries really were decommissioning their weapons – and that took years more to settle – but this time too much work had been done, too many risks had been taken, for the principals to walk away, or for the momentum to be stalled. The overwhelming majority of people in Northern Ireland supported it – 71 per cent in a referendum – and nearly 95 per cent in a referendum in the Republic of Ireland. They voted 'Yes' in the south, they said, because they had no interest in maintaining their historic claim to sovereignty over the north which had stayed in place after partition of the island in the 1920s. With those votes, a chapter closed.

And another opened. A devolved government had been agreed but it took years to take office. Unionists said they would not sit with Republicans who were still bearing arms; Republicans would not acknowledge a police service which they still saw as defending 'the other side'. And Hume and Trimble were exhausted. Hume's health was deteriorating quite fast, and Trimble's position in the Unionist Party was weakening. Paisley's Democratic Unionist Party was still calling it a treacherous deal, and as the IRA's commitment to arms decommissioning seemed to ebb and flow, Trimble found it hard to hold his party's trust. He was First Minister until he resigned in 2001, when the government in London suspended the Assembly to try to shake all parties into action, and progress was painfully slow. By the general election of 2005 Unionists were frustrated, and their support shifted decisively to Paisley's Democratic Unionists. Trimble's party – the dominant force in Northern Ireland since its foundation – had one seat out of eighteen. He resigned as leader.

His ten years in that post had begun with a show of traditional unionism in 1995, when he marched hand in hand with Paisley with the Orangemen in Drumcree, one of the traditional demonstrations that nationalists and the minority Catholic population in general saw as a piece of swaggering provocation. For unionists like Trimble it was a show of loyalty to the crown, accompanied by the cry of 'No Surrender' and flutes playing songs of war from the seventeenth century. Yet within three years he was signing the Good Friday Agreement with Sinn Fein, the political wing of the IRA, to the sound of Paisley's taunt that it was the most treacherous act in the history of Northern Ireland.

Trimble – who accepted a peerage in 2006 – is a lawyer, educated at Queen's University, Belfast, and called to the bar in that city. He knew when he became leader of his party that he had to persuade it to take a step that it feared and resented. The IRA campaign had been going on for more than twenty-five years: how could you talk to men who were gangsters and terrorists and nothing more? But Trimble knew what the British government was doing.

It was Margaret Thatcher, in 1985, who took the courageous decision to enter into an informal agreement with the government in Dublin about the future of Northern Ireland. Many of her friends were dismayed, and claimed that after she left office she said she regretted it. They were certainly right to see it as the first step to an accommodation with Sinn Fein and the IRA. It was. Thatcher, after all, had been aware of back-door contacts between her government officials and the Republican hunger strikers in the Maze Prison in 1981 to see if there might be a way out by negotiation. There had always been a pragmatic side to her.

Under her successor, John Major, the pace quickened. For the first time a government minister, Michael Ancram, met McGuinness, a former IRA commander. London was well aware that McGuinness and Gerry Adams were on the move. It would be slow, because of their history and because many of those reared in the Republican tradition thought of a deal with Britain with the same contempt as a loyalist Orangeman would regard a member of Sinn Fein. They were fighting a war, and didn't want to stop. But by the time the Blair government arrived in 1997 the contacts were frequent and intense and, with the notable assistance of President Bill Clinton in Washington, happy to apply pressure when it was needed, an agreement started to shimmer in the distance. Blair, whose mother was from County Donegal, plunged into personal negotiations, which he always enjoyed, and it worked.

For John Hume it had been a long wait. His political life began in the streets of Derry in 1968, leading the civil rights marches

that distilled the grievances of the Catholic, nationalist community and brought British troops to the streets the following year
– brought in, first of all, to support the police but seen by many
nationalists and republicans as defenders of an unjust, Unionist,
Protestant order. The IRA mushroomed, and by the early seventies the Provisionals, who had argued for war in the streets, were
persuading young men to volunteer in considerable numbers,
their efforts greatly assisted by the British government's imposi-
tion of internment in 1971.

Hume, with Gerry Fitt, founded the Social Democratic and
Labour Party, a constitutional movement for the nationalist
community. But it was hard going. The dark years that followed
brought agony to many families in Northern Ireland and to the
streets of British cities. Soldiers and police officers died, young
men and women were blown up, public servants killed in the
course of their duties. A generation was poisoned.

Hume argued throughout as a nationalist, convinced of the
injustices of successive Unionist governments in Belfast since
partition, but one who was utterly opposed to the IRA and all its
works. For years his rumpled figure, topped by black, curly hair
and a perpetual wreath of smoke, would argue the case for ration-
ality, until another bomb blew it away.

Time played its part. When Adams and McGuinness began to
explore an alternative, the chance came. It required courage on
all sides, and – perhaps the most difficult quality of all – patience.
History couldn't be wrapped up and thrown away in a year or
two: it had to be unravelled slowly, and it would be painful.

Hume and Trimble are quite different characters, the one bookish and melancholy and dark, the other bouncy and aggressive
with a lawyer's turn of phrase and a love of the fight. By the time
their moment came in the mid-nineties, however, they were ready.
Each knew that the 1998 agreement was only the start of another
long chapter – how would they know the weapons had been
destroyed, and how could they build trust between communities
that had been divided, and sometimes at war, for a lifetime? – but

each believed that, once signed, the deal would survive. The proof was in the astonishing, and occasionally strangely comic, sight of Paisley and McGuinness sitting on a sofa, sharing a joke.

By then Hume and Trimble had retreated from the stage. But without them it wouldn't have happened.

Doreen Lawrence

DOREEN LAWRENCE HAS NEVER had any desire to be famous, nor even to be a public figure. Yet she carried the Olympic torch through the streets of south-east London for part of its last journey before the start of the 2012 Games, and was cheered all the way. Her destination was a learning centre near her home, a place close to her heart, and it turned that part of the torch relay into something of a pilgrimage. She carried it to the Stephen Lawrence Centre, named after her son, who was killed not far away when he was 18 years old.

He died in the street on 22 April 1993, after he was attacked by a gang of five youths. He managed to run about 120 yards, then bled to death. No act of violence against a single person on our streets in recent times has had a greater effect beyond his family. In the nearly nineteen years that passed before two men were found guilty of his murder, Stephen Lawrence's name haunted the Metropolitan Police, forced political leaders to address painful social questions, and changed public attitudes. And all because he was black.

The commissioner of the Met at the time, Ian Blair, said that for Britain it was a 'Rosa Parks moment'. He was referring to the American civil rights campaigner who first refused to take her seat at the back of a bus in Montgomery, Alabama, and set in train a civil rights movement that couldn't be stopped. The commissioner believed that the consequences of the Lawrence murder for his force were the most profound that it had experienced in his lifetime.

Doreen Lawrence herself became a symbol of the injustice done to her son, because of her campaign to highlight the mistakes and the delays that allowed his killers to go free for nearly two decades. The police say their investigations continue to this day, because most of the gang have not been convicted. 'We don't see this as the end of the road,' said the Met's Acting Deputy Commissioner after Gary Dobson and David Norris were jailed for life.

For the police, the Lawrence case brought a damning judgement that at the time produced hostility among officers, but passed into the language: the force was 'institutionally racist'. It came from Sir William Macpherson, a retired judge, who was asked by the government to lead a public inquiry into the case and whose report in 1999 identified failures of leadership in the police, professional incompetence, and an attitude to the case that, it concluded, would not have been present if the victim had been white.

Mrs Lawrence pursued her case with dignity. She and her husband, Neville – they divorced in 1999 – fought to make public their despair at what they believed to be inadequate efforts to catch the killers. They pursued a private prosecution against five men, raising the money in a public campaign because they were not entitled to legal aid. The charges against two of the five were dropped before the trial because of lack of evidence, and the three others were acquitted at the Old Bailey in 1996, because the judge ruled that the evidence of a key witness was unreliable. But, after an inquest the following year recorded a verdict of 'unlawful killing by five white youths', the Lawrences fought on, making a formal complaint against the Metropolitan Police and arguing that the case had not been properly investigated.

The government then set up the Macpherson Inquiry, and following publication of the report the Met apologized publicly to the family and announced that it was instituting reforms to try to purge itself of racism. Mrs Lawrence had become the public face of a campaign in which she had overwhelming public support.

The strength of that support was most powerfully demonstrated when, in 1997, the *Daily Mail* published an extraordinary front page. There were pictures of the five suspects in the case – including the two who were eventually convicted fifteen years later – and the headline: 'Murderers: The Mail accuses these men of killing. If we are wrong, let them sue us.' None of them did. Such a wave of support in a case of this kind was unprecedented, and it helped the Lawrences' effort to sustain pressure on the authorities. By 1999 the Met had announced its third investigation into the case and ten years later, by the use of improved scientific tests on a speck of blood from the jacket of one of the suspects, a case was made that would eventually convince a jury.

The Lawrence case was a landmark for the black community in Britain, because it seemed to many Afro-Caribbeans an eloquent and tragic example of attitudes with which they had long been familiar in daily life. In particular, it challenged the police. In his report Macpherson said: 'The need to re-establish trust between minority ethnic communities and the police is paramount ... seeking to achieve trust and confidence through a demonstration of fairness will not in itself be sufficient. It must be accompanied by a vigorous pursuit of openness and accountability.'

The black community in which the Lawrences lived was about half a million strong by the 1980s. Doreen Lawrence came to London in 1961, when she was 9, and joined a growing population from the West Indies that had come to Britain since the 1948 Nationality Act gave citizenship, and therefore the right to settle here, to those who lived in the Commonwealth. The first arrivals came on the *Empire Windrush*, a famous ship whose name would always be associated with the community that grew up in South London, where they settled. By 1961 the number was 172,000, concentrated in London.

West Indians had been attracted by the prospect of work, but many found it difficult. They were hindered by casual discrimination which from time to time became a political issue, as when the property developer Peter Rachman became notorious for the exploitation of immigrants in the flats and mansion blocks that he owned in West London in the late fifties. But, most of the time, life in the black community was quite separate, lived under different rules. Resentment was rife, tensions with the police were exacerbated by the use of stop-and-search powers, and troubles in the street, like the violence in Brixton in 1981, were divisive.

Stephen Lawrence's murder forced everyone to take notice. Imran Khan, Doreen Lawrence's solicitor, said that the case made racial discrimination something that the community as a whole had to recognize as real. 'Before that, it was something that the left and liberals talked about as a fringe issue. Now suburban England had to accept that race existed.'

Doreen Lawrence succeeded in making her case with dignity. During the Macpherson Inquiry, when she was facing persistent questioning from the barrister representing the Metropolitan Police, she said: 'Am I on trial or something here? From the time of my son's murder, I have been treated not as a victim ... For me to be questioned in this way – I do not appreciate it.'

The combination of her dignity, and the evidence of brazen contempt from the men who had been accused of the attack but then were released, seemed to paint a vivid picture of injustice. What could she do? She fought. When their private prosecution failed, the family insisted that the police – humbled by the Macpherson Report – should keep the investigation going, which they did. Had the campaign not continued, the scientific analysis that was the key to conviction would probably not have been done: it was only because the case had become a *cause célèbre* that every avenue was explored, again and again.

Brian Cathcart, author of *The Case of Stephen Lawrence*, says that it would have been easy for the fight to stop, and everyone give up. 'The idea that there might one day by a conviction was at one point nothing but a fantasy.' And the Chief Crown Prosecutor for London, Alison Saunders, acknowledged that it was 'one of the most significant cases of this generation – changing attitudes, policing and the law'. That change in the law came in 2005 when the government repealed the 'double jeopardy' rule, which prevented someone from being tried twice for the same crime. The argument in favour of this change was that advances in science, particularly with respect to DNA, meant that cases could sometimes be reopened successfully many years after the original investigation, and safe convictions could be secured long after they had been thought impossible. In the end, that is exactly what happened to two of Stephen Lawrence's killers. They were found guilty on evidence that had once been undetectable, and thought that after the collapse of the original trial they were safe.

Doreen Lawrence became a symbol of iron determination. She wouldn't give up, even when the odds were stacked against her. She still campaigns for an inquiry into allegations of corruption involving some of the officers in the investigation. After the conviction of two members of the gang, she said that it was not a day for celebration. 'How can I celebrate when my son lies buried? When I cannot see him or speak to him?'

Her success was that she achieved this by revealing how she and her family had suffered precisely because Stephen wasn't seen as a 'bright, beautiful boy' but as a black teenager whose death in a violent street attack did not attract the same attention or effort as it might have done had he been born a different colour. The Metropolitan Police acknowledge that; so did political leaders of every hue; and so did the community at large.

The first memorial to Stephen on the site of his death was defaced and destroyed in a grotesque reminder of why he died. Its replacement is still there, and for many people it is a memorial not only to a 'bright, beautiful boy' but a reminder of how daunting it can be for even a brave mother to get justice for her son.

Tim Berners-Lee

TIM BERNERS-LEE IS A HERO in a competitive, cut-throat world that moves at a dizzying speed, but he is different. He has been described as an archetypal English country vicar, trying to make people happy and to spread a little harmony in the community of battling software giants. He has always been like that. When he was a young physicist he took a job at CERN in Switzerland, which is in the business of smashing atoms to smithereens. He took time off because he wanted to build something instead. And he invented the World Wide Web.

The size of the web is nearly impossible to measure, so no one can agree how big it is. But if you sat down at a computer at the end of 1993 there were probably 620 or so websites. Five years later Google said that it had indexed 26 million pages. Ten years later that figure was a trillion – a million million.

It was Berners-Lee who made that possible. What is more, when he had worked out a way of spinning a web that would encircle the world he had no interest in turning it into an idea that would be to his own financial benefit. You could say that he gave it away: he wanted everyone to have it.

Every time you click on a universal resource locator – the web signature that we know as a URL, which gives each page its own address – you are benefiting from the work of Berners-Lee, the man who took the fledgling internet and turned it into the most revolutionary form of communication since the invention of the printing press in the middle of the fifteenth century.

He was born in London in 1955, to parents who were both mathematicians who worked on the Ferranti Mark 1, the world's first commercially available general-purpose electronic computer. He went to Emanuel School in Wandsworth and then studied physics at Oxford. While he was an undergraduate there he got a soldering iron and built a primitive computer of his own from an old television set, using a simple processor. He was also caught hacking and banned from using the university's computer. He went to work for the telecom equipment manufacturer Plessey and then D.G. Nash in Dorset, where among other things he developed typesetting software for intelligent printers.

On a six-month attachment to CERN he started putting together the elements of what would be his breakthrough discovery. He had the idea of writing a program that could store information with a revolutionary ingredient: it would handle random associations. And that was the embryo from which the World Wide Web grew. Remembering the Victorian almanac called *Enquire Within upon Everything*, he called it, simply, Enquire. This was 'a musty old book of Victorian advice', he said, which 'I noticed as a child in my parents' house outside London. With its title suggestive of magic, the book served as a portal to a world of information, everything from how to remove clothing stains to tips on investing money. Not a perfect analogy for the Web, but a primitive starting point.'

Enquire allowed many people to access the same data. The idea, he said at the time, was to allow 'users to store snippets of information, and to link related pieces together in any way. To find information, one progressed via the links from one sheet to another, rather like in the old computer game "Adventure".'

He spent three years working at Image Computer Systems back in Britain, then returned to CERN on a fellowship in 1984 when he was ready for the next step. 'Anyone who has lost track of time when using a computer knows the propensity to dream,' he once said. 'The urge to make dreams come true and the tendency to miss lunch.' His idea was to develop a single information network that would help CERN physicists share all the computer-stored information at the laboratory, connecting hypertext with the internet and personal computers. The World Wide Web is now a synonym for the internet, but in the early eighties the difference was easier to grasp. The principles of the internet were being laid down – a system of powerful computer networks that could exchange information – but it could not yet access the web, an information space in which every item had a unique identifier and acted as part of a connected system, linking people and things that had common characteristics – a place where you could browse from your own computer and see it all.

By 1989 Berners-Lee had drawn up a plan to put to his boss, Mike Sendall. It was called prosaically 'Information Management – A Proposal'. Sendall gave him two months to go away and work on it and described the plan as 'vague … but exciting'.

It certainly was. Berners-Lee decided to call the project the World Wide Web. In autumn 1990 he was joined by a colleague, Robert Caillau. By Christmas they had built the first web browser, web server and web pages, but the World Wide Web was still a tiny network that didn't really stretch beyond the confines of the CERN lab itself. Thanks to a technical student named Nicola Pellow, who wrote a simple browser programme that could run on any computer, it became possible for anyone with an internet connection to access the web.

And the great day, which surely must have its place in history, was 6 August 1991. On that day the first website, info.cern.ch, went online, and it's still there. The principle of what-you-see-is-what-you-get was established: what was on the screen was what could be printed out. The days of technological gobbledygook were beginning to pass away.

A colleague who later worked with Berners-Lee, Wendy Hall, Professor of Computer Science at the University of Southampton, said: 'I don't think he realized what they were doing at CERN would change the world this much. I think this is as big, if not bigger, than the printing press.'

Quite soon it became clear how much the world could change. In the year the world began to recognize the existence of the web, 1992, Bill Clinton was elected president of the United States. He says: 'When I took office, only high-energy physicists had heard of what is called the World Wide Web. Now even my cat has its own Web page.'

And from the start Berners-Lee was determined that everyone should have access to the power that he had harnessed with the invention of the web. He had no time for the idea of a closed space, in which you needed knowledge to be able to navigate. Marc Andreessen, one of the early web pioneers, who co-authored the Mosaic browser released in 1994 (subsequently renamed Netscape Navigator), says that there was reluctance. 'Back then the key technical people didn't want the internet to become easy to use or graphical because that would pollute the environment. Only smart people could use the internet – that was the theory, so we needed to keep it hard to use. We fundamentally disagreed with that. We thought it should be easy to use.'

Berners-Lee is notable for not having wanted to enrich himself from his work. In an age of web billionaires, he remains the pioneer whose principal satisfaction was the opportunity he created, rather than the property he amassed and could sell. In 1994 he helped to establish the World Wide Web Consortium, which was independent of government or any other organization and was intended to promote research, to share knowledge and to mediate between web companies. It was a remarkable demonstration of his commitment to the idea rather than the product.

Berners-Lee is one of the most remarkable innovators of the twentieth century, with an impact that matches that in sciences such as physics, medicine, biology. His vision in taking the embryonic internet and creating a template in which its power could be truly exercised was the making of a revolution. Yet everyone who knows him says he remains a modest, undemonstrative man, although one with strong views. He was knighted in 2004, became one of the twenty-four members of the Order of Merit in 2007, and alongside many academic honours was named by *Time* magazine as one of the 100 greatest minds of the twentieth century. In 2012 he was elected to the Internet Hall of Fame, which probably wouldn't have existed without him.

It remains true that, for a man who helped to change the world, Berners-Lee is a quiet revolutionary. How many people would recognize him in the street? Very few, and that's how he likes it, which is another of his remarkable features.

He is still campaigning, leading the charge in trying to persuade individuals, governments, academic institutions – everyone – to make more 'raw data available' on the web because he thinks it will be good, encouraging people 'to do wonderful things'.

When he was asked a few years ago why, when he designed the URL, he decided – to the irritation of future web users – to put two slashes at the front of every web address, he admitted that he now thought they were unnecessary. 'There you go,' he said. 'It seemed like a good idea at the time.'

Diana, Princess of Wales

WHEN LADY DIANA SPENCER married the Prince of Wales in July 1981, the Archbishop of Canterbury said in his sermon that the scene was the stuff of which fairy tales were made. Robert Runcie was right, because theirs was a marriage which was turned into a story that seemed to have no limits, conceived as a modern fable and collapsing in acrimony after years of public melodrama played out in the press, all the while stirring up excitement and admiration, jealousy and fantasy. Together they created moments of public scandal and sadness, and for years after her death the Princess retained, through her name alone, the ability to perplex and tantalize. She was a whirlwind and a gentle spirit, a victim but a fighter too.

In the week after she died in a car crash in Paris in August 1997, the Princess of Wales was at the centre of a national frenzy. The preparations for her funeral had the air of a fantastical wake, with mountains of flowers in the Mall in London, vigils and candlelit processions, and the rumbling of popular antagonism to the royal family. The Prime Minister's phrase used a few hours after her death – 'she was the people's princess' – was quick and accurate: to the amazement of those who didn't share it, an obsession with her personality was let loose on the country to work its magic. For the Queen and her family the alarm was greater than anything since the abdication crisis in 1936.

Everything had been managed to avoid such dangers. The third daughter of the 8th Earl Spencer could trace her ancestry back to King Charles II – from whom the Queen is not directly descended – and it was likely from the moment of her birth, in July 1961, that she would move in a world that would offer her an aristocratic, even a royal, marriage. She would be prepared for it.

The accepted story is that she met Prince Charles in a muddy field at the Spencers' family seat when he was staying with one of her sisters, in 1977. It was announced in February 1981 that they were engaged, after a year in which she'd joined that long line of young women photographed and pursued as possible consorts for the heir to the throne. The conventions, however, were changing. They couldn't be a distant couple, protected from personal questions. They met the press and, naturally, were asked if they were in love. Prince Charles's response, 'Whatever "in love" means', would be played retrospectively, after the failure of the marriage, as a portent.

They were different characters. She was young, not yet 20, and still girlish in style. He was 32, used to the wearisome pressures of his role, and already a man who preferred to give subtle answers, perhaps letting his emotions show. Since his teens he had been used to having a chorus line of potential wives foisted on him by the press and had got used to the difficulty of keeping a private life private while accepting his duty as a public figure. He had a close circle of friends who helped him, and for Lady Diana the transition to life alongside him was always going to be a shock.

They faced the difficulty that the royal family had adapted in the previous two decades to the irresistible pressure to be more open, allowing glimpses through the glass, and therefore invited public comment that in a previous age would have been thought inappropriate. With the arrival of Diana – beautiful, charming, personable – the problems multiplied. She wasn't so much the wife of the heir to the throne as a star, and one who took to the role with gusto. She shone and sparkled, and the breathless writers spoke of a reinvention of the monarchy.

The princes arrived, William in 1982 and Harry in 1984, and the family was bathed in light. The trouble is that there was darkness underneath. Diana was suffering emotionally and physically. The marriage was troubled, though how and when it began to break apart is the subject of painful disagreements of the sort that attach to every nightmare of this kind. She later acknowledged her mid-eighties affair with a guardsman, James Hewitt, citing a continuation of the relationship between the Prince and Camilla Parker Bowles as the provocation, but the rights and wrongs, and the dates, of their respective bursts of admitted unfaithfulness were lost in the public arguments at the time of their separation in 1992. The papers called it, predictably and not entirely inaccurately, 'The War of the Waleses'.

They had become a soap opera, and maybe it was unavoidable. A fairy-tale marriage had been arranged, and took place. It couldn't survive the ways of the world.

By 1990, Fleet Street was ready for a cataclysm. A radio ham recorded a telephone call between the Princess and someone who was clearly a lover, and hawked it around the newspapers. It wasn't published, but its existence was known. Friends of the couple began to talk of their misery: Diana's loneliness and distance from her husband; his despair at her behaviour, and sadness. They couldn't remain together.

Nineteen ninety-two was the breaking point. In the spring Diana made the decision to cooperate with the journalist Andrew Morton. She insisted that her involvement had to stay secret – she would deny it publicly if asked – but she taped interviews with him and encouraged friends to do the same. This was happening when the couple made one of their last tours together – a fact which the Prince's friends would find unforgivable – and she posed for a memorable picture, alone in the fading light at the Taj Mahal.

Morton's book was serialized in the *Sunday Times* in June and told a story of eating disorders and suicide attempts, her hatred of a royal life, her complaints against her husband for alleged unfaithfulness. She was portrayed as a victim, and drank deep at the well of public sympathy. The Press Complaints Commission denounced the book as 'odious' for its invasion of Diana's life and was then humiliated to discover that she had been the source of much of the material. Two months later her taped phone conversation with an old lover was published – her nickname was Squidgy, we all learned – and when she and Prince Charles made their last tour together, to South Korea, they were a picture of sadness.

The Prince asked for a separation in November, and then had the terrible experience of reading in the newspapers some of his own intimate phone conversations with Camilla Parker Bowles. For the next two years the public was invited to take sides, with Diana managing the press battle with ease. She was the wronged woman, and the victim. The Prince found it hard to fight back, trying to explain his side of the troubled story to Jonathan Dimbleby for a book and a film in which he admitted unfaithfulness.

He never, however, talked critically about his wife in public. The same could not be said on the other side. So Diana was always ahead. She announced in 1993 that she was withdrawing from public life, but she was more prized than ever by the paparazzi and the gossip writers, whose ways she understood well.

One of the reasons for her success was her natural ability to make connections with people through her charity work. Whether shaking the hand of a man with HIV/AIDS – a remarkable event at the time – or talking about the homeless, landmines or children with disabilities, she displayed a caring face which touched many people, because they knew it to be genuine. It countered the suggestion that she might have been manipulative or cruel in her handling of the marriage break-up, and she secured a place in public affection that would last.

The climax to this awful passage of arms came at the end of 1995 when Diana gave an interview to *Panorama* on BBC1. Twenty-three million people watched her saying that she wouldn't go quietly, casting doubts on the capacity of her husband to be king, declaring she wanted to be 'queen of people's hearts', and speaking about her unhappy marriage, which she described as 'crowded'. Nothing of this kind had been broadcast before. It was either a cry of pain or a vicious, choreographed attack, depending on where your sympathies lay. But there was no doubt that it was the announcement that the marriage – the fairy tale that never was – had ended. The Queen agreed, no doubt with great reluctance, that divorce was inevitable. It came in 1996.

Diana's charity work kept her in the public eye. Her last high-profile visit was with the Red Cross to Angola to highlight the devastation and misery caused by landmines. And she was also whizzing around on the glamour circuit: she auctioned part of her wardrobe for charity in New York in June 1997 for $3 million. Hers was probably the best-known face in the world.

Then came a holiday with Dodi Fayed on the yacht owned by his father, the owner of Harrods, in the Mediterranean. Then Paris and the Ritz Hotel, a car dash along the Seine and, about half an hour after midnight on 31 August, the crash. Three and a half hours later she was pronounced dead.

The conspiracists began to spin their yarns, ushering in a new era of Diana melodrama, but she was gone. The last act before her burial at the family home in Northamptonshire was a calculated attack by her brother, Earl Spencer, at her funeral in Westminster Abbey, against those whom he thought had let her down.

But there was another notable speech, on the previous evening, broadcast live from Buckingham Palace. The Queen, persuaded of the weight of emotion stirred up by Diana's death, addressed her memory directly.

The two epitaphs were fitting: one, from her brother, still antagonistic, carefully aimed; the other, from the Queen, acknowledging a woman of natural gifts whose life plunged from fame and adulation to tragedy. They were both part of the Diana story, of the Princess and her public. Her life was sometimes sad and often puzzling, but she changed everything she touched.

Alex Salmond

A LEX SALMOND IS PROBABLY the most successful national-ist to sit in the House of Commons since Charles Stuart Parnell. No one has come closer to winning the argument for a country to leave the United Kingdom. But for all his success, and the fear he engenders in his opponents, he is not someone who can say with confidence that he *will* win in the end. He claims inevitability for his idea. He has yet to prove it.

When he was in his teens the idea of Scottish independence floated on the fringe. Nationalism in Scotland had a history, but few thought that it had much of a future. The Scottish National Party had one seat in Parliament from the Hamilton by-election in 1967, and for most Scots of Salmond's age – he was born in 1954 – talk of independence seemed fanciful. The Labour Party, set implacably against it, was dominant. And most who didn't vote Labour supported a party called the Conservative *and Unionist* Party. Yet circumstances would change everything in the course of a year or two, and Salmond's generation – to its surprise – was thrown into a constitutional argument that, forty years on, would lead to a promised referendum on independence.

Two events conspired to change the political landscape, with all the force of a volcanic eruption. They were British accession to the Common Market in January 1973 and the discovery of

North Sea oil. The consequences for Scotland were profound, and they came quickly.

Many farmers and fishermen were dismayed by the European terms negotiated by Ted Heath's government, believing themselves to have been sold too cheaply. There was great anger, and in the fishing villages of the north-east, particularly, the Conservatives found the support they had long enjoyed turning to hostility. At just the same time the realization was taking hold that North Sea oil was going to pour money into Scotland. Aberdeen was being transformed month by month: the biggest heliport in Europe, Texan accents on the golf courses, a whiff of the Wild West in the bars down at the harbour, and the promise of work and prosperity from the oil. It was Klondyke.

A political revolution began. With its tantalizing slogan 'It's Scotland's Oil' the Scottish National Party began to take on the establishment: the Conservative government in London and the Labour Party in Scotland, which, it said, knew nothing of the country beyond the city. The effect was electric. In the election of February 1974 the SNP won seven seats; in the second election in that year, in October, eleven. And fate dealt it a happy card. Harold Wilson's government had a paper-thin majority. The nationalists had a sniff of power.

This was the Scotland in which Salmond was a student of economics and history at St Andrews, at a time when politics was bracing. When he got his first job in 1978, in the civil service in Edinburgh, the stage was set for a confrontation between Labour and the SNP which would determine the course of the constitutional argument.

The government had lost its tiny majority thanks to a string of by-elections and some defections and was living day to day with the prop of a limited pact agreed with the Liberal Party led by David Steel. But Steel believed, of course, in the same Home Rule that Mr Gladstone had campaigned for a century earlier, and the cacophony for devolution was impossible for the Prime Minister,

Jim Callaghan, to ignore. He legislated for elected assemblies in Scotland and Wales.

Polls showed that a comfortable majority of Scots believed that the administrative functions that had been devolved to Edinburgh in the 1880s should be scrutinized by a legislature there rather than in London. Some of those thought of it as a stepping stone to independence; many did not. But Labour, to the obvious discomfort of a majority of its Scottish MPs, who loathed the nationalists and called them 'Tartan Tories', spent two years of parliamentary agony in passing the Scotland Act 1978, which would be put to a vote in a referendum. Did Scotland want a parliament or not?

A majority of Scots voted 'Yes' on 1 March 1979 – the government chose St David's Day in a hopeless effort to avoid a 'No' vote to the same question in Wales. But opponents of devolution had inserted a clause in the bill to annul the vote if 40 per cent of those who were *entitled to vote* did not say 'Yes'. The threshold wasn't reached, and it was in the subsequent parliamentary arguments on that particular point that the SNP – followed an hour later by Margaret Thatcher – slapped down a motion of no confidence that the government lost and brought the Conservatives to power.

In the turmoil of that 1979 election, the SNP suffered badly. But underneath it was building a movement that wouldn't be weakened by what had happened to devolution, but greatly strengthened. Alex Salmond was in the thick of it, so much so that by 1980, when he became an energy economist in the Royal Bank of Scotland, he found himself expelled from his own party.

After the heady excitement of the seventies, when there was overblown expectation in the SNP that independence might be just around the corner, the party went through a convulsion. Salmond was one of those – they called themselves the ''79 Group' – who saw its future as a social-democratic party on European lines, with a distinct left-of-centre tilt on economic and social policy. To the old guard who preferred to define its character entirely in terms of independence, that was radicalism in the wrong way. There were splits and expulsions, and Salmond was out.

Through the Thatcher years, however, the SNP settled into precisely the kind of posture that the '79 Group had envisaged. It dropped its historic opposition to the EEC and became enthusiastic about joining other small nations at the table in Brussels. It capitalized on Labour's weakness brought on by its own internal ideological battles, and when Salmond was elected MP for Banff and Buchan in 1987 it was starting to grow again.

Devolution was on the back burner at Westminster, but in opposition Labour had turned a corner. Neil Kinnock, the leader, had become a convert, egged on by John Smith, who had steered the Scotland Act through Parliament.

It was an enticing prospect for the new leader of the SNP in 1990, Alex Salmond, only three years an MP. He was quick on his feet, at home with statistics, and had the great political gift of rarely seeming to lose his temper. He always seemed to be smiling. It was a fair reflection of an easygoing personality – he is naturally gregarious, loves sport, especially horse-racing – and he had the extra advantage of irritating his opponents, who would always call him smug but found him devastating to deal with in debate.

In his first ten years as leader – he resigned in 2000 and was re-elected to the post in 2004 – he saw the Scottish Parliament come into being. Tony Blair's government got overwhelming support for it in the referendum in 1997 and the new parliament opened in 1999 when the oldest of its newly elected members, the former SNP MP Winnie Ewing, took the chair and said: 'The Scottish Parliament, adjourned on the 25th day of March in the year 1707, is hereby reconvened.'

Labour, however, had devised an electoral system of proportional representation which had one, undeclared, aim. It made it unlikely that the SNP would be able to win a majority on its own, and indeed the first two administrations were Labour–Liberal

Democrat coalitions. Then – to the other parties' horror – the SNP established a minority administration in 2007, and to cap it all, three years later, Salmond led his party to an outright win, humiliating Labour and changing the face of Scotland.

The First Minister took to his role with gusto, capitalizing on his popularity as a fixer and a tough dealer who could drive a hard bargain with Whitehall. The parliament was much more popular as an institution than it had been at the start – and Salmond had high personal ratings. But he knew that those who had voted for his party had done so for a mixture of reasons – many were disillusioned Labour voters, many thought he'd done a reasonable job with a minority and deserved a majority, and not all, by any means, equated voting SNP with independence.

Salmond had spent most of his career in a party that had peaked in the seventies and had failed over the next two decades to turn that moment into something lasting. Exploiting the fading of the Blair era in 2007 – he used Iraq to paint the Prime Minister as out of touch with Scots – he became a First Minister who was bouncy and active, though careful to avoid legislation that might be controversial.

Sometimes the other parties seemed hypnotized: What's he up to now? What did that sentence mean? He became bold enough, with his majority, to propose gay marriage legislation in 2012, arguing that it was another step towards a modern Scotland, and remained a leader who not only seemed relaxed in handling power but who evidently, openly and boyishly enjoyed it. In an era when power has tended to age politicians quickly, it has given Salmond an ever-abundant source of adrenalin.

That energy has shaped the debate about independence, because he has set the pace and some of the rules of the game. He cannot know, however, whether it will be enough. It's more than twenty years since he first led his party and, as well as experience, that longevity brings the danger of too much familiarity. To people outside Scotland tuning in to the debate he may seem the bright young thing who seems to carry all before him. To many

Scots, he is 'wee 'Eck' – our old friend Alex whom they've known for long enough.

So he began to prepare for his referendum, which he would like to hold in 2014. Battle is joined on the nature of the questions, the timing, the competence of Westminster in organizing the vote, and an intense struggle between the parties has begun. Salmond knows he goes into the fight with one historic weakness: never, since the SNP came back to prominence in the seventies, have a majority of Scots voters expressed a settled desire for independence what his opponents call 'separation' and what he calls a new kind of 'social union' with the rest of the UK in which Scotland would remain a friend, but run its own affairs. The series of arguments about money, welfare, defence, Europe and NATO is just beginning.

These are the arguments that have dominated Alex Salmond's political life, but he cannot yet know, any better than the Scots who have watched him all these years, voted for him and opposed him, how they want them to be settled. He only knows that the hour is coming.

Tony Blair

Tony Blair was the youngest Prime Minister since William Pitt, and came to office with no experience of government. He had never opened a red box of ministerial papers until the day he arrived in Downing Street. But he commanded a majority in the House of Commons bigger than any single party had known for more than seventy years, and he created another record: apart from his predecessors in the two world wars, he found himself involved in more military conflicts than any other Prime Minister of the twentieth century.

His relative youth and lack of a ministerial past were an important part of his character in office, and so was war. When he arrived in 1997, on a tide that swept John Major out of office and crushed the Conservative Party, there was no talk of it. His was a domestic programme, a promise of modernization and renewal. When he left in 2007, handing over power to Gordon Brown two years into his third term, he was as much a war leader as the man who had shaken up schools, the railways and even the NHS. His commitment to war in Iraq alongside the United States was the decision that would define his premiership for many people, and remain the most vivid illustration of his political persona.

With Margaret Thatcher, Blair was the dominating leader of the second half of the twentieth century. He says he learned from her the need to move fast and to stay the course. A few months after he became leader of the Labour Party in 1994 he set about removing Clause 4 from its constitution, preferring to have it stripped of socialist ambitions for common ownership, and began to talk of New Labour, as a studied break with the past. He changed his party and its political outlook, persuaded Rupert Murdoch that he was the leader who spoke for readers of the *Sun* and fashioned a style of government that proved successful enough to leave the Conservatives floundering in the next two general elections.

Blair's years in power, however, had pain running through them. The rivalry between him and Gordon Brown, fellow aspirants to the crown when John Smith died unexpectedly in 1994, disturbed the government he led and gave it an edgy emotional life. They fretted and fought, and their two courts of supporters engaged in a permanent argument that swung to and fro and, by the end, drained the government of enough authority to damage greatly Brown's much briefer period as Prime Minister, which he had always wanted to come along rather sooner.

Brown was the one who had political ambitions as a young man, and it was one of the irritants in the relationship that Blair seemed to float into the game by chance. He picked up the nomination for Sedgefield in County Durham at the last gasp before the 1983 election, and he learned much of the business of politics, the rough and the smooth, from Brown, in the cramped, windowless office that they shared in the Palace of Westminster in their early days as opposition MPs. Blair was 30 and Brown 32 when they were elected on the same night, and it quickly became clear to their colleagues that – like it or not – they were the faces of the future. In particular they convinced their party's director of communications, who arrived in the mid-eighties, a young man called Peter Mandelson.

From then until Smith's death, Brown's decision not to stand against Blair and the election victory in 1997, that trio dominated the party. For the two years before that election there was a bitter rift in the gang, Brown breaking off any relationship with Mandelson over his support for Blair as leader, which was betrayal in his eyes, but in power the three of them were in charge.

Blair never saw himself as a leader who would rule as if a Labour government had simply been interrupted by the Conservatives for eighteen years after 1979. He wanted something different, being a politician who didn't conform to his party's mould. Indeed, on the very day of the poll, 1 May 1997, he was talking to Paddy Ashdown, leader of the Liberal Democrats, about the desirability of coalition, even if there was to be a Labour majority. In the end that majority was so huge – 179 – that even Blair could not take the risk of denying his party its triumph.

With the comfort of that majority, New Labour – the name that Brown couldn't bear to use – developed a style that defined the Blair years. With Alastair Campbell directing the media operation at No. 10 and Mandelson, in a variety of ministerial jobs, operating as persuader and enforcer in the byways of the Westminster village, 'Blairite' came to mean slickness, a silky ways with words and a determination to fashion the story. The pair were seen as the masters of spin, turning things their way with ease and ruthlessness.

It would come to haunt them all, but in the first years there were achievements. Most of all, perhaps, there was the Good Friday Agreement in Belfast in 1998, when Blair managed to negotiate a settlement between Sinn Fein, on behalf of the IRA, and the mainstream parties. More time would have to pass before an acceptable level of arms decommissioning was achieved and the power-sharing assembly could take office, but it was an achievement that justifiably gave Blair great stature. It cemented his relationship, too, with Bill Clinton in the White House, the first of his presidential friends.

Brown, as Chancellor, was running an economic policy – with a guarantee of no interference from Blair – that he said would put an end to the cycle of 'boom and bust', and they were relatively prosperous times. The Bank of England had been given independent authority over interest rates and much of the City quite liked New Labour. The world had turned upside down. Devolution to Scotland and Wales had been approved in referendums, and Blair was cutting a dashing figure on the European stage. He was a confident Prime Minister, who now turned his attention to the Balkans.

After years of conflict in the wake of the fall of communism in eastern Europe, Blair was faced in 1999 with a crisis in Kosovo. Refugees were fleeing from Serbian troops operating under one of the last hardline regimes on the continent, that of Slobodan Milosevic. Blair sent British troops in and – in a manoeuvre which had a profound effect on him – he persuaded Clinton to commit American forces. It was the Russians in the end who persuaded their old ally Milosevic to desist, but when the Serbian leader eventually ended up at the International Criminal Court at The Hague, Blair believed that he had been the moving force.

By the time he faced the crisis of 9/11 in 2001 Blair was brimming with confidence in the international arena, and for the Americans – under their new President, George W. Bush – he found exactly the right words to express his solidarity. From that day forward he became convinced that Middle East terrorism was the great threat to civilization and would require stamina and guts to resist, even if it meant repressive legislation at home. He sent British troops to Afghanistan in October 2001 and was established, without question, as Bush's loyal ally.

That led him directly to the crisis in Iraq, which had been alarming Europe and the United States since the First Gulf War of 1991, as Saddam Hussein blustered and convinced the West that he was developing weapons of mass destruction. Throughout 2002 Blair marched in step with the White House and left Bush in no doubt of his commitment to war if it came. The precise nature of his commitment is disputed by many of those most closely involved – some think he gave guarantees nine months before the invasion, others say that until the end he was looking for a diplomatic way out in good faith – but anyway, by spring

2003 there was no doubt. Having failed to get the United Nations Security Council to authorize an attack, a 'coalition of the willing' led by Bush and Blair invaded, raced to Baghdad and deposed Saddam Hussein in days.

Blair remains convinced that he was right; much of his party that he was wrong. The weapons of mass destruction were never found – they turned out to be a will o' the wisp – but British and US troops had to fight for years, as their colleagues were doing in the vicious struggle against the Taliban in Afghanistan. Blair was grievously damaged, particularly by the view widely shared by Labour supporters that Saddam's arsenal had been an excuse for war rather than a reality. A tragic spotlight was shone on that argument by the apparent suicide of a government scientist, Dr David Kelly, accused of leaks to the press. His death came just at the moment that Blair triumphantly addressed both houses of Congress in Washington, and basked in seventeen standing ovations.

That contrast came to haunt his later years in power, and he could not escape the shadow of war.

How different it seemed at the beginning. Blair was the puppy-dog Prime Minister, cheery and fresh-faced, the forty-something representative of a new generation, whose campaign song had been 'Things Can Only Get Better'. He wasn't afraid to talk about his religious faith, he raised children in Downing Street, he wore jeans at Chequers. And his government did change the life of the country – whether in the constitution, in the introduction of civil partnerships for gay men and women or in the way schools and hospitals were run. As Thatcher had mesmerized him with her determination and verve, so his style was passed on – after Brown – to David Cameron, some of whose Downing Street staff after 2010 could be heard calling Blair the master – not as an ideological touchstone, but as the consummate political operator.

Blair gave his name to his time in power, and it is indelible. But he will remain the Prime Minister whose first election brought the country together, and then divided it.

Fred Goodwin

O N THE MORNING OF TUESDAY, 7 OCTOBER 2008, the Chancellor of the Exchequer, Alistair Darling, was pulled out of a meeting of European finance ministers in Luxembourg to take a call from the chairman of the Royal Bank of Scotland. Its shares were collapsing. Darling asked how long the bank could keep going. The answer was: 'A couple of hours, maybe.' The Chancellor told his Treasury officials: 'It's going bust this after-noon.' A bank that once boasted that it was the biggest in the world was broke. Without tens of billions in guarantees from the government, on the instant, it would have to close its cash machines.

When Darling spoke to the Prime Minister, Gordon Brown, back in London, they faced the prospect of a cataclysm, not for one bank but for the whole British banking system. A run on one would be a run on all, and it would happen that afternoon. So the government would have to take control of the Royal Bank of Scotland, which it did. And that was the end of the highest flyer of them all, the financial wizard of RBS, Fred Goodwin.

Bad stories need their villains, and he fitted the role perfectly. He even had a bad guy's nickname, 'Fred the Shred', because he had a reputation for pulling off aggressive takeovers, after which the minnow was swallowed up like a tasty bait fish on the end of a line. You turned round, and your job was gone. That was the story told about him afterwards, by everyone. But before 2008 Fred Goodwin was the golden boy of British banking, the man who could work magic. RBS just grew and grew.

There is no better figure through whom to follow the story of the banking collapse. His friends still see Goodwin as a victim, the man who was blamed for all the ills and the moneylenders' misdeeds, because he did become a lightning rod for all the anger about bankers' salaries and pensions and had to take the heat that some others were able to shrink from. But there was a reason for the odium. No one had behaved with quite the hubris that Goodwin managed, always going further, always taking one more risk, always reaching for the deal that he was determined not to let slip. Just before the fall, he had the aura of an untouchable.

Outside Edinburgh, near the airport, sits the £350 million headquarters he built for his bank: buildings that seem to form a grandiose village of their own, rather showy and shining with confidence. They were opened by the Queen in 2005, as a symbol of success. They call it 'Fred's Folly' now, and it has turned into a sad monument to the people who lost their jobs and the financial consequences of collapse: a reminder of the bank that got too big.

Goodwin became chief executive of RBS in 2000, having run Yorkshire Bank and the Clydesdale in the four years before he joined the bank. He was schooled in Paisley and read law at Glasgow University before he became an accountant with Touche Ross, where he rose fast. When he arrived at RBS he embarked on an astonishing expansion that made him feared and famous, the man who turned a modest regional bank into a global force. Within seven years he had been involved in the take-over of twenty-six other institutions – most notably NatWest – he'd been knighted and the bank's share price was rising and rising. For Goodwin, there was always another target.

In 2007, few people outside the world of financial services had heard of sub-prime mortgages, the American loans that turned out to be toxic, spreading their poison throughout the system. When the housing bubble burst in the United States in that year, sub-prime – risky – loans which had been bundled up with regular mortgages became almost worthless, and the banks scrambled to recover from a gamble which they'd thought a one-way bet but which turned out to be the biggest loser of all. In spring 2007 sub-prime loans in the United States were estimated at $1.3 trillion dollars.

The credit crunch was beginning to bite, and unfortunately for Goodwin it was just at the moment when he thought he was about to pull off a coup which, even for him, was spectacular. Throughout 2007 he battled to get control, as part of a consortium, of the Dutch bank ABN Amro, which was already talking to Barclays about a friendly takeover. Goodwin, no friend, was determined to snatch the prize away. He paid £49 billion to get it, in the biggest banking takeover Europe had ever seen.

There was rumbling in the City of London, where Goodwin had always aroused scepticism as well as a degree of wonder, and as the credit squeeze began to hurt in the United States RBS's assets were beginning to look much less attractive than they had when ABN Amro was a gleam in Goodwin's eye. Only six months after the takeover in April 2008, the shares had dropped by nearly half and the bank was forced to ask investors for £12 billion to shore up its capital. That, however, was a mere taste of the crisis to come.

Goodwin continued to insist that his plans were on track. There had been hiccups before, and this would pass. It didn't. When Alistair Darling wrote his memoir of his years as Chancellor he recalled with amazement a conversation with an unnamed banker at the height of the crisis who told him – with pride, according to Darling – that his bank had just decided that it would no longer take on any risk that it didn't understand. 'It horrified me,' says Darling. He had not known how blithely the risks had been ignored. He added that when Goodwin came to see him at his home in Edinburgh he told the Chancellor that he didn't think the financial regulator, the FSA, understood his bank. 'I don't think they were the only ones,' says Darling.

ABN Amro turned out to be the toxic asset to top them all, a bank that cost nearly £50 billion to buy and was sitting in a vast, stagnant pond of bad debt. So complicated had some of the financial instruments become, in the United States and across Europe, that banks were unsure of how to calculate the level of their exposure to the risks. They didn't have to wait long to find out. By October 2008 it was clear that a crisis was gripping banks across the developed world and governments were working on an international rescue plan in the hope that it could be implemented before one institution collapsed and the dominoes crashed down one by one.

When Sir Tom McKillop, RBS's chairman, spoke to Darling in Luxembourg on 7 October the government was forced to make available £20 billion on the spot, knowing that more would probably be needed. The figure for RBS alone ended up at more than £45 billion. Goodwin, however, insisted when he came to the Treasury late that afternoon that he didn't need as much as that: it might suggest to people that there was a reason to panic. There was. Darling and the big bankers negotiated late into the evening about how far the government would have to move into the banks. 'We either do something or we don't,' said Darling. 'If we don't and I have nothing else, then God help all of us.' With that, he says, Goodwin – whom he describes as 'the big beast of the financial services industry' – strolled out as if he were off for a game of golf.

It was characteristic. Goodwin is a man who shows little emotion. Coolness is all, but underneath there was an ambition that wouldn't be stilled. By some measures he could say at one stage that he was indeed leading the biggest bank in the world – with a balance sheet of loans and investments worth £2 trillion – having taken a little fish in the sea and turned it into a shark. Now, by the end of 2008, it was a toothless and weak beast, and the epitome of disaster. Goodwin resigned. Shares that had been worth nearly £6 were on the way down fast. They would eventually be worth around 20p. And the bank that had once seemed the pride of the industry – getting Goodwin his knighthood and carrying all before it – had to be taken over by the taxpayer if it was going to survive. McKillop and Goodwin had a humiliating encounter with shareholders in November during which they had to apologize for bringing down the bank.

As with all such scandals there was a public search for a banker who might look good in sackcloth and ashes. Well, you didn't have to look far to find a bulging bonus or a mind-boggling salary, but Goodwin was the man. When the scale of his pension became known – he had a 'pot' of more than £16 million and an annual pension of £700,000 for life when the bank went down – it was contrasted with the wreck of an institution that was now a burden on the state, with losses of £24 billion in 2008.

The public, much of it, concluded that the bankers had been enriching themselves as they headed down the primrose path to destruction.

The morality tale played itself out. Goodwin resisted government pressure to reduce his pension voluntarily, then had to give in. And in 2012 came the humiliation of having his knighthood stripped from him. Some thought that was petty, and that a precedent for removing honours for subsequent misdeeds would produce endless complications. But in respect of Goodwin, the public appetite had to be satisfied.

No one represented more clearly the collapse in confidence in banking. Tom Wolfe's 'Masters of the Universe', who made money as if it was pouring out of the magic porridge pot, were now the men you couldn't believe. Down the road, Bob Diamond at Barclays would suffer a similar fate over the LIBOR rate-fixing scandal. They'd fallen like ninepins, and their day was done. There were still riches in the City, but the crash that started with Lehman Brothers in New York and Northern Rock in Newcastle upon Tyne brought an end to the era of endless optimism and guaranteed riches, an end to the era of bankers' faith in their infallibity.

Fred Goodwin was the man who fell to earth. Others flew after him, but perhaps not quite so close to the sun.

Rupert Murdoch

R UPERT MURDOCH has been described by one of his British editors as the most inventive and bravest deal-maker the world has ever known, and by another of them as 'evil incarnate'. His buccaneering presence changed the face of newspapers and television, taunted and seduced governments across the world, provoked fear and admiration, and turned him into a real-life Citizen Kane whose writ runs round the globe, and whose personality throbs at the heart of his empire. There is always a special frisson in Fleet Street, even now, when the word goes out: 'Rupert's in town.'

No newspaper proprietor of his time has matched his power, and probably none has taken more risks. In Britain, for more than four decades he has had more influence on the press than any other individual, inventing styles and changing the rules, turning his iconoclastic zeal on traditions and conventions and ripping them up. And now, in 2012, he finds himself like a Gulliver tied down by a thousand ropes, caught in the biggest journalistic scandal of our age and unable to break free, however hard he tries.

The press before the hacking scandal was fashioned in his image; the press after the Leveson Inquiry will have to adapt to the regime that he has created, though it is the last thing he ever wanted. In 2011 he apologized to a parliamentary committee for wrongdoing in his organization, and this was the moment when his power in Britain began to ebb for the first time since he smelt Fleet Street ink and set to work.

The *News of the World* makes bookends for the story, its start and its finish. Murdoch took the paper over in 1969 in a typical raid. Despite its sure-fire menu of scandal and populist outrage it was floundering, and Murdoch saw his opportunity. He had newspapers in Adelaide, inherited from his father, and the Mirror group in Sydney, and in 1964 founded Australia's first national newspaper, *The Australian*. The *News of the World* was a perfect opportunity and later that year he picked up the *Sun*, a floundering successor to the old *Daily Herald*, for less than a million pounds, and this could use the Sunday paper's presses in Bouverie Street for the rest of the week. Murdoch later remarked that he was amazed at the ease with which he entered the newspaper business in Britain.

It took him just under a decade to knock the *Daily Mirror* off its perch as the biggest-selling daily newspaper, with a combination of sharp writing, brilliant tabloid presentation, and gimmicks: when the first Page Three girl appeared, half naked, in 1970, Murdoch was delighted at the fuss in Parliament and the suggestion that his paper should be prosecuted. What more could he ask for? Time and again the *Sun* was ahead of the game and by 1979, firmly in the Conservative camp, it became the cheerleader for Thatcherism. With her victory, Murdoch was blessed.

After a union crisis forced the closure of *The Times* for a year in 1978 and the Thomson organization decided to sell it, Murdoch outmanoeuvred his rivals Robert Maxwell, Tiny Rowland, and Lord Rothermere of the *Daily Mail* to get the prize. He had his hands on one of the world's great newspapers and already dominated the tabloid market. The Murdoch Era was established, and he was starting to expand his operations in the United States, where he already owned several newspapers and had his eye on television.

From the start, Murdoch was seen rather differently inside and outside his business. To those who worked with him in London he was as much editor-in-chief as proprietor, relishing the rolling presses, gossiping about the news, rewriting headlines, and on his editors' backs in a way that Lord Beaverbrook himself would have admired. As he transformed the *Sun* from its Labour-supporting posture in the 1970 general election to embrace the right-wing populism that would become its trademark, his critics on the left began to see him as The Enemy. But to many of his journalists he always seemed less of an ideologue than a swashbuckling freebooter, with no overweening set of views that guided his editors. He just liked stories that sold newspapers.

But after he pulled *The Times* into his stable, Murdoch's political power began to be a question of public debate. Sir Harold Evans, famous crusading editor at the *Sunday Times*, was given charge of *The Times*, fought with Murdoch and lost. He said, after he was forced out in 1982, that guarantees of editorial independence meant nothing to that proprietor, and said later that Murdoch never made a promise he didn't break. Then in 1986 Murdoch engineered a Fleet Street coup that once again made him hero and villain all at once, his favourite role.

Union troubles had dogged newspapers for a generation, and the game was up. There were regular unofficial strikes, relations with managements were bad, the costs were too much for the proprietors. Murdoch secretly built an entire new plant for his papers at Wapping in east London, moved in overnight, locked the unions out, and settled down behind the barbed wire for a prolonged siege.

He knew that he had the (often unspoken) gratitude of other newspaper owners, although as far as the unions and Labour were concerned he now bore the mark of the beast. In the mid-nineties, much later, the playwright Dennis Potter gave a famous television interview when he was dying of cancer in which he said that he called his disease Rupert so that he could get close to it:

if he had the time, he said, he would shoot him for the pollution of the British press.

By then Murdoch was a mogul. Wapping had come just after he had done a remarkable deal in America, getting hold of 20th Century Fox in Hollywood and becoming a naturalized American so that he would be allowed to move into television there. The regulatory changes made by the Reagan administration meant that eventually Murdoch was able to found Fox News, the first news service in the United States to have an aggressive political tone, and throughout the nineties his power increased on both sides of the Atlantic.

In Britain, his BSkyB satellite television service became a powerful weapon, being the single most important force in reviving football when he decided to invest heavily in live matches. It also poured money into live golf, rugby and cricket, but it was with football – the cash-rich, high-rolling, celebrity-driven game of the nineties – that Murdoch scored.

That influence brought him close to political leaders, who wanted to be close to him. Their party didn't matter so much as their power. By the time Tony Blair came along Murdoch was ready to see if he could make friends, although he said that if they did end up making love it would be like porcupines: very, very carefully. Nonetheless, they managed it. Murdoch's newspapers backed Blair in 1997, a historic shift that infuriated the Conservatives, just as Gordon Brown, Blair's successor, was dismayed when Murdoch switched back to the Conservatives after he became Prime Minister, although when Murdoch was asked once what he thought of David Cameron, he replied, with characteristic brevity: 'Not much.'

Behind all this, of course, lay the question of how his papers used their power. In 2007 the royal editor of the *News of the World* and a private investigator were jailed for intercepting voicemail messages left for royal aides. News International, the Murdoch newspaper group in Britain, threw a blanket over the smoking gun but, gradually, despite two years of obfuscation and denial, enough of the truth seeped out to set in train the biggest scandal the British press had ever seen.

The Metropolitan Police, embarrassed by its failure to follow up evidence of wrongdoing, was forced into action after a gap of about four years, and a long series of arrests began, featuring, at the head of the queue, Rebckah Brooks, chief executive of News International and former editor of the *Sun*, and Andy Coulson, former editor of the *News of the World* and subsequently communications director to David Cameron in 10 Downing Street. The court proceedings would be a long time coming, but Murdoch had to acknowledge that his papers had been involved in wrongdoing, on a gigantic scale. Hundreds of public figures were lining up to complain that their phones had been hacked, and a story that at the beginning had seemed to pass the public by – they'd never had a high opinion of journalists – produced outrage, and parliamentary hearings at the Leveson Inquiry into the press, ordered by Cameron, with a brief to advise on a new regulatory regime.

Murdoch's son James had to leave the chairmanship of the broadcaster BSkyB as a consequence of the scandal. In the process, Murdoch lost one of the biggest deals he'd sought: the full control of BSkyB that would have allowed a lucrative expansion of his worldwide television interests, a massive step for his global enterprise, News Corporation. As it was, by mid-2012 News Corp was fighting in the United States to stem a vast tide of criticism and to protect its assets. Murdoch, at the age of 81, was well past his zenith, and on the defensive, even humiliated.

How long could it last? None of his children has a passion for newspapers to match his own, and the interest of News Corporation in keeping its British newspapers when the cases are heard and the courts have spoken must be in doubt.

For a whole generation Murdoch was the man who set the pace and sounded the horn. When he did, everyone followed. He was irresistible, to journalists, politicians who couldn't let him go – whether they were dazzled or repelled – and his public, whose tastes he knew so well.

Yet the whisper of an answerphone message on a mobile phone sounded the end of it all. The empire will surely survive in some form, and Murdoch will remain an enigmatic powerhouse, as he has always been, teasing and threatening, laughing and growling. But the glory days are gone.

Simon Cowell

SIMON COWELL SAYS HE THINKS the reason his television shows have been a success is that we are living through a 'fame epidemic'. He is also quite content to take credit for spreading the virus. The achievement may be one of the few things that makes him happy.

No one epitomizes the business of the twenty-first-century celebrity more than Cowell. He makes and breaks young careers with the flick of an eyebrow or a pout; he thrives on instant stardom, and likes the feeling that it could all come unstuck a moment later, because that drives him on. 'I'm always striving for something else,' he says. 'I don't relax. I've tried to, and I can't.'

He became a celebrity himself, and a national irritant, with the arrival of *Pop Idol* on ITV in 2001, when he was largely unknown outside the music business. Ten years later he was in the top ten of the *Sunday Times* music rich list, worth something over £200 million. His face was a picture of the age: determined, focused on success, a little cruel. 'I'm very, very competitive,' he says. 'I like winning. It's not the money. I like winning – I don't like being in second or third place.' Most of the time, so far, he has won.

As a judge on *Pop Idol*, then with his own *The X Factor*, and later *Britain's Got Talent* – all of them franchised around the world – he made a fast fortune. His own production company,

Syco, has sometimes accounted for three-quarters of the profits of its parent, Sony UK. And that financial success was accompanied by a cultural imprint that he stamped on everything he touched: the idea that fame is around the corner and there's nothing more valuable. In an interview in 2011 he recalled that when he was growing up there was no such thing as a designer watch, the celebrity culture hadn't really arrived, and life was slower. 'But now – and I'm part of the reason, I accept that – you've just got too many people, because of the lottery, because of the internet boom, wanting fame; who want to go from nought to 60 in an instant.'

When he says he accepts some responsibility, it is with no sense of guilt. He says he did wonder after the singer Susan Boyle was built up as a wildly unlikely star on *Britain's Got Talent*, then came second and broke down, whether he had failed to exercise any duty of care. But that is about as far as it has gone. He negotiated his way through the jungle of the music business – he says it's full of people who are sharks, 'vile, absolutely vile, vile people' – and believes it to be a reflection of life in general – a little more frenzied, driven by exceptional egotism, but nonetheless revealing how human beings instinctively want to behave.

Some of those 'vile people' think the same of him. He divides opinion among television viewers because he doesn't give you much choice: he's either a beast with a warm heart concealed somewhere inside, or just a beast. And he angers people in the business too, because he's associated with the kind of talent he promotes: safe, easily marketable, derivative. His music industry critics don't like his power, and they think his taste works against originality and daring because he has to sell it on television, and more, they say the people produced by his system crowd out more interesting talent. He doesn't care. He'll point to his creations – Will Young, whom at first he didn't like, Leona Lewis, JLS, One Direction – and say: there you are. But he's still resented.

This fame machine was born in 1959. His mother was a ballet dancer and his father worked for EMI as a property executive. He left school with two O-levels and found his way onto the set of

Stanley Kubrick's film *The Shining* – as a runner, doing odd jobs – when he was still a teenager. A couple of years later he was taken into the mailroom of EMI at the bottom of the heap, but he was in the industry that had always lured him. 'From my first day on the job I began planning and scheming my way to the top of the business.'

Cowell jokes about his single-mindedness and his vanity – his luxury object when he was a guest on *Desert Island Discs* was a mirror – but acknowledges that it isn't all a pose. He recalls as a boy throwing the Monopoly board on the floor if he realized he wasn't going to win in a family game, speaks of his unhappiness when somebody he knows gets ahead of him, and describes dark moods that last for days. 'Things might have gone really well and then I torture myself,' he once told the *Daily Mail*. 'I cannot believe it. I have to find something to make me miserable.'

It's almost unnecessary for him to add that if he had a session with a psychiatrist he thinks it would be a long one, because, by his own description, he is 'odd'. You can see it in the houses he likes to rent, on both sides of the Atlantic, and adapt to his tastes. Everything is black or white or beige, the lines sharp, not a hint of clutter. The garden will be shaped and manicured so that it looks as if nothing would dare to grow there. There are shiny black surfaces everywhere, and he enjoys the order and simplicity.

It may not be very odd, but it is certainly unusual, for someone to arrange to have an intravenous drip once a week with a cock-tail of vitamins – he's quite happy to have it put in while he is working – and he was reported to have told the former Prime Minister, Gordon Brown, over dinner that he was planning to have himself frozen after his death. He can't remember saying it, but does think it's a good idea. He eats the same breakfast every day – sometime in the middle of the day – runs a business that prizes hard work and detail, and he is unforgiving of those who don't accept the rules.

Cowell has had the good fortune to invent a style as well as a money-making machine. *Pop Idol* was a talent show that blended for the first time the sight of raw talent being forced into shape – sometimes with excruciating results – in front of waspish and ruthless judges who were not only putting on a performance for the cameras, but offering the prospect of fame and riches to people who were encouraged to believe that their lives could be changed almost overnight. Some were, most weren't.

A huge audience built up, and when *The X Factor* replaced the show after three years, building on the successes and failures of *Pop Idol* performers, the format was given another twist. Those who found it manipulative or vulgar, and there were plenty of those, were outnumbered by the millions who watched, and voted. Gone was the cosy folksiness of *Opportunity Knocks* of a generation before: this was for big money, national tours, the chance of international celebrity and riches, with Cowell as the guaranteed Mr Bountiful who would introduce the winner to his world.

They were shows made for an age of prosperity, where dreams were dangled in front of young performers invited to make a contrast between their upbringing – almost always modest, and without the prospect of financial success – and the nirvana that their talent could bring them. All they had to do was conquer the terror of the stage, get their voices in shape, and somehow deliver to a phalanx of celebrity judges, led by Cowell, the idea that they had the hidden ingredient that only that programme could discover and exploit.

There are dozens of versions of his shows around the world. When *Britain's Got Talent* came along in 2007 – having been launched in the United States the year before – Cowell was executive producer and judge, selling the idea to every continent. It became one of the most successful television franchises of its time. Cowell said of his shows: 'I have an instinct for what the public want and there are very few people who have it in my area.'

Ten years after his first talent show appeared on Saturday night, riding high, he was justified in making that claim. He'd known failure – he nearly went bust when he was 30 and had to move back in with his parents for a time – but he caught a tide that was running just after the turn of the century, when stories of fabulous wealth in entertainment, and a popular obsession with celebrity, matched the tales of the financial miracles that they were performing in the City of London, stoking up the boom that would never end. Whether it was a belief that the bubble would never burst, or whether it was in large part the old desire to escape from a life that seemed so dull by comparison with the fairy-tale world of the stars, who can say? But it worked.

Cowell attributes it to gut instinct. 'I'm not that musical,' he says. 'I don't really know how a record is produced, and funnily enough I don't want to. I listen from a punter's perspective, as somebody would buy a track.' But, of course, he is also a fighter. For years he has battled with Simon Fuller, the artist manager and entrepreneur with whom the *Pop Idol* format was devised, about earnings from the worldwide use of their shows, and for a share of the American market. When he says the music business is 'not a very nice business' he knows exactly what he's talking about. 'I take more pleasure out of my own success than other people's success. It's just one of those things,' he told *GQ* magazine.

Cowell is one of those people who come along and find that their style and personality fit their time. He is brash, shameless about ambition and ruthlessness, happy to sell dreams and, if they evaporate, say: 'That's life.'

He is well aware that he managed to invent a form of TV hypnotism in which every twitch of his face, every gesture, seemed to be transmitted to the performer in front of him: someone either shivering in fear or enjoying the blissful feeling that fame is on the way. Like Cowell, the shows are brittle but powerful, edgy and sometimes troubling.

Try and imagine Saturday night over the past decade without him.

The Queen

A TWENTIETH-CENTURY MONARCH would never have to
ride into battle, nor find stratagems and spoils to outwit
other kings and queens. Survival on the throne, however, could
not be guaranteed: the waters had risen and many had been swept
away. It was an advantage to the Queen, maybe not obvious at
the time of her accession in 1952, that she grew up with the
abdication of her uncle frighteningly fresh in her family's mind,
and with a feeling, therefore, for the fragility always lurking
underneath. When Edward VIII left the country before his coronation in 1936, the monarchy trembled. When the young Queen
swore her coronation oath, she committed herself to a life of
service that was, in part, a guarantee that it would never happen
again.

She was told she was Queen in Kenya on 6 February 1952.
Duty was the watchword. The royal court had unshakeable ways,
and still operated under the influence of Queen Mary, who
married the future George V in the last decade of the nineteenth
century and died only a few months before her granddaughter's
coronation as Elizabeth II on 2 June 1953. The past was ever-
present. Nothing must change, and the solemnity of the ceremony
– the first coronation to be seen on television – was a statement
of continuity.

Yet, inescapably, the appearance of a 27-year-old Queen at a time when the austerity of the post-war years was beginning to lift, stirred up a breeze for the celebrations. This was change. The Festival of Britain in 1951 was a boast about a country that had not only survived the threat of invasion from Nazi Germany but was now creative and confident. The very name 'Elizabeth' encouraged memories of the age of gold: of Shakespeare and Spenser, Drake and Raleigh, and all the adventurers who'd spun the web of empire. Optimism was in the air. With the conquest of Everest by Hillary and Tenzing announced on the very day of her crowning, the Queen could expect to emerge as a personality of the kind that once would have been unthinkable. But she never had an appetite to rush it. The apparatus of court, the iron commitment to continuity with which she'd grown up, meant that it had to be gradual

The Queen had been introduced to the country as a young princess, aged 14, speaking on the radio for *Children's Hour* in 1940 to address those who had been evacuated from the cities in the war.

She and her sister Margaret were more familiar to the public than their predecessors could ever have been. The story of the first years of her reign – which we've followed through the first portraits in this series – was one of gradualism. The fifties was not the dull decade it has often been labelled – fridges, washing machines, televisions were popping up in every household – but socially the landscape remained familiar.

Sir Winston Churchill was the first of the twelve Prime Ministers who served her through to her Diamond Jubilee, then deep in the autumn of his political life, and his successors through the fifties, Anthony Eden and Harold Macmillan, had both been born in the 1890s, when Queen Victoria was on the throne. Public life still practised the politics of deference and it was a conservative age, preserving the social strata that a previous generation would recognize. When Princess Margaret wanted to marry Group Captain Peter Townsend in 1953, royal consent was withheld. He was divorced, and the Church of England was implacably hostile. The public seemed on Margaret's side. No matter.

But change was welling up. The Queen stopped the presentation of debutantes at court in 1958 and the first faint signs of loosening were seen. The Prince of Wales, born in 1948, went to schools with other boys; once he would have been educated by a governess at home. And then the sixties took a hand. Everything speeded up. Televisions were in every front room, more people were flying the Atlantic than going by ship, youth culture was rampant. The Queen found herself making the Beatles MBE, on the recommendation of the Prime Minister, Harold Wilson. In the shires they roared with horror, but it was done. And by 1968 the royal household was persuaded to do a more daring thing than it had ever imagined, to let the cameras in.

Royal Family, first broadcast in June 1969, showed the Queen, the Duke of Edinburgh and their four children at Windsor and Balmoral, appearing to behave in a reasonably normal human way. Would that be reassuring, or would it smash the magic glass through which royal highnesses should be seen and admired? The jury of courtiers was out; the public had decided. They wanted more, so the Palace obliged with the now familiar 'walkabout'. The idea that it hadn't happened before would seem bizarre to the generation that followed.

The trouble was in judging how fast change could be safely engineered in an institution that believed it had to stay solid, especially when things were dissolving around it. As we've seen in these portraits, the seventies were tumultuous: industrial prosperity was waning, inflation was going up, striking workers were in the streets. European accession in 1973 was a jab of confidence for some, a betrayal for others, and an act that would trouble the political parties for a generation. The Queen was cast in the role of stabilizer. When she made her Silver Jubilee speech in Westminster Hall in 1977 she decided to say, in the face of the devolution debate that was gripping politics, that she could not forget she had been crowned Queen of the United Kingdom. And she went on to say: 'Perhaps this Jubilee is a time to remind ourselves of the benefits which union has conferred, at home and in our international dealings, on the inhabitants of all parts of this United Kingdom.' Her words, always government-approved as a rigid constitutional practice, sounded personal. Indeed they were. The Prime Minister's office at the time said they were 'entirely the product of the Palace'.

And in the eighties the monarchy had no choice but to become more personal, because events such as the marriage of the Prince of Wales to Lady Diana Spencer in 1981 whipped up an interest that had to be satisfied. Caught in a culture that wanted more and more – pictures, interviews, intimacies – the royal ship had to find a way of staying steady in a storm. It was difficult. The fairy-tale marriage became an elongated crisis that buffeted everyone, and encouraged the public appetite. Rupert Murdoch, in particular, whose Republicanism has been one of his few unchanging political attitudes, was happy to oblige, particularly through the revelations in the *Sunday Times* about the state of that marriage, with the willing help of the Princess herself.

The royal family was splintering. By 1992 the marriages of three of the Queen's four children had broken and soon after a fire at her beloved first home, Windsor Castle, she spoke of her pain, calling the year her 'annus horribilis'.

The most horrible time of all, as we recalled through the story of the Princess of Wales, was Diana's death and funeral, when a wave of anger seemed to spring up against the royal family and its perceived coldness. Why had the flag not been lowered at Buckingham Palace? An explanation of long-standing protocols was not good enough. So the Queen – who had spoken to the crowds with red, swollen eyes and in a breaking voice outside the chapel where the Princess's body lay – spoke live on television to express her personal feelings. It would have been inconceivable at the time she came to the throne.

Yet an extraordinary change did occur. The reasons are obscure, and they are for historians, but in the years leading to her Golden and then Diamond Jubilee, the Queen's position did not weaken, but strengthened. It remained a remarkable fact that after she had been on the throne for sixty years the Republican voice did not seem any louder than it had been a couple of generations earlier and the Queen, in her mid-eighties, was still able to perform acts of deep symbolism that carried great national weight. In 2011 she went to Ireland, the first monarch to set foot in the Republic since the Rising of 1916 and the war of independence, and one whose close kinsman, Lord Mountbatten of Burma, had been murdered by the IRA in 1979.

The head of state was speaking powerfully, with a force that was a direct consequence of the length of her reign and the care with which she had negotiated the rocks and shoals of politics throughout those six decades. Its authenticity could not be denied.

At the Diamond Jubilee, the celebrations – which were repeated in a different way six weeks later for the Olympic Games in London – were a conscious acknowledgement of the *good* things that had happened, thanks to the innovators, the brave people, the artists and entertainers, the thinkers and doers who had made sure that despite everything – recessions, terrorism, social problems of all kind, the weather – here was a country that could still have a sense of itself and a certain resilience. The connection between that feeling and history is inescapable and in her sheer dedicated *steadiness*, her seeming permanence, the Queen was able to represent that link, from the here-and-now to a past that for a moment at least did not seem distant, but a living inheritance.

There was enough confidence for the monarch to agree to play a part, for fun, to participate in the history of entertainment in her time. She met her most famous spy. When she said in a filmed performance, 'Good evening, Mr Bond', it was the most surprising thing anyone had ever heard her say.

It was an exhibition of confidence. Why not? Maybe they have been good years, after all. The characters we've met on the journey through this series have played many different parts, rising high and falling low, and painting the canvas in their own distinctive colours. They are the people who have made the Queen's time, begun the rolling changes that have shaped her age, slowly, often too quickly to be understood, sometimes violently. At the centre of it all, placed there by birth and not by choice, she has absorbed everything, a figure obliged as a matter of duty to try to find the most elusive balance of all, between continuity and change.

Acknowledgements

Tʜᴇ ꜱᴇʀɪᴇꜱ ɪɴ ᴡʜɪᴄʜ ᴛʜᴇꜱᴇ ᴘᴏʀᴛʀᴀɪᴛꜱ were broadcast in summer 2012 was a joy to write, because I worked with producers who love radio and the way it deals with words. I am immensely grateful to James Cook, Sukey Firth, Alison Hughes, Sarah Taylor, Mike Tighe, Clare Walker, for their commitment and friendship, and, for part of the series, Poppy Goodheart and Kate Howells. Ania Wigmore helped to keep the show on the road. We were working against a clock that sometimes seemed to tick very loudly, but it was fun. Andrew Smith supervised the project meticulously, under Rob Ketteridge and Graham Ellis, controller of production in BBC Audio and Music, whose idea it was. They assembled a formidable team in the best BBC tradition. I have acknowledged in the Introduction the commitment and work of the panel which produced the names of our New Elizabethans, because they gave me a list with which it was possible to spin a good story. Those of us who work for BBC Radio 4 are often reminded of what it means, and our listeners deserve their own vote of thanks for their nominations, which they produced with typical fervour. I am grateful to Iain MacGregor, publishing director at Collins, for producing a book at lightning speed when it would have been easier not to, and, as always, to my wife Ellie for her forbearance and unflinching support when summer seemed to be slipping away from us.

JN, September 2012

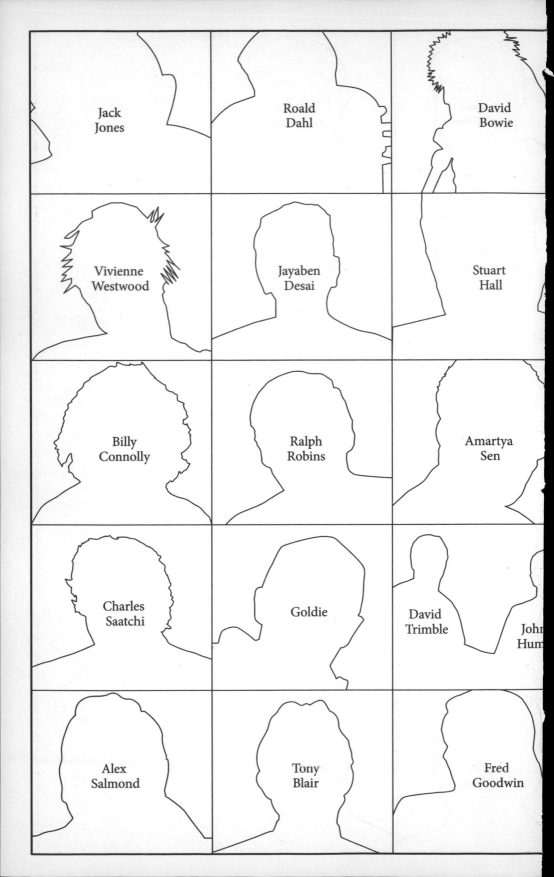

Jack
Jones

Roald
Dahl

David
Bowie

Vivienne
Westwood

Jayaben
Desai

Stuart
Hall

Billy
Connolly

Ralph
Robins

Amartya
Sen

Charles
Saatchi

Goldie

David
Trimble

John
Hum

Alex
Salmond

Tony
Blair

Fred
Goodwin

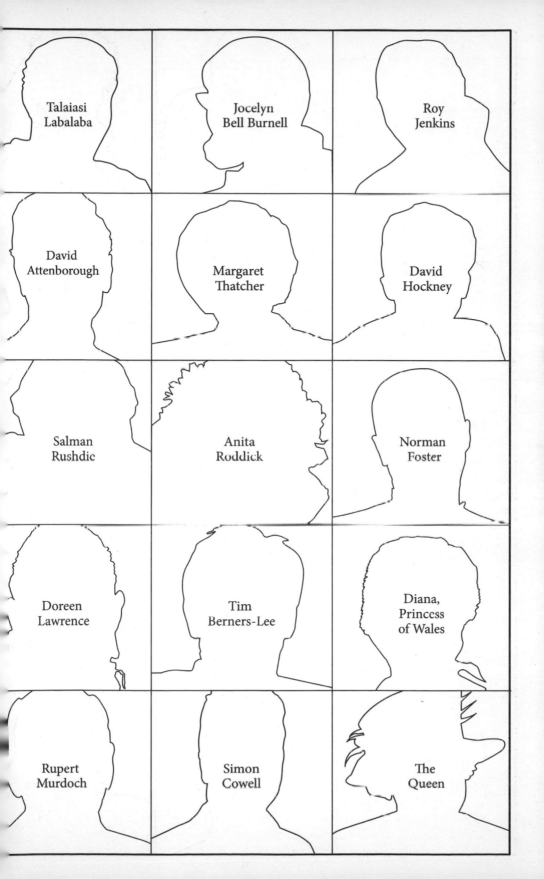

Talaiasi
Labalaba

Jocelyn
Bell Burnell

Roy
Jenkins

David
Attenborough

Margaret
Thatcher

David
Hockney

Salman
Rushdie

Anita
Roddick

Norman
Foster

Doreen
Lawrence

Tim
Berners-Lee

Diana,
Princess
of Wales

Rupert
Murdoch

Simon
Cowell

The
Queen